teach yourself...

Access
for Windows 95

Charles Siegel

MIS:
PRESS

A Subsidiary of
Henry Holt and Company, Inc.

First Edition—1996

Library of Congress Information

```
Siegel, Charles
    Teach yourself… Access for Windows 95 / by Charles Siegel.
        p. cm.
    ISBN 1-55828-441-9
        1. Microsoft Access for Windows.    2. Microsoft Windows 95.
3. Database management.    I. Title.
CA76.9.D3S563338 1995
005.75'65--dc20                                        95-25020
                                                          CIP
```

Printed in the United States of America.

10 9 8 7 6 5 4 3 2

MIS:Press books are available at special discounts for bulk purchases for sales promotions, premiums, fund-raising, or educational use. Special editions or book excerpts can also be created to specification.

For details contact: Special Sales Director
                          MIS:Press
                          a subsidiary of Henry Holt and Company, Inc.
                          115 West 18th Street
                          New York, New York 10011

Associate Publisher: Paul Farrell   **Production Editor:** Patricia Wallenburg
Managing Editor: Cary Sullivan   **Technical Editor:** Christine Ruana
Development Editor: Judy Brief   **Copy Editor:** Gwynne Jackson

Dedication

To my son, Beni

Acknowledgments

Thanks to all the people at MIS:Press who helped on this book,
particularly to my developmental editor, Judy Brief;
my layout editor, Patty Wallenburg; and
the technical reviewer, Christine Ruana.

TABLE OF CONTENTS

Chapter 2

Chapter 3

Chapter 4

Chapter 5

Fast Forms, Reports, and Mailing Labels 151

Chapter 6

Part II

Chapter 7

Chapter 10

Chapter 11

Chapter 12

INTRODUCTION

Is This Book for You?

Access is such a rich and powerful application that most people do not know where to begin when they start using it.

Access makes it easy for users to work with databases. You can create tables, edit data, and use queries to find the data you want with very little effort. The Form and Report Wizards can do the work of designing data entry forms, reports, and mailing labels for you.

Access also makes it easy for developers to create applications. Though it includes an entire programming language, Visual BASIC for Applications, its interface is so versatile that developers can create many custom applications without writing a single line of code. Access' queries, forms, reports, and macros are powerful enough to do most of the tasks that used to require programming. You should note that this book does not cover designing or programming applications. Visual BASIC and the theory of computer programming require a book of their own.

When users read the standard Access manuals, they often have to wade through long discussions of power features to learn about the simple features they need to work with on their own data. The online Help system is also so extensive and complex that sometimes it is hard to use it just to get started. The average user needs to know the basics of creating tables, simple forms, reports, and mailing labels. The sophisticated user needs to understand the basics as well as other advanced features such as properties and expressions.

This book is designed for people who want to get started with Access quickly and for people who want to learn the power features of Access.

The book is divided into two parts. It begins with "Access The Easy Way," which introduces all the basic features of Access. It teaches you how to create databases and tables, how to add and edit data, and how to do basic queries to find the data you want. It covers both Form Wizards and Report Wizards, which you can use to design and display all your forms and reports. Part I concludes with a chapter on relational databases that teaches you how to use these basic features of Access to deal with more complex data. Even when a database program is very simple, the actual data being used is often complex. This is when knowing how to manipulate relational databases comes in handy. After using Access' basic features and reading Chapter 6, "Relational Databases," you will be able to deal with almost any complex practical application.

After you have learned the necessary basics of Access, you can go on to the second part of this book, Power Features. Part II teaches you how to use action queries to update your data with less effort, how to use Access expressions to calculate values, how to create custom forms and reports, and how to use simple but powerful macros to automate tasks that you do repeatedly. These are all features that can increase your power and efficiency, and, most importantly, save you time.

The features of Access covered in this book take you to the edge of being a developer, because Access makes it easy even for nonprogrammers to create state-of-the-art database applications that anyone can use.

PART I

Access the Easy Way

CHAPTER 1

A Quick Tour of Access

A ccess has become the best-selling database management program because of its combination of power and ease of use. On one hand, Access is powerful enough that developers can use it to create entire applications that require little or no programming. It also contains an entire programming language, Visual BASIC for Applications, which can be used to develop richer and more advanced applications. On the other hand, Access is easy enough to use that in a short time beginners can learn to manage their own data.

It is easy for you to get started with Access by taking a quick look at how it is organized. This chapter gives you a quick tour of Access. It covers:

* starting Access
* opening a database file
* using the Database window to view different types of Access objects
* opening a table in Datasheet View and Design View
* opening a query in Datasheet View and Design View

1

- ✳ opening a form in Form View, Datasheet View, and Design View
- ✳ opening a report in the Print Preview window
- ✳ creating new objects
- ✳ understanding when multitable databases are needed
- ✳ using the online Access help system
- ✳ quitting Access

Before You Begin

This chapter includes a few exercises to give you a feel for the basic features of Access. To do them, you must already have Access 7.0 installed on your computer and you must know the basic ways of using Windows applications.

This book assumes that you know only the most basic Windows techniques, such as how to use the mouse, make selections from drop-down menus, and scroll through a window. If you have ever used a Windows program, you should have no trouble doing the exercises in this book.

The Access Database and Its Objects

In other database management programs, the term *database* is sometimes used to refer only to the tables that hold data. Access uses the term more broadly. An Access database consists of the tables that hold the data and all the related objects, such as queries, forms, and reports, that are used to manage the data in the tables.

In this chapter, you will take a quick tour of a sample database distributed with Access so you can see the different types of objects it includes. You will learn more about how to create and use these objects in the rest of Part I of this book.

This chapter is meant to give you a quick overview of an Access database. You should not try to memorize what is covered here. You need not worry about understanding the details of the objects you look at. Everything mentioned here is covered thoroughly in later chapters. For now, you will simply open an Access database and look through it quickly to see how it is organized.

Starting Access

To start Access, first click **Start** on the Windows Task Bar and then move the mouse pointer to **Programs** on the menu that is displayed. Windows will display another menu to the right with all of the program groups available. You may be able to select **Microsoft Access** from this program menu or you may have to select a program group that displays yet another menu with **Microsoft Access** as one of its options.

By default, Access will be in the Microsoft Office program group, but it may have been installed in or moved to another group in the computer you are working on. For example, it may be in the Applications, Startup, or a special Microsoft Access program group.

 If Access is in the Startup program group, it will start automatically every time you start your computer. If you close it, you can always restart it again by selecting it from the Task Bar menu system as described above.

Start Access now, so you can do the rest of the exercises in this chapter. Follow these steps:

1. Click **Start** on the Windows Task Bar and move the pointer to **Programs**.
2. If Microsoft Access is available on the menu, click it. Otherwise, move the pointer to the **Microsoft Office** program group on the right to see if the menu that is displayed includes **Microsoft Access**. If necessary, move the pointer over other program groups to display other menus, until you find the **Microsoft Access** menu item. Select this menu item to start Access.

After starting, Access displays a dialog box that lets you create a new database or open an existing one.

Opening a Database

Try opening a sample database distributed with Access. After you have become more familiar with Access, you can open a database in the same way you open files in other Windows applications, by choosing **Open** from the File menu. For now, it is easier to use the initial Microsoft Access dialog box to open one:

1. The **Open an Existing Database** radio button should be selected, and **More Files** should be selected in the list below it; if they are not, select them. Click **OK**. Access displays the Open dialog box. Make sure that the My Documents folder is open (displayed in the Look in drop-down list, which is at the top of the dialog box), as shown in Figure 1.1.

2. Select **Shortcut to Northwind** and click **Open** to open it—or simply double-click **nwind** to open it.

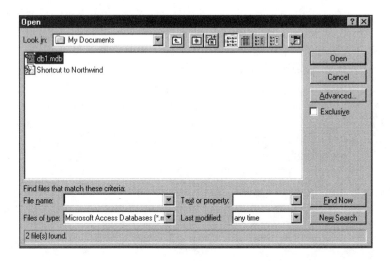

FIGURE 1.1   OPENING A SAMPLE DATABASE FILE IN ACCESS.

3. The Northwind Traders dialog box is displayed to introduce this sample database. Select the checkbox so this dialog box is not displayed again, and then click **OK**.

Databases that you open are added to the list in the dialog box displayed when you start Access, making it easy to open them again in the future.

The Database Window

When you open a database, Access displays the Database window, shown in Figure 1.2, which lets you work with all the objects in the database. This window is sometimes called the *database container*, because it contains all the objects that make up the database.

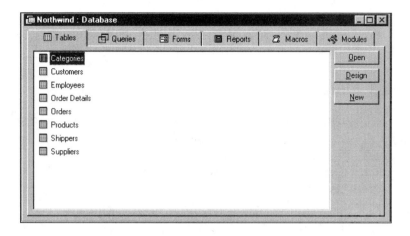

FIGURE 1.2   THE DATABASE WINDOW.

As you can see, this window has tabs across its top edge, with the names of different types of Access objects. Click one of these tabs to display the names of all objects of that type in the list box in this window. In the illustration, the **Tables** tab is selected, and all the tables in the database are displayed in the list box. All these types of objects are described later in this chapter.

You can use the buttons on the right side of the Database window to work with these objects in different ways:

✻ Select the **New** button to create a new object of the type that is displayed.

✻ Click an object in the list to select (*highlight*) it, and select the **Open** button to view and enter data. You can also double-click an object in the list instead of using its Open button.

✻ Click an object in the list to select it, and select the **Design** button to change the object's design.

When you work with Access, you will probably find that you use the menu system less than with other applications, because you can do so many things simply by using the Database window.

Reports, macros, and modules have different buttons instead of the Open button, but all objects, like Tables, have New and Design buttons.

Once you have opened a window to display an object, you can switch between views of most objects to display their data or change their design, either by using the View menu or the toolbar.

Using a Table

Tables are the most fundamental objects in Access, the first object that you must design. Display one of the tables in the sample application:

1. If necessary, click the **Tables** tab to display the Tables list. Click the **Products** table to select it.

2. Once the Products table is selected, click the **Open** button to display the table, shown in Figure 1.3.

You can also open the table simply by double-clicking its name in the list or by selecting its name and pressing **Enter**.

SHORTCUT

Product ID	Product Name	Supplier
1	Chai	Exotic Liquids
2	Chang	Exotic Liquids
3	Aniseed Syrup	Exotic Liquids
4	Chef Anton's Cajun Seasoning	New Orleans Cajun Delights
5	Chef Anton's Gumbo Mix	New Orleans Cajun Delights
6	Grandma's Boysenberry Spread	Grandma Kelly's Homestead
7	Uncle Bob's Organic Dried Pears	Grandma Kelly's Homestead
8	Northwoods Cranberry Sauce	Grandma Kelly's Homestead
9	Mishi Kobe Niku	Tokyo Traders
10	Ikura	Tokyo Traders
11	Queso Cabrales	Cooperativa de Quesos 'Las Cabras'
12	Queso Manchego La Pastora	Cooperativa de Quesos 'Las Cabras'
13	Konbu	Mayumi's
14	Tofu	Mayumi's
15	Genen Shouyu	Mayumi's
16	Pavlova	Pavlova, Ltd.

Products : Table

Record: 1 of 77

FIGURE 1.3   THE PRODUCTS TABLE.

HOW A TABLE IS ORGANIZED

You can see that an Access table holds a list of repetitive data. In the rest of this book, you will create a table to hold a list of names and addresses, which is the most common use of a database management program. This sample table holds a list of products. This sort of repetitive data was kept in a file cabinet, a rolodex, or a box of index cards before recordkeeping was computerized.

There are two terms you should know, as they are almost always used when computerized databases are discussed. They are simply new names for familiar things.

✳ A *record* is all the data on a single entity. For example, if you have a list of names and addresses, each record includes the name and address of one person. In the sample table, where you have a list of products, each record includes the name and other details for one product.

✳ A *field* is one piece of data that appears in each record. For example, if you have a list of names and addresses, the first name might be the first field, the last name might be the second field, and the street address might be the third field. In the sample table, there are fields for Product ID, Product Name, Supplier, and others.

NOTE Because of the way they are arranged in the table, records are also called *rows* and fields are often called *columns.*

A *table* is made up of all the similar records that you want to work on together. For example, you might want to keep the names and addresses of all your clients in one table and the names and addresses of all your friends in a second table.

SWITCHING TO DESIGN VIEW

Before you can use a table, you should specify what fields it will include. You can use the View tool at the left of the toolbar, as shown in Figure 1.4, to switch between the Design View of a table, which lets you define its fields, and Datasheet View, which lets you see the data in those fields.

FIGURE 1.4   THE VIEW TOOL.

You are looking at the table in Datasheet View, and you should glance at it in Design View before going on to look at other objects. Because you are in Datasheet View, the **Design** option of the View tool is displayed on the toolbar button, so you do not have to use the drop-down menu to switch views.

1. Click the **View** tool to display this table in Design View, as shown in Figure 1.5.

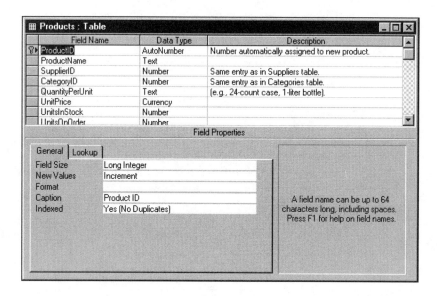

FIGURE 1.5   A TABLE IN DESIGN VIEW.

2. When you are done looking at it, click the **Close** box in the upper-right corner of the Table window to close it.

You can see that the design of the table includes a name and a definition of each field in the table. You will learn to design a table in Chapter 2 and to work with data in it in Chapter 3.

Using a Query

A *Select Query*, the simplest and most important sort of query, lets you select which data from a table is displayed. You can specify which fields are displayed, enter criteria to specify which records are displayed, and specify the sort order of these records.

Like the Table window, the Query window can be displayed in Datasheet View or Design View. The toolbar for a Query window also includes an SQL View button, which displays the underlying programming code that is used to create this query, but this advanced feature of Access is not covered in this book.

Try displaying a very simple query based on the Products table, which you just looked at, in both of these views:

1. Click the **Queries** tab of the Database window to display the Queries list. Double-click the query named **Products Above Average Price** (or click this query and click the **Open** button) to open it in Datasheet View, as shown in Figure 1.6. You can see that this query includes just two fields from the Products table—the Product Name and the Unit Price.

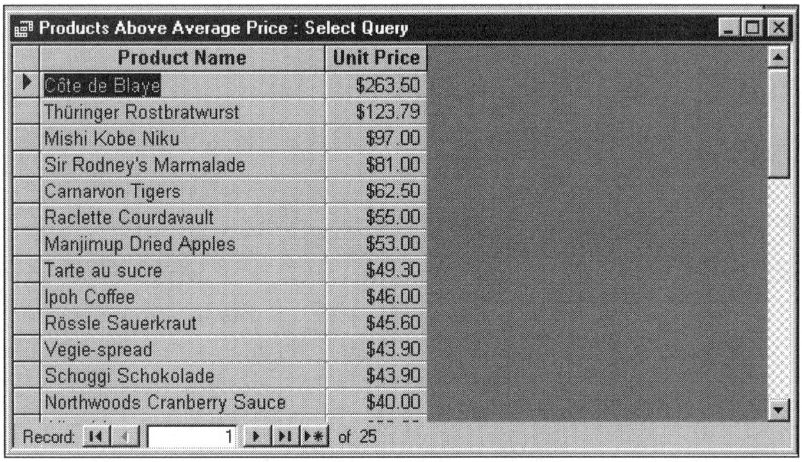

Product Name	Unit Price
Côte de Blaye	$263.50
Thüringer Rostbratwurst	$123.79
Mishi Kobe Niku	$97.00
Sir Rodney's Marmalade	$81.00
Carnarvon Tigers	$62.50
Raclette Courdavault	$55.00
Manjimup Dried Apples	$53.00
Tarte au sucre	$49.30
Ipoh Coffee	$46.00
Rössle Sauerkraut	$45.60
Vegie-spread	$43.90
Schoggi Schokolade	$43.90
Northwoods Cranberry Sauce	$40.00

Products Above Average Price : Select Query

Record: 1 of 25

FIGURE 1.6   A QUERY IN DATASHEET VIEW.

2. Now, click the **View** tool to display the design of this query, as shown in Figure 1.7. You can easily see that the Design View lets you specify which fields are included by selecting the checkboxes under the field names. You can also see that it has cells where you can enter criteria to specify which records are displayed, used in this sample query to include only records with a Unit Price field that is greater than the average unit price.

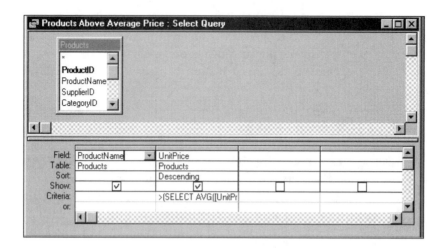

FIGURE 1.7   A QUERY IN DESIGN VIEW.

3. When you are finished looking at it, click the Query window's **Close** box.

Select queries are fundamental to Access because you can use them instead of tables as the source of forms or reports in order to specify which records the forms or reports include. In fact, you can use a select query instead of a table as the basis of another query.

You will learn more about select queries in Chapter 4. Select queries that include more than one table are covered in Chapter 6. More advanced select queries and other types of queries (such as action queries, which let you change the data in a table) are covered in Chapter 10.

Using a Form

Forms let you control how data is displayed on the screen.

As you learned earlier, a table displays each record on a single line and each field in a column. The table format lets you look at a number of records at the same time, but it generally does not let you see all of the information on each record, because there is usually too much to fit across the screen.

A form usually displays one record at a time. You can select which fields to include in the form, and you can usually arrange the fields on the screen in a way that lets you see them all at once. You can also make a form much more interesting visually than a table, and you can display pictures in it.

When you open the Form window, the View tool at the left of its toolbar includes three options, as shown in Figure 1.8.

FIGURE 1.8   THE VIEW TOOL FOR A FORM.

These buttons let you do the following:

✳ *Design View* lets you change the design of the form.

✳ *Form View* lets you view the data in the form.

✳ *Datasheet* View lets you view the fields included in the form as a table.

When you are using a form, it is often convenient to switch back and forth between Form View and Datasheet View in order to look at one record or many.

Try looking at a sample form based on the Products table in all these views:

1. Click the **Forms** tab of the Database window to display the Forms list. Double-click **Products** in the list to display the Products form shown in Figure 1.9. You can see that the form gives you a much more attractive way of viewing the data in the table.

2. Now, click the **View tool drop-down arrow** and select **Datasheet View** to display this form as a table, as shown in Figure 1.10. This datasheet contains only the fields included in the form, not necessarily all the fields in the table on which it is based.

3. Finally, click the **View** tool (which is now displayed as the **Design View** tool) to see this form in Design View, as shown in Figure 1.11. When you are finished looking at it, close the Form window by clicking its **Close** box or choosing **Close** from the File menu.

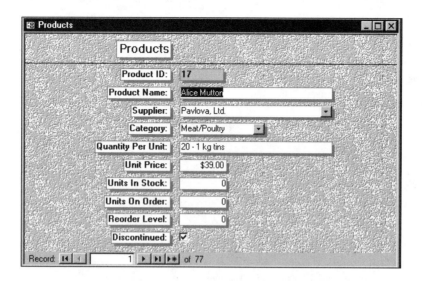

FIGURE 1.9 **THE PRODUCTS FORM IN FORM VIEW.**

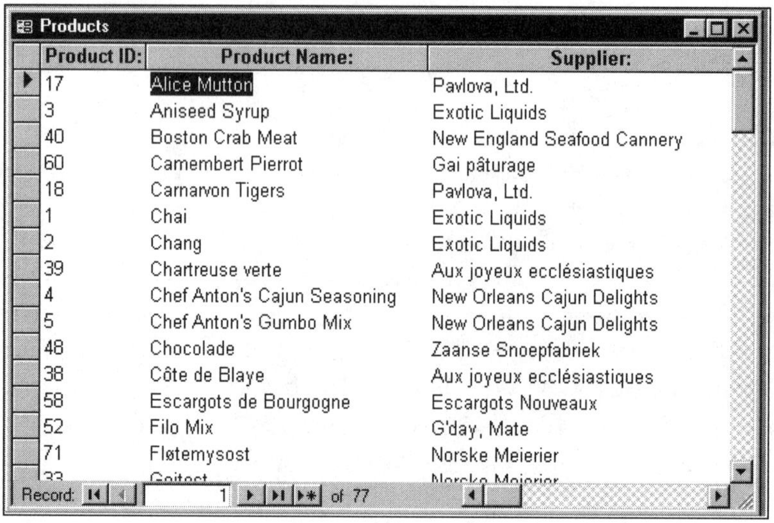

FIGURE 1.10 **THE PRODUCTS FORM IN DATASHEET VIEW.**

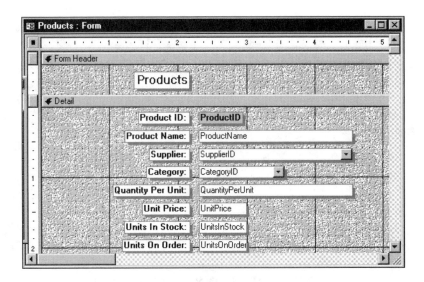

FIGURE 1.11   THE PRODUCTS FORM IN DESIGN VIEW.

Access includes easy-to-use Form Wizards that let you answer simple questions so it can automatically design forms for you. These Wizards are powerful enough that many users find they do not need to use Design View to create custom forms. Chapter 5 covers forms and Form Wizards. Chapter 7 discusses how to design custom forms.

Using a Report

Though they can be printed, the objects you have looked at so far are usually used to display data on the screen. Reports are meant specifically for printing data.

For this reason, when you display the Reports list, the Database window button has a Preview button instead of the Open button, as shown in Figure 1.12. You can display reports in either the Print Preview window or in Design View.

You can simply double-click a report in the Reports list or select it and press **Enter** to display it in the Print Preview window.

You cannot edit data displayed in reports as you can in tables, queries, and forms. Instead, the Print Preview window displays them in a way that makes it easy for you to see how they will appear when they are printed. You just have to click the window to switch between viewing the report full size and viewing an entire page.

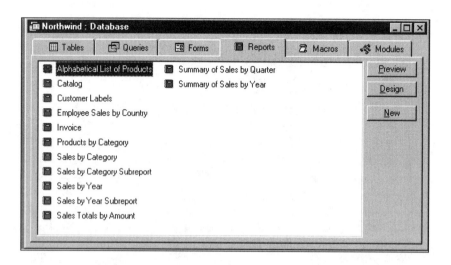

FIGURE 1.12   THE DATABASE WINDOW FOR REPORTS.

The Print Preview window is a separate Access window. It is not a view of a Report in Design View. When you close it, Access will display the window under it, which is either the Database window or the Report Design window, depending on which you opened the Print Preview window from.

The Report window in Design View is very similar to the Form window. Access includes a Report Wizard that designs reports for you, and many users can get by without designing custom reports. For now, you can just look at a report in the Print Preview window.

1.   Click the **Reports** tab of the Database window to display the Reports list. Double-click **Alphabetical List of Products** to display it in the Print Preview window. You might want to scroll downward, so you can see more of the report, as shown in Figure 1.13.

2.   Now move the mouse pointer to the Print Preview window. The pointer is displayed as a magnifying glass. Click to view a full page of the report, as shown in Figure 1.14. Click on the report again to display the report full size. When you are finished looking at it, press **Esc** to close the Print Preview window.

Chapter 5 teaches you how to use the Report Wizards to generate reports and mailing labels. Chapter 9, in Part II of this book, covers how to use the Report window in Design View to create custom reports and mailing labels.

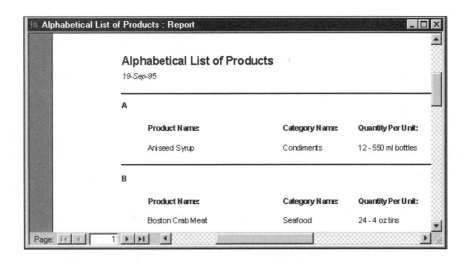

FIGURE 1.13   PREVIEWING A REPORT.

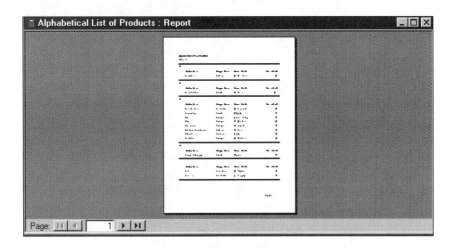

FIGURE 1.14   ZOOMING THE PRINT PREVIEW WINDOW.

Macros and Modules

The next two objects in the Database window are power features of Access:

✳ *Macros* let you automate and speed up your work and are used when
you develop applications. A macro is a list of actions. Access performs

all the actions in the list when you run the macro. Macros can save time for Access users; they are covered in Chapter 11 of this book.

✳ *Modules* let you write programs in Visual BASIC to develop advanced applications. This book does not cover programming.

It is not necessary to look at these tabs to get oriented in Access.

Creating New Objects

You can create a new object of any of these types by displaying the panel for that object type and clicking the **New** button. When you do this, Access displays a dialog box like the one shown in Figure 1.15.

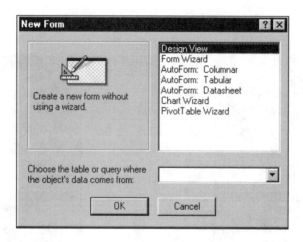

FIGURE 1.15   CREATING A NEW OBJECT.

All New Object dialog boxes have options similar to the first two options in this dialog box:

✳ **DesignView** displays the object in Design View, so you can create it from scratch.

✳ **Form Wizard** (or other type of Wizard) displays a series of steps that let you create a new object by answering simple questions.

New dialog boxes also have specialized options, such as the specialized Form types listed here, but creating an object from scratch in Design View or creating the object using the appropriate Wizard are the two fundamental options that are available.

Using a Wizard

Since you have already looked at Design View, you should take a moment to look at a typical Wizard.

All Wizards are made up of a series of steps with instructions in plain English, such as the step of the Form Wizard shown in Figure 1.16. Each of these lets you make choices to specify certain features of the object. Many Wizards include directions on how they work and use pictures that change to illustrate your choices.

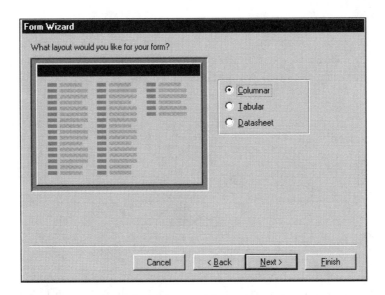

FIGURE 1.16   USING A WIZARD.

Each dialog box in all of the Wizards has the same buttons at the bottom, which you use to navigate among all the dialog boxes.

✳   **Next>** displays the next dialog box. Select this button after you have filled out each dialog box. When you get to the last one in the sequence, this button is dimmed.

✳ **<Back** displays the previous dialog box, so you can go back and change specifications you entered earlier.

✳ **Finish** leaves the Wizard and creates the form or other object.

✳ **Cancel** leaves the Wizard and discards your work.

The final dialog box of any Wizard has option buttons that let you specify how the object should be displayed when it is created. Usually, you can display the object with data or display it in Design View, so you can customize the design generated by the Wizard. For some types of objects, such as Forms and Reports, even if you are creating a custom design, it is easiest to use the Wizard to create the basic layout and then customize it in Design View.

Auto Forms and Auto Reports

You can also create new objects using the New Object tool, shown in Figure 1.17. Most of the options on this tool's drop-down list let you use the New dialog box that you just looked at; they are equivalent to displaying the appropriate panel in the Database window and clicking its **New** button.

FIGURE 1.17   THE NEW OBJECT TOOL.

You can also use the first two options of this tool's drop-down list, Auto Form or Auto Report, to instantly create a form or report on the table or query that is currently selected in the Database window. This form or report includes all the fields and records in the table or query, arranged in a standard layout.

NOTE The New Form and New Report dialog boxes let you create Auto Forms and Auto Reports, as does using Design View or the Wizard, and they give you several standard layouts from which to choose.

Naming Objects

Object names can be edited directly in the Database window. Select an object and choose **Rename** from the File menu to make the file name into editable text. Alternatively, select the object and simply click the name of it again to make it editable text.

The easiest way to name an object after creating it is to slowly click it twice in the Database window.

Why You Need Multiple Tables

Some of the objects in the database you looked at in this chapter are based on more than one Access table. This is an example of a *multiple table* or *relational database*. Most business applications require relational databases because there are many types of data that you cannot store effectively in a single table.

When businesses first began to use computers, they discovered they could eliminate repetitious data by breaking up some databases into multiple tables. When businesses kept records on paper, for example, the Payroll Department had a file with each employee's name, address, social security number, and data on how much each was paid. Likewise, the Benefits Department had a file with each employee's name, address, social security number, and data on the benefits each was entitled to. The Training Department also had a file with each employee's name, address, social security number, and data on the training courses each had taken.

You can see that a large company with many departments could easily have had many copies of the same basic information on each employee, such as name, address, and social security number, stored in many different files. All this data would have to be entered several times, and then, if an employee moved, the address would have to be changed several times.

This repetition was impossible to avoid when records were kept on paper. When you computerize, however, you can break up this data into several tables. One table may have basic information, such as name, address, and social security number. Another may contain data on payroll, and still others may have data on benefits training, and so on.

The computer can look up the name and address that goes with each payroll record. It can retrieve data so quickly that it can display the name and address from one table and the payroll data from another table as quickly as if they were in a single table.

You only have to enter the basic data once, however. When someone moves, you only have to change the address in one table, and it will automatically be changed in all the forms used by all the departments.

Relational databases are not needed for very simple data, such as a mailing list, but they are needed for most business applications. Chapter 6 covers relational databases in more detail, and Chapter 2 includes more details on the type of data you can store in a single table.

WARNING

For now, you should simply realize that you cannot deal with complex data without breaking it up into multiple tables. The most common error people make when using database programs is to try to create a single table to hold data that should be kept in multiple tables. If you try to do this, it causes problems later. It is best to design tables properly from the beginning.

Getting Help

Access has the same sort of help system used by other Windows applications. Choose **Microsoft Access Help Topics** from the Help menu to display the Help window, shown in Figure 1.18. This window has several tabs that give you different ways of searching for help. We will take a look at the two most important.

To use the Contents tab, double-click one of the General topics to display more specific subtopics, and double-click one of these to display still more specific topics; you can also double-click an open topic to close it.

General topics are displayed with book icons: keep opening these until you reach actual help topics, displayed with page icons, as shown in Figure 1.19. Double-click a topic with a page icon (or select one and click **Display**) to view help on that topic.

The Index tab, shown in Figure 1.20, lets you search for help alphabetically. Simply type the initial letters of a topic to display it in the list. Double-click an item in the list (or select it and click **Display**) to view help on that topic.

Once you are looking at a help topic, shown in Figure 1.21, you will see that some words are displayed in green and underlined with a dotted line. You can click them to temporarily display a help window, which disappears when you click again.

FIGURE 1.18   THE HELP WINDOW.

FIGURE 1.19   USING THE CONTENTS TAB.

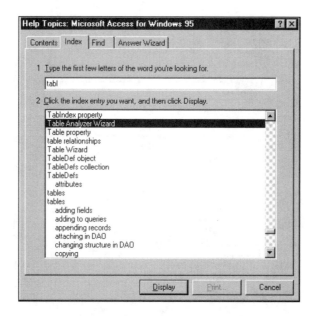

FIGURE 1.20   USING THE INDEX TAB.

FIGURE 1.21   A HELP TOPIC.

As you are viewing help topics, you can click **Back** to display the previous topic you viewed, or click **Help topics** to return to the Main Help window.

In addition to the usual help system, which is so extensive that it is sometimes difficult to use, Access gives you some quick methods of getting help described below.

Quick Help for Menus and Toolbars

It is easy to get quick help on the Access menu and toolbar:

✳ Help on menu commands is available as you move the highlight through the menu. Just scroll through the commands of a menu; either hold the mouse button down or use the **Up** and **Down Arrow** keys. Access displays a help line in the status bar at the bottom of the screen describing the function of the highlighted menu option.

✳ Help on Toolbar tools is available if you move the mouse pointer to any of the Toolbar tools. Access displays a help line in the status bar describing the function of that tool. After you keep the pointer on it for a moment, Access also displays the name of the tool in a box next to the pointer; this is called a *tool tip*.

Interface Help

Interface Help is a special feature of the Access Help System that lets you get more extensive context-sensitive help on menus, toolbars, windows, and other features of the Access interface.

 To use it, click the **Help on Interface** tool at the far right of the main toolbar. When you are using a dialog box, the toolbar is not accessible, but you can click the **?** button on the dialog box's title bar instead.

In either case, the mouse pointer is displayed with a question mark next to it. You can then click any feature of the Access interface or choose any menu item to display the Access Help System with help on that feature.

To restore the pointer to its normal appearance without using Interface Help, click the **Help on Interface** tool (or the **?** button of the dialog box) a second time.

Quitting Access

WARNING

When you are finished working with Access, choose **Exit** from the File menu or click the **Close** box at the far right of its title bar to close Access. You should always close Access or other database applications when you are done working with them to avoid loss of data.

If you want to turn off your computer when you are finished with Access, you can be sure to avoid losing data if you select **Start** and then **Shutdown** from the Windows Task Bar.

To Sum Up

In this chapter, you learned to start Access and to open a database. You also used the buttons of the Database window to display the most important Access objects—tables, queries, forms, and reports. You learned how to look at different views of these objects, including Datasheet View, Design View, Form View, and Print Preview, by using either the toolbar or the Database window buttons, and you learned that you can create objects using Design View or Wizards.

Now that you have gotten a general idea of how Access is organized, you can go on to learn how to create and work with each of its objects. In Chapter 2 you will begin by designing a sample table.

CHAPTER 2

Creating a Database and Table

A simple database table holds repetitive data. Before you store this data in a computer, the first step is to design the table. This is a bit like deciding what blank spaces you should include on a paper form—one line for a name, two lines for an address, and so on—except that you must be more precise when you design the fields of a computerized database table.

You must specify a name for each field, the type of data it will hold, and sometimes the length of the field. You must decide in advance, for example, whether a field will hold text or numbers and the maximum size of the text or numbers the field can hold.

When you design a table in Access, you can also define properties of fields. For example, you can create an input mask that includes characters in the field in every record—such as the hyphens in a social security number—so you do not have to enter them by hand.

In this chapter, you begin by creating a database to hold the sample application you will create in this book, then learn to create a table and get hands-on experience by creating a sample table. You learn how to:

✳ create a database using the Database Wizard

✳ create a database from scratch

✳ create a table using the Table Wizard

✳ create a table using the Table window in Design View

✳ define field names and data types

✳ define field properties for the different data types

✳ create a primary key field

✳ use a table in Design View and Datasheet View

✳ modify the design of an existing table

The table you create in these exercises will be used again in later chapters.

Creating a Database

As you learned in Chapter 1, an Access database is a collection of all the related objects you use to manage data, including tables, queries, forms, reports, macros, and modules. Every object must be part of a database.

Most of this chapter discusses how to design tables. Before you create a table, however, you must create a database to hold it.

How to Create a Database

When you start Access, it displays a box that gives you the option of creating a new database or opening an existing one. In the last chapter, you used this dialog box to open an existing database. You can select one of its other option buttons to create a new database using the Database Wizard or to create one from scratch.

THE FILE NEW DATABASE DIALOG BOX

The quickest way to create a new database is to select the **Blank Database** option button in this box and click **OK**. Access displays the File New Database dialog box, shown in Figure 2.1, to let you specify the name and folder of the new database. After you have used this dialog box, it immediately displays the Database window with a new, empty database.

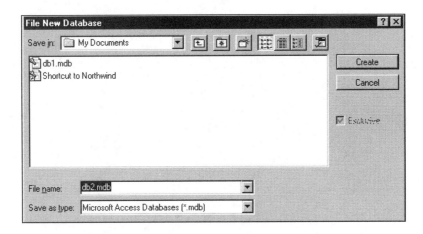

FIGURE 2.1   THE FILE NEW DATABASE DIALOG BOX.

The list in the center of this dialog box includes the names of all the files and folders in the current folder, whose name is in the Save in drop-down. You can use the List, Details and Properties buttons to control how these are displayed:

 List: displays only the names and a small icon of the folders and files, so as many of them as possible can be displayed in this box.

 Details: displays the name, type, and date last modified of both files and folders, and the file size.

 Properties: displays a list of files and folders in the left half of the box, and also displays some properties of the currently selected file or folder in the right half of the box.

You can also display the properties of an individual file or folder by right-clicking it and selecting **Properties** from its pop-up shortcut menu, to display a Properties dialog box such as the one shown in Figure 2.2, but beginner do not have to worry about these properties.

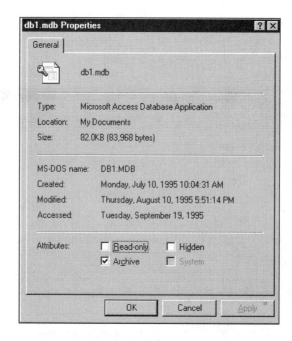

FIGURE 2.2   A PROPERTIES DIALOG BOX.

NAMING THE DATABASE

To name the new database, simply enter a name in the File name box of the File New Database dialog box.

If you want a name similar to that of an existing file, you can click that file in the list to display its name in this box, and then edit its name. You can also create a new file with the same name as an existing file, but this will overwrite the existing file and destroy all the data in it. Access asks for confirmation before overwriting a file.

 Use the same naming conventions that you use to name other files in Windows 95: names may be up to 255 characters long (including the folder and file names) and may include blank spaces.

Access automatically gives the file the extension .MDB (Microsoft Database). Access suggests names such as DB1.MDB or DB2.MDB for new databases that you create, but you should use a meaningful name to make it easier to keep track of the file.

The Save as type drop-down lets you display only Databases or databases and other files in this list. It is included for compatibility with other File New dialog boxes, and you should always leave Database selected as the type, unless you have some special reason to change it.

SELECTING THE DATABASE'S FOLDER

As you can see in Figure 2.3, the Save in drop-down lets you select any of the disk drives of your computer or any folder that is above the current folder. To open folders that are in the current folder, double-click on them in the list of files and folders. As a quick method of opening the folder that is above the current folder, click the **Up One Level** button.

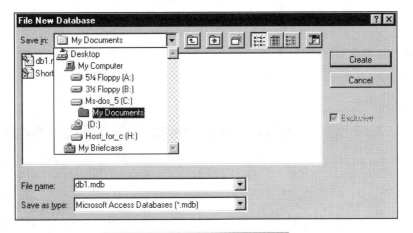

FIGURE 2.3   THE SAVE IN DROP-DOWN.

To create a new folder, click the **Create New Folder** button to display the New Folder dialog box, shown in Figure 2.4. Simply enter the name of the new folder in this dialog box. The new folder is automatically located in the current folder, whose name is displayed in the Save in drop-down. Be sure to open the correct folder before clicking the **Create New Folder** button.

N O T E

In other Windows database applications, it is usually best to create a new folder for every database you work with, to keep all of its files organized in one place. In Access, though, because all the objects of the database are kept in a single file, it is not necessary to create a directory to keep them organized. The .MDB file in Access does the work that the folder does in other database management programs.

You can keep a number of databases in a single folder, without creating confusion about which tables, queries, reports and forms belong to which database: you simply open one .MDB file to use all the objects from that database.

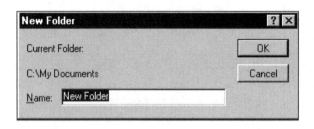

FIGURE 2.4   THE NEW FOLDER DIALOG BOX.

USING THE DATABASE WIZARD

You can also create a new database by using the database wizard, shown in Figure 2.5.

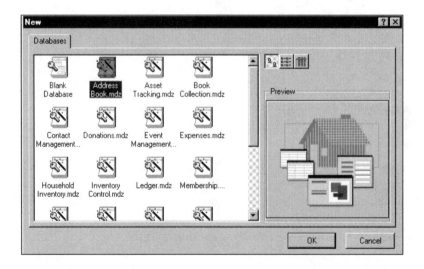

FIGURE 2.5   THE DATABASE WIZARD.

To display this wizard, select the **Database Wizard** button of the dialog box displayed when you start Access or, if you are already using Access, choose **New Database** from the File menu or click the New Database tool.

This wizard lets you choose among and customize a number of databases that are distributed with Access. These are designed for specific purposes, such as an address book, a household inventory, and a membership list, and they include typical tables, queries, forms, and reports that you might need for each of these.

Simply select one of these icons and click OK to create it. Access displays the File New Database dialog box, described **above**, to let you name it, and displays dialog boxes to let you customize it. For example, Figure 2.6 shows the dialog box that lets you choose which fields are included in the sample address book database.

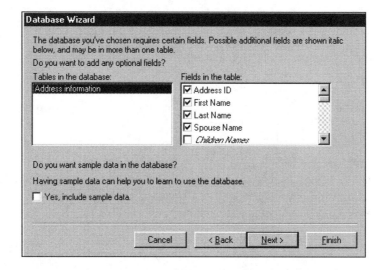

FIGURE 2.6 **CREATING A DATABASE USING THE WIZARD.**

After you have learned the basics of using Access in Part I of this book, you may want to create some of the databases included in the wizard to see which of them might be useful to you.

CREATING A BLANK DATABASE FROM WITHIN ACCESS

You can create a blank database when you are already working in Access. After choosing **New** from the File menu or clicking the **New Database** tool to display this wizard, be sure that **Blank Database** is selected and click **OK**. Access displays the File New Database dialog box, which you use to name the new database, as described earlier.

A Sample Database

Now, let's create a sample database to use in the exercises in this book. In practice, you may want to use the Wizard to help create databases, but when you are learning, it is best to create a blank database and then add objects to it yourself. Once you have learned to work with a blank database in this way, it will be easy for you to work with databases created using the Wizard.

Since you have already used the box displayed when you start Access to open a database, you should try creating the new database from within Access. You can name the database Teach Yourself, after the book, and give the folder that you keep it in a name that indicates that you will use it to store all your own Access applications:

1. If necessary, start Access. When the box is displayed to let you open or create a database, click **Cancel** to open Access without a database open. (If you are already working in Access, skip this step. When you create a new database, any database you already have open will automatically be closed.)

2. Choose **New Database** from the File menu or click the **New Database** tool. When Access displays the New Wizard, be sure that **Blank Database** is selected, and click **OK**.

3. Access displays the File New Database dialog box. The File Name text box is highlighted, so you can simply type **Teach Yourself** to replace the suggested name. It is not necessary to type the MDB extension.

4. The My Documents folder should be the open folder by default. If it is not, make it the current folder displayed in the Save in drop-down.

5. The dialog box should look like Figure 2.7. Then click **Create** to create the file. Access displays the new Database window, shown in Figure 2.8.

N O T E

All the work you do in this book will be held in this database, and you can archive it or simply delete it when you are done with the book.

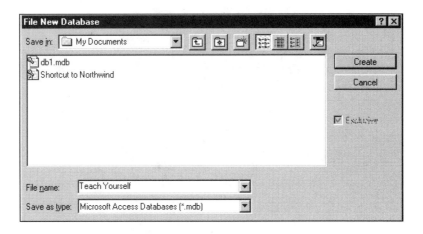

FIGURE 2.7   CREATING THE NEW DATABASE.

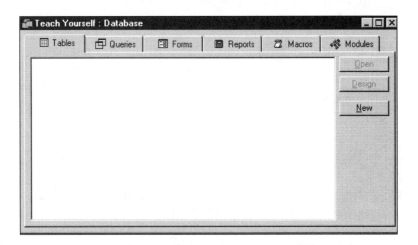

FIGURE 2.8   DISPLAYING THE NEW DATABASE WINDOW.

Creating a Table

The Database window you have created is ready for you to create a table. Notice that the **Tables** tab is selected by default, so that it appears in front of the other tabs at the top of the Database window.

If you click the **New** button, Access displays the New Table dialog box shown in Figure 2.9, which gives you the following choices:

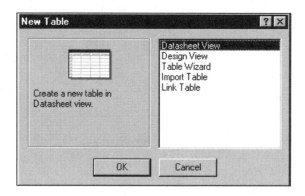

FIGURE 2.9   THE NEW TABLE DIALOG BOX.

✳ **Datasheet View**: creates a new table and displays it in Datasheet View, so you can enter data immediately. The new table has twenty fields with names from Field1 to Field20, as shown in Figure 2.10, but you can rename them by double-clicking the column header and editing their names. Then enter data in the table. When you first save it, Access determines the data type (for example, text or numbers) of each field on the basis of the data you entered. You can change the definition of these fields any time, using the methods covered in the section on "Modifying the Design of a Table" later in this chapter.

WARNING

This Datasheet View feature is occasionally convenient if you want to enter data quickly, but it can lead to problems in the long run. If the data you enter is not a complete sampling of the data you need, or if you do not break down the data into the fields you will actually need in your work, then the default field type will be wrong. It is better to analyze and design the table before entering data, to make sure you break it down into the fields you need and have the right data type for each. As you will learn later in this chapter in the section on "Planning the Table," failure to design the table properly can cause many problems in your later work.

✳ **Table Wizard**: lets you create the table using the Wizard described in the next section.

✳ **Design View**: displays the new table in Design View so you can define its fields, using the methods described later in this chapter.

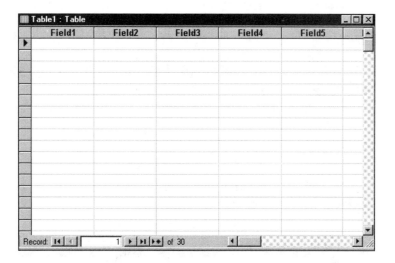

FIGURE 2.10 CREATING A NEW TABLE IN DATASHEET VIEW.

✳ **Import Table and Link Table**: let you work with data from other applications. These wizards will be discussed in Chapter 12, which covers sharing data with other applications.

After looking briefly at how to use the Table Wizard, you will look in more detail at how to use Design View to create a new table from scratch.

Once you know how to create a table in Design View, it will be easy for you to create one using all of the other methods.

N O T E

The Table Wizard

Like the Database Wizard, the Table Wizard lets you choose among and customize a number of ready-made tables that are distributed with Access, which are designed for specific purposes.

Figure 2.11 shows the first step of this wizard, which lets you choose among a sample table and choose which fields from it are included in the table you create. In the illustration, the Mailing List table is selected in the list of Sample Tables on the left. All the fields available for this table are included in the list of Sample Fields in the center.

To include these fields in the table, you must move them to the list on the right using the following methods:

✳ To move a field from the Sample Fields list to the Fields in my new table list, select it and click the **>** button or double-click it.

✳ To move all the fields from the Sample Fields list to the Fields in my new table list, click the **>>** button.

✳ To move a field from the Fields in my new table list back to the Sample Fields list, select it and click the **<** button or double-click it.

✳ To move all the fields from the Fields in my new table list back to the Sample Fields list, click the **<<** button.

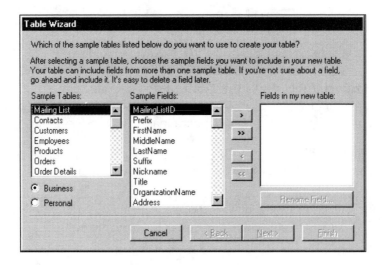

FIGURE 2.11   THE TABLE WIZARD.

The next step of the wizard lets you enter a name for the table, and the following step lets you create the table.

After you have learned to create a table in Design View, in the following section, you will find this wizard an easy-to-use shortcut for creating tables, which you then can use Design View to customize to fit your own needs.

The Table Window in Design View

If you select **Design View** in the New Table dialog box, Access displays the Table window, as shown in Figure 2.12. When you use this window in Design View, the Datasheet View tool is displayed as the first button on the toolbar, so you can click it at any time to switch to Datasheet View.

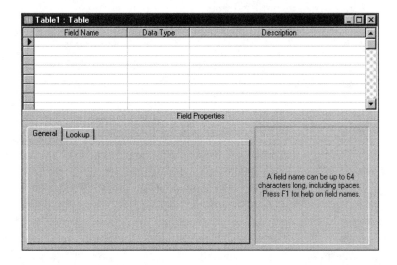

FIGURE 2.12 THE TABLE WINDOW IN DESIGN VIEW.

When you design a table, you specify the names of its fields and the type of data each field holds. Some fields hold only numbers, some only text, and some other types of data. All the available data types are discussed below. This is called *defining the structure of a table* or simply *designing a table*.

DESIGNING THE TABLE

As you can see, the Table window contains columns named Field Name, Data Type, and Description. You can move among columns by clicking them with the mouse or using the arrow keys. You can also press the **Tab** key to move a column right and **Shift-Tab** to move a column left. When you design a table, you use the same editing keys that you use to enter and edit data. These are described in detail in Chapter 3, which discusses editing data.

To enter the name of each field, type the field name in the Field Name column. When you move the cursor to the Data Type column, Access adds a drop-down arrow to that column, which you can click to display list of data types.

Use of the Description column is optional. If you enter a description, it is displayed as a help line in the status bar when that field is selected in the table or in a form. If you do enter information in this column, you should use descriptions that will be helpful during data entry.

INSERTING AND DELETING FIELDS

✳ To insert a new field between already defined fields, move the cursor into any row and choose **Insert Row** from the Edit menu, or click the **Insert Row** tool to add a new blank row above the cursor.

✳ To delete a field, move the cursor anywhere in the row and choose **Delete Row** from the Edit menu, or click the **Delete Row** tool.

FIELD PROPERTIES

When you specify a data type, Access displays the field properties available for that data type in the Field Properties panel in the lower half of the window, as shown in Figure 2.13. You can select properties such as the maximum size of the data that can be entered in the field, the format of the field, and validation rules that check the data. You can move the focus to this panel by pressing **F6** or by clicking it with the mouse. Field Properties are discussed later in this chapter.

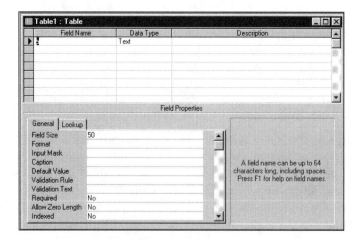

FIGURE 2.13   FIELD PROPERTIES FOR A TEXT FIELD.

THE HELP PANEL

The Table window also includes a help panel on its lower right, with brief context-sensitive help. Press **F1** to display the help system with more extensive context-sensitive help.

SAVING AND NAMING THE TABLE

 You can save changes at any time when you are defining the table by choosing **Save** from the File menu, or clicking the **Save** tool.

SHORTCUT

Alternatively, when you are done defining the table, you can simply close the Table window by as you would close any other Document Window in Windows 95. If you have not already saved it, Access prompts you to save and name the Table.

The first time you save the table, Access displays the Save As dialog box, shown in Figure 2.14, to let you name the table. This dialog box is not like the Save As dialog box that you are familiar with from other Windows applications, because it does not let you select drive and folder where the table is located. You specified the drive and folder of the database file when you first created it. This table is part of this database file, so it does not have its own drive and directory. You just need to enter a name for it.

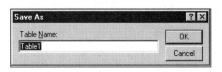

FIGURE 2.14   THE SAVE AS DIALOG BOX.

Access suggests the name Table1, Table2, or the like, but you should give the table a meaningful name in order to make it easier to identify and use it in the future.

ACCESS NAMING CONVENTIONS

All Access objects, including tables, must be given names that follow these Access naming conventions:

✳   Names can be up to 64 characters long.

✷ Names can include any characters except the square brackets ([and]), the period (.), the exclamation point (!), and the backquote (`; not included on most keyboards).

✷ Names cannot include control characters (ASCII values 0 through 31, which cannot be entered by typing in the ordinary way).

✷ Names can include spaces but cannot begin with a space.

These conventions let you give Access tables and other objects complete and meaningful names.

Defining Fields

To define the structure of the table, you must enter at least the name and data type of all fields. For fields of certain data types, such as Text and Number fields, you should also specify the field size in the Field Properties list.

FIELD NAMES

Use the same naming conventions for fields as for other Access objects. Names can include up to 64 characters, as described in the previous section, "Access Naming Conventions."

DATA TYPES

Access, like other database management systems, requires you to specify the type of data that each field holds, as shown in Figure 2.15.

SHORTCUT

Rather than using the drop-down, you can choose a data type simply by entering its first letter once you have moved the highlight to this column.

You can choose among the following data types:

✷ **Text** holds up to 255 characters, including letters, numbers, and special characters.

✷ **Memo** holds text of variable length and is used to hold more text than you would keep in a text field. To store memos, Access uses only the disk space that is needed to hold the text you entered.

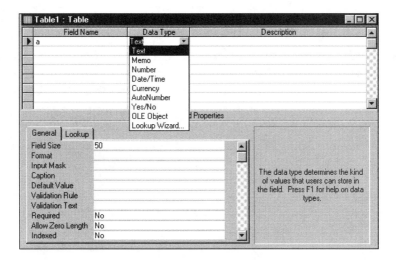

FIGURE 2.15 **SELECTING A DATA TYPE.**

✳ **Number** holds numbers actually used in calculations. The type of number it can hold and accuracy of calculations depends on the size you give to the number field. Number field properties are covered later in this chapter. Some number fields hold only integers and others can hold numbers with many decimal places.

✳ **Date/Time** holds dates and times. Whether you can enter a date, a time, or both depends on the format you give to the field, described later in this chapter.

✳ **Currency** holds numbers used as amounts of money, or any numbers used in calculations with up to four decimal places of accuracy.

✳ **AutoNumber** holds sequential numbers that Access automatically enters. Access places the number 1 in this field in the first record you add to the table, the number 2 in the second record, and so on. You cannot change the numbers that Access enters in this field.

✳ **Yes/No** holds only two values, displayed as Yes and No, True and False, or On and Off depending on the format you give it in the Field Properties panel.

✳ **OLE Object** holds data from other Window applications that support Object Linking and Embedding (OLE). This field can be used to display pictures, sound, or any other type of data available in other applications that support OLE. OLE objects are an advanced feature of Access, and are covered in Chapter 12 of this book.

✳ **Lookup Wizard** lets you create a field that lets the user choose values from a list. People who are using Part I of this book to get up and running as quickly as possible do not need to use this advanced field type, and so it is covered in a separate section on "Advanced Topics" at the end of this chapter.

Access validates data entry based on field type. For example, you can only enter numbers in number fields, and you can only enter valid dates in date fields. You cannot enter 02/30/95 as a date, because February does not have thirty days. You can control data entry more precisely using the Validation Rule and Validation Text Field properties, discussed below.

FIELD PROPERTIES

As you know, when you specify the data type of a field, Access displays a panel with field properties allowed for that type of data. You can move between this panel and the main panel by pressing **F6** or clicking the panel with the mouse.

It is important to set some field properties, such as the size of text fields. Others such as Caption, which lets you specify the label used for the field in a form, are optional but can be convenient, even for beginners. Some properties are meant for more advanced users and are covered later in this book; for example, validation rules require you to use Access Expressions, which are covered in Chapter 8.

Most properties work similarly when they are used with different data types, but there are a few very important exceptions:

✳ Field Size applies only to text and number fields, and works differently for the two.

✳ Decimal Places applies only to number and currency fields.

✳ Format also works differently for different types of fields since the formats you use to display text, numbers, and dates (for example) are obviously very different.

After looking at Field Size, Decimal Places, Format, and other General properties for each data type, you will begin to understand the General properties common to many data types.

In addition to the General tab, the Field Properties panel has a Lookup tab that lets you create an edit control, a list box, or a combo box, so the user can either type in a value or choose one from a drop-down list. Like the Lookup Wizard, the Lookup properties of Fields are covered in the section on "Advanced Topics" at the end of this chapter.

TEXT PROPERTIES

The Field Size property should always be set for text fields. You may also want to use the Format property.

FIELD SIZE

The size of a text field is the maximum number of characters it can hold. Text fields can contain from 1 to 255 characters.

By default, Access makes a text field large enough to hold 50 characters, but this is more space than you need for most fields. If you have a field that holds just one character—such as a middle initial or a code letter—and you leave the Field Size at the default, you are wasting disk space.

> You should generally make text fields no larger than the length they need to hold the data you will be entering in them.

N O T E

You should use the smallest number that will hold all the data in a given field, in order to save disk space and to let Access read your data as quickly as possible. If you give a text field the size 50, Access will always store 50 characters for that field: if the actual name in it is only 10 characters long, for example, it will store 40 blank space characters in addition to the name. Then, Access will have to take the extra time to read through all these blank spaces whenever it reads your file from disk.

FORMAT

You can specify the Format property of text fields by using the symbols shown in Table 2.1.

For example, you might want to enter > as the format of a State field, so the characters are displayed in capital letters.

Apart from these four symbols, other characters are used literally and inserted in the data. For example, if you have a social security number entered in a text field with only numbers, you can display it with hyphens in the appropriate places by using the format **@@@-@@-@@@@**. The @ symbol represents any character, and the hyphens are inserted literally.

TABLE 2.1 SYMBOLS FOR FORMATTING TEXT FIELDS.

Symbol	Meaning
@	Character is required
&	Character is not required
<	Convert letters to lowercase
>	Convert letters to uppercase
Other characters	Used literally

NOTE The Format property determines only how fields are displayed. To control how data is entered, use an input mask, described later in this chapter.

MEMO PROPERTIES

Memo fields do not have a Field Size property. They can hold up to 1.2 gigabytes of data, but Access uses only as much disk space to store them as it needs to hold what is entered.

Memo fields can be formatted in the same way as text fields, using the symbols listed in Table 2.1. It is less common to format memo fields than text fields, however.

NUMBER PROPERTIES

You should always specify the size of number fields, because the size of a number field determines what sort of number it can hold. You may also find it convenient to use Format and Decimal Places properties for number fields.

FIELD SIZE FOR NUMBER FIELDS

The size of a number field is based on the amount of computer memory needed to work with different types of numbers. You can select any of these options from the Field Size list:

✳   **Byte** holds numbers between 0 and 255, with no fractions or decimals.

- ✳ **Integer** holds numbers between approximately –32,000 and 32,000, with no fractions or decimals.

- ✳ **Long Integer** holds numbers between approximately –2 billion and 2 billion, with no fractions or decimals.

- ✳ **Single** holds numbers between approximately -3.4×10^{38} and 3.4×10^{38}. Calculations are accurate to 6 decimal places.

- ✳ **Double** holds numbers between approximately -1.7×10^{308} and 1.7×10^{308}. Calculations are accurate to ten decimal places.

- ✳ **ReplicationID** is used as a unique identifier when you are replicating the table. Beginners do not need to worry about this advanced feature of Access.

Choose the data type of a number field depending on what use you want to make of it. For example, calculations on the Double type can be slow because of the additional precision of their results, and it is better to use Single unless you need the extra precision or the larger numbers that Double offers. Calculations are much faster on Integer and Long Integer than on Single or Double, but the field and the results of calculations will not include any decimals.

NOTE If you are doing calculations that must be accurate to no more than four decimal places, it is best to use the Currency data type rather than the Number data type, even if the numbers do not represent amounts of money. Calculations with currency data use fixed point calculations that avoid rounding errors, rather than the floating-point calculations used with single and double number data, and so they can be performed more quickly.

FORMAT

By default, number fields are displayed as you enter them. You can also give both number and currency fields these standard formats, which you select from their Format property lists:

- ✳ **General Number** is the default selection. The number is displayed as entered.

- ✳ **Currency** displays negative numbers in parentheses and in red. Two decimal places are displayed, and a comma (or other separator) is used to separate every three digits.

✳ **Fixed** displays at least one digit. Two decimal places are displayed if the Decimal Places property is not changed.

✳ **Standard** uses a comma (or other separator) to separate every three digits, and two decimal places are displayed if the Decimal Places property is not changed.

✳ **Percent** displays the value as a percentage. This involves multiplying it by 100 and adding a percent sign. For example, 1 is displayed as 100% and .5 is displayed as 50%.

✳ **Scientific** displays the value in scientific notation, as a number between zero and ten multiplied by some power of 10.

Some of these formats include a comma or some other separator between every three digits. The comma is used as the separator in the United States, but other characters are used in other countries. By default, Access uses the separator specified in the Windows Regional Settings Window, which you can display by double-clicking the **My Computer** icon on the Windows desktop, double-clicking the **Control Panel** in the My Computer window, and then double-clicking the **Regional Settings** icon in the Control Panel Window. Alternatively, you can click on the **Start** menu on the bottom Windows task bar, select the **Settings** menu item, and click twice on **Control Panel**. You can also create custom number formats, but most users do not need them. For more information, see the Help topic "Formatting Numbers" in the Index tab of the Access Help System.

DECIMAL PLACES

The Decimal Places Property list includes the option Auto, which displays the number of decimal places defined by the Format property. It also allows you to select the number of decimal places to display, from 0 to 15. If you select a number, it overrides the number of decimal places defined by the Format property.

DATE/TIME PROPERTIES

Format is the only property of Date/Time fields that we will discuss. You can use the following standard formats for Date/Time fields by selecting them from the Format properties list box:

✳ **General Date** displays the date and/or time depending on your entry. If you entered only a date, the time is not displayed. If you entered only a time, the date is not displayed. If you entered both, they're both displayed, and the date appears first.

- ✳ **Long Date** displays the date with the day of the week and the month written out—for example, Tuesday, September 6, 1994.

- ✳ **Medium Date** displays the date with the month abbreviated and placed before the day and the year—for example, 06-Sept-94.

- ✳ **Short Date** displays the date as numbers separated by slashes—for example, 9/6/94.

- ✳ **Long Time** displays the time as hours, minutes, and seconds separated by colons and followed by AM or PM—for example, 2:45:26 PM.

- ✳ **Medium Time** displays the time in hour and minutes, separated by a colon and followed by AM or PM—for example, 02:45 PM.

- ✳ **Short Time** displays hours and minutes as a twenty-four hour clock—for example, 14:45.

You can also create custom Date and Time formats, but most users do not need them. For more information, see the Help topic "Formatting Numbers" in the Index tab of the Access Help System.

CURRENCY PROPERTIES

The Currency data type can be thought of as a special case of the Number data type, which has a fixed size. You can format currency fields in the same ways you do number fields: to display any of the numeric format listed previously, such as currency, fixed, and percentage.

NOTE The difference between the two data types is that currency fields perform decimal calculations more quickly than number fields because they use fixed point rather than floating point arithmetic. They should be used for extensive calculations that do not require more than four decimal places of accuracy, even if they do not involve amounts of money.

SIZE

You do not specify the size of a currency field. It can hold up to fifteen digits to the left of the decimal point and is accurate to four digits to the right of the decimal point.

FORMAT AND DECIMAL PLACES

A currency field can have the same Format and Decimal Place properties as a number field.

AUTONUMBER PROPERTIES

AutoNumbers are integers that are automatically entered when you add records. By default, their Field Size property is Long Integer.

Their default New Values property is Increment, which enters new values in sequence. You can also select **Random** to enter random numbers in this field.

You can give AutoNumber fields the same formats as number fields.

YES/NO PROPERTIES

Yes/No fields can have three formats:

✳ Yes and No

✳ True and False

✳ On and Off

Simply select one of these three from the Format drop-down: the first option will be displayed for Yes and the second for No.

OLE OBJECT PROPERTIES

OLE objects can have captions, validation rules, and validation text. They are created in other Windows applications and can be many different types of objects, such as pictures or sounds. OLE Objects are discussed in Chapter 12.

Common Properties

Now that you have looked at the special features of individual data types, you can look at properties that apply to different data types in similar ways.

INPUT MASK

A number of field types can have a field Input Mask property that specifies the format in which data is entered. Because this advanced property is not needed for people who are using Part I of this book to get up and running as quickly as possible, it is covered in a separate section at the end of this chapter.

CAPTION

All fields have a Caption property. The caption is used as the heading of that field's column in the Datasheet View. The caption can be any text up to 255 characters.

DEFAULT VALUE

Fields of all data types, except AutoNumber and OLE Object, have a Default Value property. The value you enter is displayed as the default value of this field in every record. For example, if most of your customers live in California, you can enter CA as the Default Value property of the State field. CA is automatically displayed as the field's default value in each record. Access allows you to edit this field if you need to enter a different value: simply type over the highlighted default value.

Advanced users can also use an expression as a field's default value. Chapter 8 discusses expressions in detail.

VALIDATION RULE AND VALIDATION TEXT PROPERTIES

All fields have Validation Rule and Validation Text properties, which let you test the data entered. The Validation Rule is an expression that is evaluated whenever data is entered or edited in the field. The Validation Text is displayed if the entry does not conform to the Validation Rule. Validation Rule and Validation Text properties are discussed in detail in Chapter 8.

REQUIRED PROPERTY

The Required property lets you specify that data is required in a field. The user will not be allowed to leave the field blank during data entry.

ALLOW ZERO LENGTH

The Allow Zero Length property lets you specify that a zero-length string can be entered in the field. To enter a zero-length string in a field, type "" (two quotation marks with nothing between them).

You can enter a zero length string to specify that there is not a value for the field to distinguish it from fields which have a value that is unknown or not yet entered. For example, if you have a field where you list the special interests of people in your mailing list, you can enter a zero length string for those who have said that they have no special interests. By contrast, a blank entry might indicate that you do not know whether a person has a special interest.

INDEXED PROPERTY

The Index property lets you create an index based on a field of any data type except Memo, Yes/No, and OLE Object. Indexes can speed up access to data but are not necessary to using Access; they are covered in Chapter 12.

Primary Key Fields

Access can retrieve data more quickly if you designate one of its fields as a primary key. This key field must always be used when you work with relational databases. It is discussed in more detail in Chapter 6 of this book.

When you use most database programs, there is no reason to create a primary key unless you are working with relational databases, but Access is designed so that it always works more effectively if a table has a primary key.

WHAT IS A PRIMARY KEY?

A *primary key* is a field or a combination of fields that uniquely identifies each record. The most common primary key is an ID field such as Employee Number or Customer Number, which is given an arbitrary value that is different for each record in the table. This field has no purpose except to be the primary key.

Though it is possible, it is not advisable to use meaningful fields as the primary key. If you use the Last Name field (or even a combination of Last Name and First Name fields) as a primary key, for example, then you cannot add a new person to the Table who has the same name as someone who has already been entered. If someone changes his or her name, you can also lose data—or create massive data entry problems—in a relational database.

A social security number is the only meaningful field that can sometimes be used as a primary key. It was designed to be a primary key for Social Security files, and it is actually an arbitrary number assigned to each American worker. No two people have the same Social Security number, so the Social Security number uniquely identifies a person.

It is best to create a primary key by using a field of the AutoNumber data type by using an additional field. For example, use an Employee Number field as a primary key, and make it the AutoNumber data type so its values are entered automatically.

CREATING THE PRIMARY KEY

It is very easy to create the primary key field in an Access table. Define a number field in Design View as you would any other field. Select the field (for example, the AutoNumber field) and either choose the **Primary Key** option of the Edit menu, or click on the **Primary Key** tool. Access displays a key graphic to the left of the primary key field. For example, the Employee Number is the primary key field in Figure 2.16.

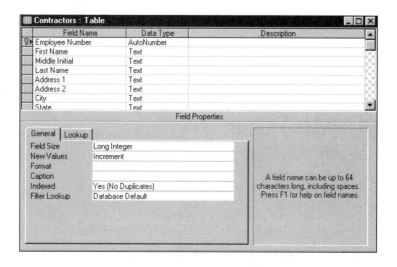

FIGURE 2.16   PRIMARY KEY FIELD.

AUTOMATICALLY CREATING A PRIMARY KEY FIELD

Access creates a primary key field for you if you do not create one yourself. When you close the Table window, Access displays the dialog box shown in Figure 2.17, and asks you if you want a primary key field defined. Click on **Yes** if you want Access to create the field.

If one of the fields in the table is the AutoNumber data type, Access designates it as the primary key. Otherwise, Access adds a new AutoNumber field to the table and gives it the name ID.

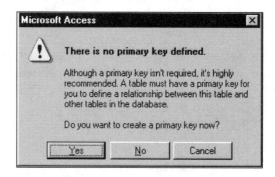

FIGURE 2.17   ACCESS CAN CREATE A PRIMARY KEY FOR YOU.

Creating a Sample Table

Now that you have learned how to design a table, you should get some hands-on experience designing and creating a sample table. The table you create in this chapter will be used again in later chapters, so you should save your work.

Our sample database will be used to record hours worked and wages paid to contractors. We will record names, addresses, hourly rate of pay, hours worked, and other basic information.

After you have learned to work with this simple database in Access, it will not be hard for you to work with a more complex relational database (covered in Chapter 6).

Planning the Table

Let's assume our company is a small software development company named "The Soft Tech Development Group." Our company has periods of heavy workloads when we need to hire contractors in addition to our regular employees. We hire three types of contractors: programmers, technical writers, and clerical help.

For each person, we must record basic data such as name and address. We will also record whether each person is a programmer, writer, or clerical. Since contractors are not always free when you call them, we will include a field to record the date when a contractor becomes available. This field can generally be left blank, but we'll fill it in when a contractor will not be available until after a certain date. We will have a field to specify whether a contractor is willing to work overtime on short notice, and finally, we'll include fields that record the hourly wage and hours worked by each contractor.

 NOTE To save data entry time as you do the exercises in this book, the sample data does not include fields for telephone number, social security number, or fax number, and they use only a five-digit zip code rather than the extended zip code.

Our company is in New York City, and most of the employees live in the New York area, but some of the contract programmers and writers live elsewhere and communicate by modem and Federal Express.

BREAKING DOWN THE DATA

It is easier to search and sort a value if it is in a field by itself. When you have the option, it is generally a good idea to break down and organize the data into more fields rather than fewer.

For example, if you create a single City/State/Zip field, you cannot produce mailing labels that are sorted by ZIP Code, and it is difficult to search for all the records from a single state or city. It is always best to have three separate fields for city, state, and ZIP code.

Likewise, if you create a single field to hold first and last names, then you cannot produce a report that is sorted by last name.

Sometimes you can create a single field for first name and middle initial, though this depends on how you want to use the data. If you want to send form letters that address the people by first name, for example, you should have a separate field for middle initial. This allows you to produce letters with the salutation *Dear John* instead of *Dear John Q.* You may also want to consider whether you need a title field for titles such as Mr., Ms., or Dr. You need this field, for example, if you want to do a mailing with a salutation like *Dear Mr. Smith*.

In the sample application, let's assume our mailings will use the first name only. Therefore, we need to put the middle initial in a separate field, and we will not use a title field.

It takes more time to work with your table if it has an extra field, but it can cause you hours of trouble later if you do not include a field you need from the start.

ONE-TO-ONE RELATIONSHIPS

You should look for one-to-one relationships of each field to each record when designing a table.

In our sample database, for example, you must consider whether there is only one of each of the fields that you plan to use in the table for each contractor. You know that each person has one first name, one last name, one address, one wage rate, and so on. All of these have a one-to-one relationship with the record.

Let's assume, also, that everyone works as either a programmer, a writer, or clerical help, but not as more than one of these. Thus, this information is in a one-to-one relationship with the record and can be kept in a single field. The easiest way to store the information is in a one-character text field, where you enter the code letter **P** for programmer, **W** for writer, or **C** for clerical.

If some contractors did more than one of these jobs, you would have to design the table differently. You could create three Yes/No fields—one for Programmer, one for Writer, and one for Clerical—and enter yes in each that applies to a given person. This would make data entry a bit harder than keeping this information in one field because you would have to move through two extra fields as you typed each record. It is best not to use this method unless it is necessary.

There is some information you must store in this database, however, that does not have a one-to-one relationship with the records in the Contractor table. You must enter the time worked more than once for each person. For example, each contractor may send in a bill and timesheet every month. You have to enter the billing date, the number of hours worked, and the amount billed each time you get a bill. All this billing data is in a many-to-one relationship with the records in your contractor file.

Think about trying to enter this data in the same table that contains fields for the contractor's name and address. You could include a billing date, hours worked, and amount billed field in each record. You would have no problem entering this data when you got your first bill, but what would you do when you got your second bill?

Would you add a new record for the contractor, so that you had to re-enter all the basic data for a contractor each time you got a bill? That would create a large table, filled with repetitive data.

Would you add new fields called Billing Date 2, Hours Worked 2, and Amount Billed 2? Soon, you would have so many fields that your table would be unwieldy. Keeping similar data in fields with different names also makes it difficult to produce a report that sums the total amount billed by each contractor.

In fact, the only viable way to record this data is by creating a separate table for it, which you could call the Billing table. This Billing table would have fields for the billing date, the number of hours worked, and the amount billed, and it would also have a key field—the Employee Number. Each record in the Contractor table also has an Employee Number field, and you would use these key fields to relate the two tables so you know which contractor each billing record applies to.

In Chapter 6, you will learn about relational databases and create a second table to store billing data. At this point, however, you cannot store this billing data in the single-table database you are working with.

Exercise: Creating a Table

Now that we have done the analysis needed to design your table, let's do the following exercise to create it. To save data entry time, we won't include some of the fields you would normally have in a table like ours, such as social security number and telephone number. The purpose of this sample table is to teach you the features of Access, rather than to give an example of an actual application.

To create the table, follow these steps:

1. If necessary, start Access and open the sample database, Teach Yourself, which you created in the exercise at the beginning of this chapter.

2. Make sure the Tables tab is displayed, and click the **New** button. Access displays the New Table dialog box. Select **Design View** and click **OK** to display the Table window in Design View.

3. The first field is the primary key. As the field name, type **Employee Number**. As the Data Type, select **AutoNumber**. Then, to make it the primary key, choose **Primary Key** from the Edit menu (or click the **Primary Key** tool). Notice that a key icon appears to the left of the field.

4. Begin adding fields for name and address. As the next field name, type **First Name**. Press **Tab** to move to the Data Type column. It displays the default data type, Text, and Properties panel. Leave Text as the Data Type. Double-click the **Field Size** property to select its default value of 50, and type **20** to replace it, as shown in Figure 2.18. You can leave the other properties as they are.

5. For the next field, enter the field name **Middle Initial**, the data type **Text**, and a field size of **1**. For the next field, enter the field name **Last Name**, the data type **Text**, and a field size of **25**.

6. For the next field, enter the field name **Address 1**, the data type **Text**, and a field size of **30**. For the next field, enter the field name **Address 2**, the data type **Text**, and a field size of **30**. For the next field, enter the field name **City**, the data type **Text**, and a field size of **25**. For the next field, enter the field name **State**, the data type **Text**, and a field size of **2**. For the next field, enter the field name **Zip**, the data type **Text**, and the field size of **5**.

Figure 2.19 show how your table looks so far now that you have added fields for all the basic name and address data, though not all the fields are visible.

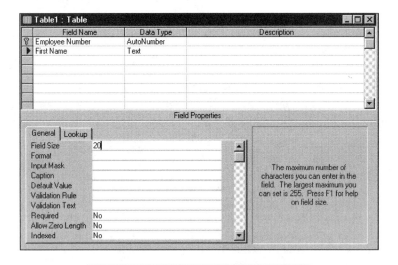

FIGURE 2.18   ADDING FIELDS TO A NEW TABLE.

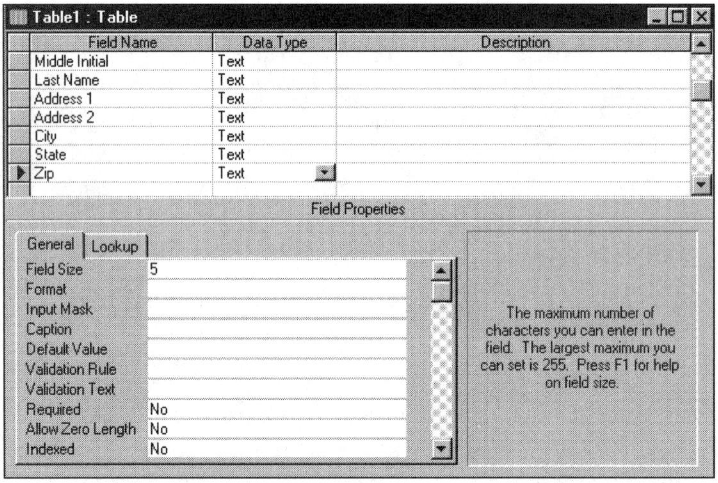

FIGURE 2.19   FIELDS FOR BASIC DATA.

Before going on, you should save your work. Choose **Save** from the File menu. In the Save As dialog box, enter the name **Contractors** and press **Enter** (or click **OK**).

Now you must add fields for the other types of data: job category (programmer, writer, or clerical), hourly wage, date available (entered only if the contractor is not currently available when you call), and whether the contractor is available for emergencies. You should also add a memo field to hold notes.

1. As the next field name, type **Job Category**. As the field type, select **Text**. Since users may need help when they are entering data in this field, enter the description **Type P for Programmer, W for Writer, or C for Clerical**. This description is displayed in the Status Bar as a help line when you enter data in this field. As the field size, enter **1**.

2. As the next field name, type **Hourly Pay**, and as the data type, select **Currency**.

3. As the next field name, type **Date Available**. As the data type, select **Date/Time**. As the description, type **Enter a date only if the Contractor is not available when you call**.

4. As the next field name, type **Emergencies**, and as the data type, select **Yes/No**.

5. As the final field name, type **Notes**, as the field type, select **Memo** as the field type. The final table design is shown in Figure 2.20, though not all fields are visible.

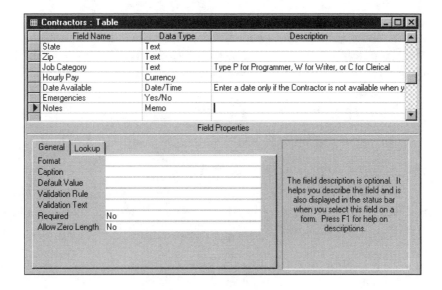

FIGURE 2.20   THE DESIGN OF THE NEW TABLE.

6. Click the Table window's **Close** button (or choose **Close** from the File menu). When Access prompts you to save changes, click **Yes**.

The new table's name is displayed in the Database window, ready for you to work on in the future.

Using Datasheet View and Design View

After you have created a table, its name is added to the Database window and you can open it at any time in either Datasheet View or Design View. You can easily switch between these two views. Datasheet View lets you add, view, or modify data. Design View lets you create or modify the design of a table.

You can open the table from the Database window in either view:

✳ Select the table and click the **Open** button to open it in Datasheet View. You can also open the table in Datasheet View simply by double-clicking on the table name.

✳ Select the table and click the **Design** button to open it in Design View, which you learned about in this chapter.

When a table is open in either of these views, the View tool is displayed on the far left of the toolbar. You can use it (or choose **Table Design** or **Datasheet** from the View menu) to switch between the two views.

Modifying the Design of a Table

You can modify the design of a table either in datasheet or design view.

MODIFYING THE DESIGN IN DATASHEET VIEW

You can make a few simple changes in the design of a table in Datasheet View—adding, deleting, or renaming fields. Simply right-click a column's heading to display its shortcut menu, shown in Figure 2.21, and then:

✳ Choose **Rename Column** to make it possible to edit the column's heading. The field will be given this new name.

✳ Choose **Insert Column** to add a new column to the left of the column whose menu you used. By default, it will be given a name such as

Field1 and will be a text field with the size 255. You can rename it using the method that was just described, and change its properties using Design View.

✳ Choose **Delete Column** to remove the column from the table.

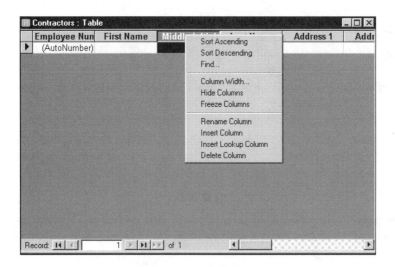

FIGURE 2.21   A COLUMN'S SHORTCUT MENU.

Rather than using the Shortcut menu, you can click a column's title to select the column, and then:

✳ Choose **Rename Column** from the Format menu to rename the column.

✳ Choose **Column** from the Insert menu to add a new column to the left of the selected column.

✳ Choose **Delete Column** from the Edit menu to remove the column.

MODIFYING THE DESIGN IN DESIGN VIEW

In Design View, you can modify the table's design using just the same methods you used to create the table initially. You can make selections from list boxes, use the usual Access editing methods to change specifications entered as text, and also select, delete, insert, or move rows in Design View just as you do when you are editing the data in a table in Datasheet View.

Because these techniques are most important in editing data, they are discussed in detail in Chapter 3. Once you have become accustomed to editing data in Access, you will find it very easy to use the same techniques to modify the table design.

DATA LOSS WHEN MODIFYING A TABLE

WARNING

When you modify the design of a table that you have already added data to, there is a danger of data loss. If you have changed the design in a way that might destroy data, Access warns you when you save the change.

If you delete a field, you will lose all data you entered in that field. The following sections describe the other changes are the most likely to cause data loss.

DATA LOSS WHEN CHANGING FIELD SIZE

If you make a field size smaller, you lose existing data that cannot fit into the new size of the field. For example, text data is truncated if you reduce the size of a text field to 20 characters from 30 characters. Fields with data longer than 20 characters retain only the first 20 characters, and discard the rest.

Number data is rounded to fit into the new size, with a loss of some decimal places. Fields that do not fit in the range of values that can be held by the new size lose their data entirely and are displayed as blank fields. For example, if you change the size of a number field to Byte, all values are rounded to the nearest integer and decimal places are lost. Any value that is not between 0 and 255 is lost completely and replaced with a blank field.

DATA LOSS WHEN CHANGING DATA TYPE

If you change the data type of a field, all data that cannot be held in the new field type is lost. For example, if you change a text field to a number field, any character in the text field that is not a number is lost.

ADDING A PRIMARY KEY

If you designate an existing field as a primary key, any records with duplicate data in that field are discarded because a Primary Key must have a unique value in each field.

Making a Backup Copy

When modifying a table design, it is good practice to copy the existing table to a temporary table to have a backup in case a mistake is made.

SHORTCUT

The easiest way to do this is to select the object name and select **Copy** from the Edit menu (or press **Ctrl-C**), then choose **Paste** from the Edit menu or press **Ctrl-V** to paste the object with a new name. Access displays the Paste Table As dialog box, shown in Figure 2.22. Leave the **Structure and Data** option buttons selected, and enter a new table name.

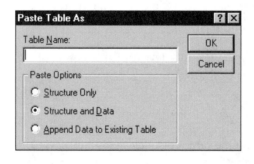

FIGURE 2.22 THE PASTE TABLE AS DIALOG BOX.

For example, highlight **Contractors**, press **Ctrl-C**, then **Ctrl-V**. Access will prompt you for a new name. Enter **Contractors 2** and press **Enter**. Now you can modify Contractors with Contractors 2 as a backup copy. This utility and others like it will be covered more systematically in Chapter 12.

Advanced Topics

The Table window has a few advanced features in Design View that are not necessary for beginners to learn. These features can be very useful because they give you more control over what data can be entered and let you reduce data-entry errors. Because beginners may not want to take the time to learn them at this stage in their study of Access, these features are placed in this separate section. Most readers should skim this section to see what these features are and either learn them now or come back to them later when you reach a point where they will be useful. Readers who are using this book to get up and running as quickly as possible can simply skip this section.

Though this section does not include exercises, you might want to try some of the features described as you read about them. If so, you should begin by creating a copy of the Contractors table, which you can use to test these features of table design.

1. In the Database window, select the **Contractors** table. Then choose **Copy** from the Edit menu and **Paste** from the Edit menu. In the Paste As dialog box, enter **Contractors 2** as the new name of the table, and click **OK**.

2. Select your Contractors 2 backup table and click **Design** to display it in Design View.

Now, you can try changing the design of this new table as you read the rest of this section.

Input Masks

Text, number, date/time, and currency fields can have a field Input Mask property that specifies the format in which data is entered. Do not confuse an input mask with a format. A format specifies the format in which data is displayed, not how it is entered.

You can create your own input masks by typing the input mask characters, shown in Table 2.2, in the Input Mask property box.

TABLE 2.2   INPUT MASK CHARACTERS.

Character	Meaning
0	Number required
9	Number or space can be entered but is not required
#	Number, plus or minus sign, or space can be entered but not required
L	Letter required

?	Letter can be entered but not required
A	Letter or number required
a	Letter or number can be entered but not required
&	Any character or a space required
C	Any character or a space can be entered but not required
<	Characters that follow converted to lowercase
>	Characters that follow converted to uppercase
!	Characters fill from right to left rather than from left to right. Can be used when characters on the left are optional, and can be included anywhere in the mask.
****	Following character is displayed literally rather than read as a code.

Other characters can be used literally in an input mask and will be inserted in the data that is entered. In addition, separators such as the decimal point (.), the thousands (,), the date (/) and the time (:) can be entered and will be used literally.

An input mask can be useful for a social security number, for example. Use the mask 000-00-0000 to require the numbers be entered and to display the hyphens literally in the appropriate places between the numbers. When you enter data in the table, the hyphens are displayed in the places you indicated, and there are spaces for the entry of the numbers.

STORING INSERTED CHARACTERS

You can also add a comma followed by a 0 after the input mask to specify that the inserted characters from the input mask should be stored in the table. If you leave out this part or enter a comma followed by a 1, Access stores only the characters that are entered, not those that are part of the input mask. For example, if you use the mask 000-00-0000,0, Access stores the hyphens as well as the numbers in the table. If you use the mask 000-00-0000 or 000-00-0000,1, Access stores only the numbers without the hyphens.

When you define the length of the field, you must take into account whether you are going to store these inserted characters. If you do not store them, you have to use the Format property to display them.

DISPLAYING SPACES

You can also enter a third part to the input mask that specifies how blank spaces are displayed. After the second part of the mask, add any character following a comma. For financial uses, for example, it is common to display spaces as asterisks for security, like this:

```
$ 00.00,0,*.
```

THE INPUT MASK WIZARD

You can also use the Input Mask Wizard to generate these input masks for you. To use this Wizard, click the **Input Mask** property to display a **...** button (called a Builder button) to its right and then click this button. Alternatively, click anywhere on this property box with the right mouse button to display the shortcut menu is displayed, and choose the **Build** option from this menu. Since you have already learned to create custom Input Masks, you will find this wizard very easy to use.

Lookup Fields

If you create a Lookup field, the user can select the value in the field from a drop-down list, rather than entering it an a text box in the usual way. There are two types of list that can be used:

* **Combo Box:** a combination of a text box and drop-down list, which lets the user enter a value in the text box or select the value from the list.
* **List Box:** requires the user to select the values from the list.

A list box restricts the user more than a combo box, and so it is useful for fields that can only take certain values.

Which of these you choose, there are two possible sources for the data displayed in the list. You can type a list of values to display in the list, or you can display the values from an existing table or query.

To create either of these, it is easiest to start by choosing **Lookup Wizard** from the Data Type drop-down of the field to display the Lookup Wizard, and use it to create a new lookup field. The properties of the Lookup field defined by the Wizard are displayed in the Lookup tab for that field, and you can modify them using the Table window in Design View.

N O T E

The most important of these is the Display Control property, which you can use to select **Combo Box** or **List Box**. The Wizard creates a Combo Box by default, and if you want to limit the user's choices, you can select **List Box** as this property. To learn about other properties, select one and press **F1** to display help on it.

When you select **Lookup Wizard** from the Data Type drop-down to display the Wizard, its first step, shown in Figure 2.23, lets you specify whether you want to get the values from an existing table or from a list you type in. The steps in the rest of the Wizard depend on which of these you choose.

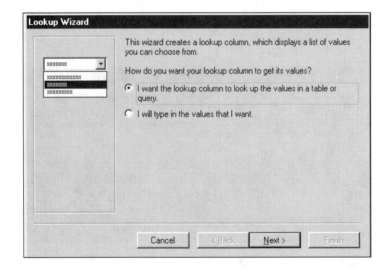

FIGURE 2.23 **CHOOSING THE TYPE OF LOOKUP.**

N O T E

If you want to try experimenting with the Lookup fields, at this point, you should try creating a field that reads values from a list: it should be easy for you to follow the illustrations below, to create a Lookup field that you can use to select a Job Category. Because it is particularly useful when you are working with relational databases, an exercise on using a lookup field that gets data from another table will be included in Chapter 6.

TYPING IN A LIST

If you choose to type in a list, the second step lets you choose how many columns to display and type in the values in those columns. A table with the number of columns that you enter is displayed below, and you can enter values in it just as you do in an ordinary Access table.

You might want to display multiple columns if the one that you want to add to the table is not clear. For example, if you are using a lookup list to enter data in the job category field of your sample table, just displaying the letters P, W, and C could be confusing for the data entry person. It would be better to display two columns, the first with these letters, and the second with the words Programmer, Writer, and Clerical, as shown in Figure 2.24. You can also click and drag the right edge of the title of one of these columns to change its width: in the illustration, Col1 has been narrowed, because it only holds one letter.

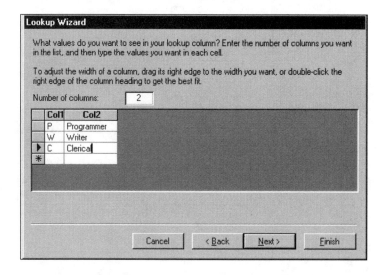

FIGURE 2.24   ENTERING VALUES DISPLAYED IN THE LOOKUP LIST.

If you use multiple columns, the next step, shown in Figure 2.25, lets you specify from which column the values should be taken that are stored in the table; this step is omitted if you include only one column. In the example using the Job Category field, you would store values from the first column, which holds the letters that are actually stored in these fields; the second column is only there to make it easier for the user.

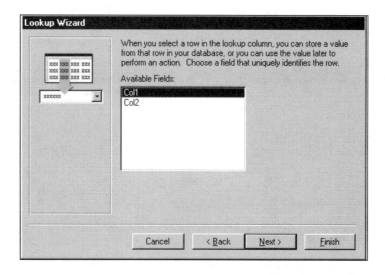

FIGURE 2.25 **CHOOSING WHICH VALUES WILL BE STORED.**

The Final step simply lets you enter the a label used for the drop-down that this wizard will generate. The name of the field is used by default and is generally the best lable.

Figure 2.26 shows Lookup properties generated by the Wizard to let you select values for the Job Category field. After generating these properties using the Wizard, you should select **List Box** (rather than the default Combo Box) as the Display Control Property (or select **Yes** as the Limit to List Property), so the user can never enter any values in this field except P, W, and C. Figure 2.27 shows how this field is used for data entry.

USING VALUES FROM A TABLE

It is particularly useful to include values from a table when you are working with a relational database. As you will learn in Chapter 6, in a relational database with two tables, the key field in one of the tables must be present in the other table. This option also has some advanced features, used only by programmers.

If you select the radio button in the first step of the wizard that has the lookup field "get values from another table," the steps that follow let you choose the table or query that the fields are taken from and let you specify which fields of the table or query are displayed in the list.

Chapter 6 discusses this type of Lookup field in more detail and shows how it can be used with a relational database.

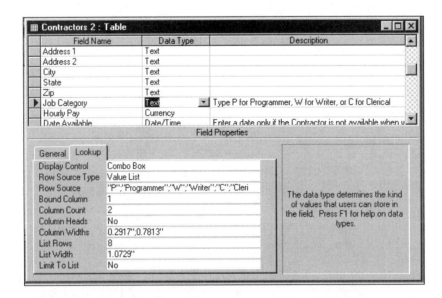

FIGURE 2.26   LOOKUP PROPERTIES FOR THE JOB CATEGORY FIELD.

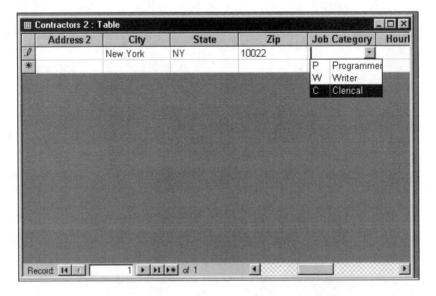

FIGURE 2.27   USING THIS LOOKUP FIELD FOR DATA ENTRY.

To Sum Up

In this chapter, you created a database file and designed a table.

You learned that you must look carefully at the application you are working with before designing the table to decide what data you need and how to break it up into fields. You now know to make sure that the fields in your table are in a one-to-one relationship, so that you do not have to use a multitable database, and that it is best to give an Access table one field that is its primary key. (In Chapter 6, you will learn to use multitable databases.)

To design the table, you used the Table window in Design View and specified what fields the table should have. You entered the name and data type of each field in the table and properties such as Field Size for some fields. After you designed the table, you saved it and named it using Access naming conventions.

Now that you have created a sample table, you can go on in the next chapter to work with data.

CHAPTER 3

Working with Data

In the last chapter, you created a sample table named Contractors, and you learned how to display it in Design View and Datasheet View. Now you are ready to work with this table in Datasheet View to add, edit, and view data. Often, you can make it easier to add data by creating data-entry forms, which you will learn about in later chapters. However, working in Datasheet View is the easiest way to work with many database applications and is a common way of working with tables. In this chapter, you will learn to:

* add and edit data
* move among records you have already added
* delete records
* use shortcuts that save data entry time
* search for records containing specific data
* search using partial values and wildcard characters
* replace data quickly
* perform a quick sort on a table

71

✳ move, hide, resize, and freeze columns for easier viewing

✳ change fonts and row sizes to create more attractive datasheets

✳ print datasheets

Adding and Editing Data

In the last chapter, you learned to open and close a table:

✳ To open a table, highlight the name of the table you want in the Database window and then click the **Open** button or press **Enter**. You can also double-click the name to open the table. If you are working with several types of objects, you may have to select the **Tables** tab in the Database window to display a list of tables.

✳ To close a table, select **Close** from the File menu or click the **Close** box of the Table window.

You also learned that you can switch between Design View and Datasheet View by using the **View** tool on the toolbar or by choosing **Table Design** or **Datasheet** from the View menu.

You already know how to work with the table in Design View to define the fields that make up the table and specify their properties. In this chapter, you will work with the table in Datasheet View to add, edit, and view data. When you first open a table, it is displayed in Datasheet View, so you can enter data.

The Basics

You use the Access editor to add new records or modify existing records. Before we go into more detail about the editor, though, you should be familiar with a few general ways of working with records.

ENTERING DATA

As you enter data, these three graphics are displayed in the record selector box, which is the farthest left of each row of the fields in the datasheet:

 Asterisk—Access automatically adds blank records or rows to the end of the table as you add data. The blank record is marked with an asterisk in the left column to indicate that it will not be saved when you close the table.

Arrowhead—If you highlight or move the cursor to a record, an arrowhead is displayed to its left, indicating that it is the current record.

Pencil—While you are entering or editing data in a record, the arrowhead is replaced by a pencil to indicate changes are being made but not yet saved.

> **NOTE** You can also make any record the current record by moving the cursor to one of its fields. The easiest way to do this is by clicking on a field.

SELECTING RECORDS

You can select a record by clicking its record selector box. When you move the pointer to this box, it is displayed as a right-pointing arrow; when you click it, all the fields in the record are highlighted, as shown in Figure 3.1. You can also select records by choosing **Select Record** from the Edit menu to select the current record or **Select All Records** from the Edit menu to select all the records.

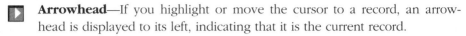

Employee Num	First Name	Middle Initial	Last Name	Address 1	Addr
1	Carla	R	Tannenbaum	1637 Fordham F	
2	Peter		Woodworth	Star Consultant	4152 Fr
3	Kevin	M	Smith	42 Elm Circle	
4	Samuel		Smalz	1701 Albemarle	
5	Jessica		Smythe	WordSmiths	910 Uni
6	Josephine	B	Estevis	47 Bleeker St.	
7	Sidney		Smithson	Computer Tool \	7943-23
(AutoNumber)					

FIGURE 3.1   SELECTING A RECORD.

You can select groups of records in the following ways:

✳ Click the record selector box of one field, hold down the mouse button, and drag up or down across the boxes of adjacent records to select all these records.

✳ Select a record, and hold down the **Shift** key while you click the record selector box of another record to select the two records and all the records between them.

NOTE

You can also select columns in much the same way as you select records. Later in this chapter, you will learn how to work with columns and to select blocks of data by clicking and dragging over them.

These methods of selection make it easy to add new records and modify or delete existing ones, once you have learned to use the Access editor.

The Access Editor

Editing data in Access is similar in many ways to editing text in other Windows applications, but it is also different in ways that make it easier to enter data.

In Access, as in other Windows applications, you can select (highlight) text, and it will be replaced by anything you type or be deleted if you press the **Delete** or the **Backspace** key. You can also place an insertion point in the text, so that text is inserted at that point. Using the insertion point also enables you to use the **Delete** key to delete a single character to its right and the **Backspace** key to delete a single character to its left.

If you are working with an insertion point and press the **Insert** key, you toggle from insert mode to overwrite mode, and each character you type replaces a character of the existing text. You can press **Insert** again to toggle back to insert mode.

SPECIAL KEYBOARD BEHAVIOR

The Access editor also allows you to use the keyboard in some ways that are different from other Windows applications, which makes it easier to move around tables of data.

In most Windows applications, if text is selected (highlighted), you deselect it by pressing any of the cursor movement keys—the **Arrow** keys, **Home**, **End**, **PgUp**, or **PgDn**. In Access, these keys are used to move among records and fields.

If you use the keyboard to move the highlight to a field, the data in that field is selected. As in other Windows applications, anything you type replaces the selected text. However, pressing any of the cursor movement keys moves the highlight to another record or field, and the highlight is not replaced with an insertion point. For example, in other Windows applications, pressing the **Left Arrow** key deselects text and places an insertion point at the left of the text. In Access, pressing the **Left Arrow** key moves the highlight one field to the left and selects all the data in that field.

By default, the data in fields is always selected as you use the keyboard to move through datasheet. To place an insertion point in the field using the keyboard, press **F2**. You can then use the cursor movement keys to move the insertion point within the field. Use the **Left** or **Right Arrow** keys to move one character left or right, and the **Home** or **End** key to move to the beginning or end of the data in the field.

The **F2** key is a toggle. If you are working with an insertion point, you can press it again to select the text in the field.

NOTE

Table 3.1 summarizes the use of all of the cursor movement keys when there is selected text or an insertion point. Whenever you use one of these keys to move to another field, the data in that field is selected, and you must press **F2** if you want to use an insertion point again.

TABLE 3.1   CURSOR MOVEMENT KEYS IN DATASHEET VIEW.

Key	Selected Data	Insertion Point
Left, **Right Arrow**	Moves one field left or right	Moves one character left or right
Up, **Down Arrow**	Moves one record up or down	Moves one record up or down
Ctrl-Left Arrow, **Ctrl-Right Arrow**	Moves one field left or right	Moves one word left or right
Ctrl-Up Arrow, **Ctrl-Down Arrow**	Moves insertion to beginning or end of field	Moves insertion point to beginning or end of field
PgUp, **PgDn**	Scrolls up or down one window	Scrolls up or down one window

continued

Key	Selected Data	Insertion Point
Ctrl-PgUp, **Ctrl-PgDn**	Scrolls left or right one window	Scrolls left or right one window
Home, **End**	Moves to first or last field of record	Moves to beginning or end of field
Ctrl-Home, **Ctrl-End**	Moves to first or last field of table	Moves to beginning or end of field
Tab	Moves to next field	Moves to next field
Shift-Tab	Moves to previous field	Moves to previous field
Enter	Moves to next field	Moves to next field

N O T E

If you are not comfortable with keyboard behavior that is different from other applications you are accustomed to, you can easily change Access' default keyboard behavior, by using the Options dialog box, covered in Chapter 12.

USING THE MOUSE

The mouse, by contrast to the keyboard, is used for editing in Access as it is in other Windows applications:

❋ To select the data in a field, double-click it.

❋ To place an insertion point in the field, click the location where you want the insertion point.

❋ To find the data you want, scroll through the table using the scroll bars at the side and bottom of the Table window.

Adding and Modifying Records

To add a new record to the table, move the highlight to the blank record that Access automatically adds to the end of the table. This is marked with an asterisk on the left. Add the data to it using the editor techniques described previously. In a table with many records, you might find it useful to use one of the following methods to move the highlight to the new record:

✳ Choose **GoTo** and then **New** from the Edit menu.

✳ Click the **New** tool (which has an asterisk on it).

✳ Press **Ctrl-+** (hold down the **Ctrl** key and press the **+** key).

To edit an existing record, move the highlight to the record and change the data in it using the editor techniques described previously. Methods for moving among existing records and finding a specific record are described later in this chapter.

> When you move to the record, a right arrowhead is displayed in the selection box to show that it is the current or active record.
>
> N O T E

USING DATA ENTRY MODE

Sometimes it is more convenient to add new records without displaying the records already in the table. To do this, choose **Data Entry** from the Records menu. Access hides all the existing records in the table and displays a blank record, as shown in Figure 3.2. You make entries in the usual way, but only the new data you enter in the table is displayed.

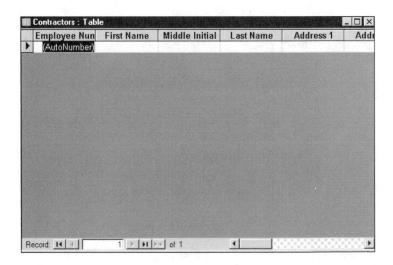

FIGURE 3.2   DATA ENTRY MODE.

CANCELING AN ENTRY

When you begin to make a new entry or edit an existing record, the pencil is displayed to the left of the record. This indicates that the record has been changed but not saved.

N O T E

As long as the pencil is displayed, you can cancel all the changes in the current field by pressing **Esc**. Pressing **Esc** a second time cancels all the changes you made in the record.

SAVING AN ENTRY

Changes you make to a record are automatically saved when you move the highlight to another record, so there is usually no need to explicitly save your data.

If you want to save the current record while you are still working on it, you can do so by choosing **Save Record** from the Record menu or by clicking the **Save** tool on the toolbar (which has a picture of a floppy disk) or by pressing **Shift-Enter**.

DELETING A RECORD

To delete a record, select the entire row and then choose **Delete** from the Edit menu or press the **Del** key. You can also select multiple records and delete them all in the same way. In either case, Access displays the dialog box shown in Figure 3.3, telling you the number of records you deleted and giving you the opportunity to confirm or cancel your change.

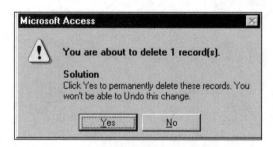

FIGURE 3.3   CONFIRMATION DIALOG BOX.

SPECIAL CONSIDERATIONS FOR DATA ENTRY

You generally enter values into fields using the Access editor described earlier in this chapter. There are a few data types that are entered differently, however.

YES/NO FIELDS

A Yes/No field is displayed as a checkbox. Click it to add or remove the checkmark. Using the keyboard, press the spacebar to add or remove the checkmark.

MEMO FIELDS

Memo fields are entered and edited in the much same way as ordinary text fields. You can enter an indefinite amount of text, and scroll through the field to view it.

If you want to enter more than one paragraph in a memo field, you can press **Ctrl-Enter** to add a line break, since pressing **Enter** will move you to the next field rather than beginning a new paragraph. Once you have added multiple paragraphs, you can use the **Up** and **Down Arrow** keys to move among them when you are working with the insertion point, and you can use the **Left** and **Right Arrow** keys to move within each paragraph.

It is difficult to work with multiparagraph memo fields in Datasheet View. If you have lengthy memo fields, you should create a form to work with them, using the methods covered in Chapters 5 and 7.

OLE OBJECT FIELDS

Object Linking and Embedding (OLE) lets you store objects from other Windows applications, such as pictures, sounds, spreadsheets, or videos, in Access databases. A common use of OLE is to store pictures of people in a database, along with their names and addresses.

Because OLE is a powerful and advanced technique that can be used in many ways, it is discussed at length in Chapter 12.

LOOKUP FIELDS

Lookup fields let you choose data from drop-down lists, and they were covered at the end of Chapter 2.

Data Entry Shortcuts

In addition to the methods described previously, there are a few shortcuts that can save you data entry time.

COPYING DATA FROM THE PREVIOUS RECORD

You can copy data from the same field of the previous record by pressing **Ctrl–'** or **Ctrl–"** (hold down the **Ctrl** key and type either a single or double quotation mark).

INSERTING THE CURRENT DATE OR TIME

To insert the current date, press **Ctrl–;**. To insert the current time, press **Ctrl–:**.

INSERTING DEFAULT VALUES

If you have defined a default value for a field (using the Default Value property described in Chapter 2), you can enter it in the field by pressing **Ctrl-Alt-Spacebar**.

The default value is entered in the field automatically when the record is created, but you may want to use this key combination to reenter the default value in a field that you edited earlier.

WINDOW EDITOR FUNCTIONS

You can also use the usual Window editor functions to save time when you are entering data.

CUTTING, COPYING, AND PASTING

To use cut and paste, first select the text you want to remove. Then choose **Cut** from the Edit menu or press **Ctrl-X**. The text is placed in the Windows clipboard, an area of memory used to store data temporarily. If you select a record or a number of records and choose **Cut** from the Edit menu, Access asks for confirmation, just as it does when you delete records, since you are removing the records from the table.

To copy text, select it and then choose **Copy** from the Edit menu or press **Ctrl-C**. The text remains in its current location, and a copy is placed in the Windows clipboard.

You can paste the contents of the clipboard in any appropriate location; for example, if a record is in the clipboard, you must select a record before pasting. Choose **Paste** from the Edit menu, or press **Ctrl-V**.

WARNING

Whenever you use cut or copy, you must remember that the clipboard holds only one piece of data at a time. When you cut or copy something else, it replaces any data that is already in the clipboard.

Copying and pasting are particularly useful if you select an entire record. Click the selection arrow to the left of a record to select all the fields of that record, then select **Copy** from the Edit menu to place the entire record in the clipboard. You can copy a name and address out of an Access table in this way, and then paste it into a letter in a Windows word processing program.

Paste Append

In addition to the ordinary **Paste** command, Access has a **Paste Append** command that creates a new record containing the contents of the clipboard.

If you are entering a new record with data similar to an existing one, you can select and copy the existing record, as described above, and then choose **Paste Append** from the Edit menu to add a second copy of that record to the end of the table. You can then edit the second record as necessary. You can also select and copy a record from a different table and then return to the current table and use the Paste Append option to add it to the table. When you append a record to a datasheet in this way, Access pastes data into the columns of the table in the same order they appear in the original table, regardless of the names of the fields. If the fields are not in the same order in the two tables, you can move the columns of the datasheet you are appending data to, so that they match the order of the columns in the datasheet that you are copying data from. These methods are described later in this chapter.

As you learned earlier, you can also select multiple records in a table by clicking and dragging the mouse through their selection boxes. You can choose **Copy** from the Edit menu to copy them all, and then choose **Paste Append** to add them all to a table.

Undoing the Last Change

 You can choose **Undo** from the Edit menu or click the **Undo** tool to undo the last change you made.

You can also undo the last change simply by pressing the **Esc** key.

Moving Among Records

After you have entered data, you can move among the fields of existing records by using the cursor movement keys and scroll bars, as described earlier in this chapter. To move quickly among records, choose **Go To** from the Edit menu to display the submenu shown in Figure 3.4, which has these choices:

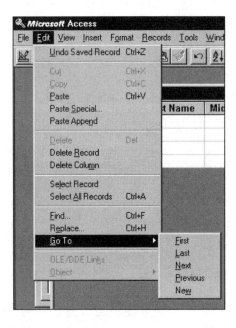

FIGURE 3.4   THE GO TO SUBMENU AND RECORD TOOLS.

✳ **First** moves to the first record in the table.

✳ **Last** moves to the last record in the table.

✳ **Next** moves to the next record after the current record.

✳ **Previous** moves to the record before the current record.

✳ **New** moves to the blank record marked by an asterisk at the end of the table.

Access also has five arrow tools on the lower border of the Table window in Datasheet View that are equivalent to the GoTo commands.

The record indicator, in the center of the record tools, displays the number of the current record. You can change this record number to move to a different record. Double-click the record number or press **F5** to select it (or click it to add an insertion point). Type a new record number and press **Enter** to make the new record the current record. Figure 3.4 above illustrates the record tools and indicator.

> If you are working with a large table, you will probably find it easier to use the **Find** option to move to the record you want.

N O T E

The **Find** option is discussed later in this chapter, but before you look at it, you should add some data to your sample table to consolidate what you have learned already.

Adding Data

Now, let's add some sample data to the table you created in Chapter 2. This will get you accustomed to the methods of data entry used in Access and will provide sample data to use for future exercises when you produce forms and reports and work with a relational database.

> This exercise assumes that you did not do the optional exercise to define the Job Category as a Lookup field in Chapter 2. If you did, there will be slight differences in data entry from what is described in the exercise.

N O T E

1. If necessary, start Access. Open the **Teach Yourself** database, then open the **Contractors** table in Datasheet View.

2. The employee number will be entered automatically. Simply press **Tab** to move the highlight to the First Name field and type **Carla**. Notice that as soon as you begin to make an entry, the pencil is displayed to the left of the first record, a new record with the asterisk to its left is added to the table, and the Employee Number 1 is entered for the first record.

3. Press **Tab** and type **R** in the Middle Initial field. Press **Tab** and type **Tannenbaum** in the Last Name field. Press **Tab** and type **1637 Fordham Rd.** in the Address 1 field. Press **Tab** twice to skip Address 2, and in the City field, type **Bronx**. Press **Tab** and in the State field, type **NY**. In the Zip field, type **10423**.

4. Press **Tab** to move to the Job Category field. Notice the field description you entered when you defined the table, "Type P for Programmer, W for Writer or C for Clerical," is displayed in the status bar. Type **P**. Press **Tab** to move to the Hourly Pay field, and type **95**. Press **Tab**. Notice this number is displayed as $95.00 because it is a currency field, and is displayed by default in this format.

5. Leave the Date Available field blank and press **Tab** to move to the Emergencies field. Press the spacebar to enter a check in this box and press **Tab**. In the Notes field, type **Low level database programming in C++ language**. Notice how the memo field scrolls to hold an indefinite amount of text, as shown in Figure 3.5. Press **Tab** to move to the next record. Access saves the first record as it makes the second record the current record.

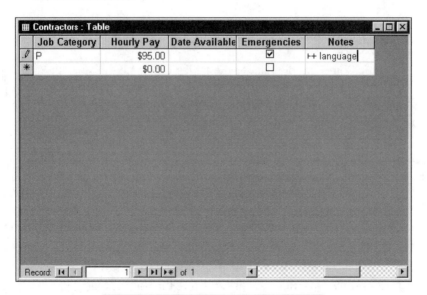

FIGURE 3.5 ENTERING TEXT IN A MEMO FIELD.

Now that you have gotten a feel for how to move among fields, you should enter the data listed below, so you have a few more sample records in the table to work with in later exercises.

Do not enter values in parentheses. The employee numbers are entered automatically in the Counter field, and they are included in parentheses to make it easier to keep track of the records as you enter them. Likewise, (none) simply means there is nothing to enter in the field.

Employee Number	(2)
First Name	Peter
Middle Initial	(none)
Last Name	Woodworth
Address 1	Star Consultants
Address 2	4152 Front St., #314
City	Hoboken
State	NJ
Zip	07030
Job Category	P
Hourly Pay	80
Date Available	7/1/96
Emergencies	(No)
Notes	Programs the user interface in C++

Employee Number	(3)
First Name	Kevin
Middle Initial	M
Last Name	Smith
Address 1	42 Elm Circle
Address 2	(none)
City	Greenwich
State	CT
Zip	06830
Job Category	W
Hourly Pay	55
Date Available	(none)
Emergencies	√(Yes)
Notes	Designed and wrote manual for our financial analysis software

Employee Number	(4)
First Name	Samuel
Middle Initial	(none)
Last Name	Smalz
Address 1	1701 Albemarle Rd. Apt. D-14
Address 2	(none)
City	Brooklyn
State	NY
Zip	11226
Job Category	C
Hourly Pay	9
Date Available	(none)
Emergencies	√(Yes)
Notes	(none)

Employee Number	(5)
First Name	Jessica
Middle Initial	(none)
Last Name	Smythe
Address 1	WordSmiths
Address 2	910 University Ave.
City	Berkeley
State	CA
Zip	94709
Job Category	W
Hourly Pay	50
Date Available	9/1/96
Emergencies	(No)
Notes	Complete manual writing service

Employee Number	(6)
First Name	Josephine
Middle Initial	B
Last Name	Estevis
Address 1	47 Bleeker St.
Address 2	(none)
City	New York
State	NY
Zip	10010
Job Category	P
Hourly Pay	90
Date Available	12/1/96
Emergencies	√(Yes)
Notes	Programs user interface in C++ or Visual BASIC

Employee Number	(7)
First Name	Sidney
Middle Initial	(none)
Last Name	Smithson
Address 1	Computer Tool Works
Address 2	7943-2301 Technology Parkway
City	Provo
State	UT
Zip	84601
Job Category	P
Hourly Pay	150
Date Available	(none)
Emergencies	(No)
Notes	Provides customized functions for financial calculations in C++, Xbase, and COBOL

After you have finished entering the data, your table should look like the one in Figure 3.6.

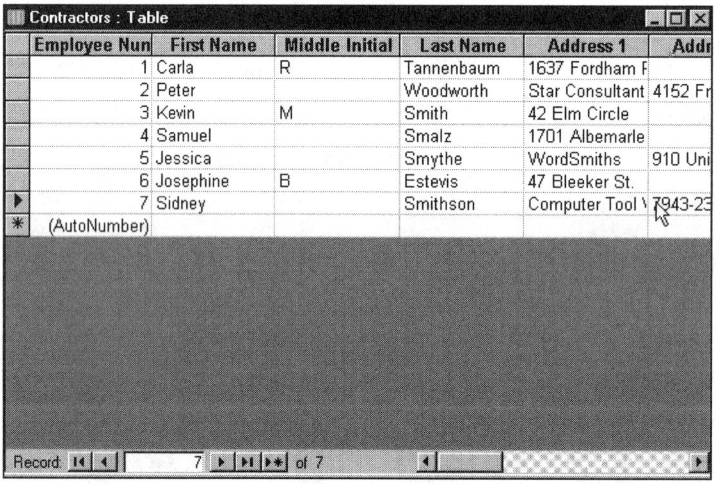
Contractors : Table
Employee Num
First Name
Middle Initial
Last Name
Address 1
Addr
1 Carla R Tannenbaum 1637 Fordham F
2 Peter Woodworth Star Consultant 4152 Fr
3 Kevin M Smith 42 Elm Circle
4 Samuel Smalz 1701 Albemarle
5 Jessica Smythe WordSmiths 910 Uni
6 Josephine B Estevis 47 Bleeker St.
7 Sidney Smithson Computer Tool \ 7943-23
(AutoNumber)
Record: 7 of 7

FIGURE 3.6 SAMPLE DATA IN THE CONTRACTORS TABLE.

Finding Records

It is common to want to find a record based on its contents. There are two ways you might want to do this:

- Find a single record—for example, look up a person by name.
- Isolate a group of records—for example, find all the people in your table who are programmers.

In this section, you look at finds, which are used to look up a single record. Chapter 4 discusses queries and filters, which are used to find a group of records.

This is the simplest way to find a single record:

1. Place the cursor in a field that contains the data you want to search for. Choose **Find** from the Edit menu to display the Find dialog box, shown in Figure 3.7. You can also click the **Find** tool, which looks like a pair of binoculars, to display the dialog box. 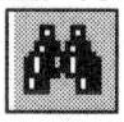

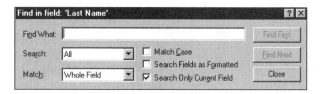

FIGURE 3.7   THE FIND DIALOG BOX.

2. Enter the value you are searching for in the Find What text box. You can enter text and/or numbers.

3. Click the **Find First** button to find the first occurrence of the value in that field, or click the **Find Next** button to find the next occurrence of the value in the field.

4. If the record you have found is not the one you want, continue to click the **Find Next** button until you reach the record you want. The dialog box remains open until you select the **Close** button.

If you begin the search by clicking **Find Next**, Access lets you continue the search at the beginning of the table after it reaches the end so that you can scan the entire table.

If you are searching for the record of someone whose last name is Smith and you think the record is near the beginning of the table, for example, place the cursor in the Last Name field, enter **Smith** in the Find What text box, and click the **Find First** button to go to the first Smith in the table. If that is not the right person, click the **Find Next** button repeatedly until you get to the right Smith. When you find the right person, click the **Close** button to close the Find dialog box and return to the table, with that record as the current record.

Find Options

In addition to this simple search, there are a few other options in the Find dialog box.

COMPLETE OR PARTIAL MATCH

By default, Access looks for a complete match. The value you enter in the Find What text box must be the same as the entire entry in the field.

You can use the Match drop-down list to search for these types of partial matches:

✳ **Start of Field** finds all records that begin with the value you entered. For example, if you search for the last name Smith, Access would find records that have Smithson or Smithe as the last name, as well as Smith.

✳ **Any Part of Field** finds records that have the value anywhere in the field. This is very useful if, for example, you are searching for an address and you remember only the street name, not the street number.

If you have changed this feature earlier, select the **Whole Field** option in this drop-down to return to the default.

SEARCHING ALL FIELDS

By default, the **Find** option searches for the value you entered only in the current field (the field where the cursor was when you began the search). To make this clear, the title of the dialog box is Find in field: followed by the field name.

If you deselect the **Search Only Current Field** checkbox, **Find** searches for the value in all the fields of the table. The title of the dialog box changes to Find (rather than including the field's name) to make this clear.

N O T E

Searching all fields is slower than searching only the current field; you should use this option only if you have some special reason to do so.

MATCH CASE

By default, finds do not distinguish between upper- and lowercase letters. If you search for Smith, for example, you will also find records with SMITH and smith in them.

Select the **Match Case** checkbox if you want to find records with the text capitalized exactly as it is where you entered it.

SEARCHES BASED ON FORMAT

By default, the value you enter must match the value in the table. Select the **Search Fields as Formatted** checkbox if you want to search for the value as it is displayed, based on the display format you specified for the field.

For example, ordinarily you would search for a date by entering something like **11/15/96** in the Find What text box. If you select this option, you could search for that same date by entering **15 Nov 96**, assuming you formatted the date field so it is displayed in that way.

N O T E

This option slows down the find, and you should use it only if you have some special reason to do so.

Finds Using Wild Cards

Rather than entering an exact value in the Find What text box, you can use the wild card characters shown in Table 3.2 as part or all of the value you are searching for.

TABLE 3.2   WILDCARD CHARACTERS FOR FINDS.

Character	Meaning	Example
?	Matches any single character	Sm?th matches Smith, Smyth, Smeth
*	Matches any number of characters	Sm* matches Smith, Smyth, Smithson, Smythers
[ ]	Matches all options enclosed in brackets	Sm[iy]th matches Smith or Smyth but not Smeth
[!]	Matches all options not enclosed in brackets	Sm[!i]th matches Smyth or Smeth but not Smith
[–]	Matches a range of characters	[a-d]* matches any value beginning with a, b, c, or d The hyphen must separate single letters only.

Find and Replace

Access includes a Find and Replace feature, which gives you a quick way of changing records on the basis of their content.

Choose **Replace** from the Edit menu to display the Replace dialog box, shown in Figure 3.8. As you can see, all the controls in this dialog box are the same as controls in the Find dialog box, with one exception. This dialog box also has a Replace With text box, where you can enter a new value to replace the one in the Find What text box.

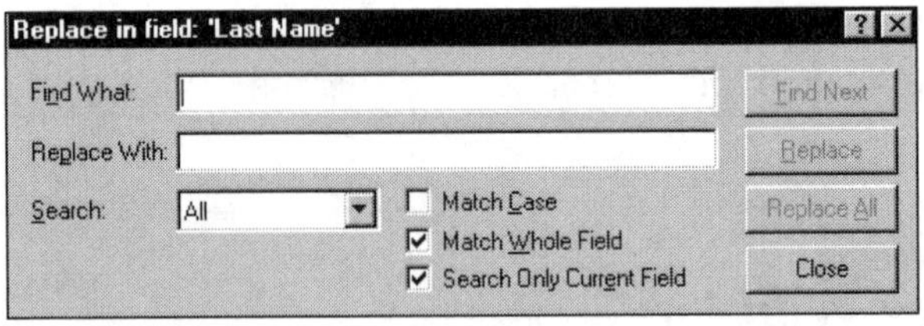

FIGURE 3.8   THE REPLACE DIALOG BOX.

You can select **Find Next** to go to each occurrence of the Find What value. When you see the value, you can select **Replace** to replace it with the Replace With value and go to the next occurrence, or you can select **Find Next** to go to the next occurrence without replacing the current one. You can select **Replace All** to replace all occurrences of the value without confirmation, or select **Close** at any time to close this dialog box.

As an example of how the Replace feature can be used, consider a telephone area code region that has added another area code. Some of the records in your database maintain the old code, while others need to be changed to the new code. You could enter **212** in the Find What text box and **718** in the Replace With text box. Then, as you go through the table, you can decide whether to select **Replace** to change the area code in the record or **Find Next** to go on without changing the area code.

Indexed Finds

Finds are faster if the field you are searching is indexed. If you often search for the last name, for example, you should create an index on the last name field.

As you saw in Chapter 2, you can create an index based on a single field by selecting **Yes** as the Indexed property for that field in Design View. Indexes are discussed in detail in Chapter 4.

Finds Versus Queries

The **Find** and **Find and Replace** options are relatively simple because they are based on a value in a single field. In contrast, queries let you find records based on much more complex criteria. For example, a query can be based on the content of many fields or on a comparison of values in fields with the criteria in the query. Queries are discussed in detail in Chapter 4. In Chapter 10, you will look at Action Queries, which provide a more powerful way to change data.

N O T E

Finds are usually the fastest way of finding a specific record when you need to look up a record by last name or by the content of some other field.

Quick Sorts

As you will see in Chapter 4, queries also let you specify the order of records based on the content of one or more fields. If you only want to change the sort order of the records based on the content of one field, the easiest way to do it is by using a quick sort. Figure 3.9 shows the table sorted alphabetically by last name.

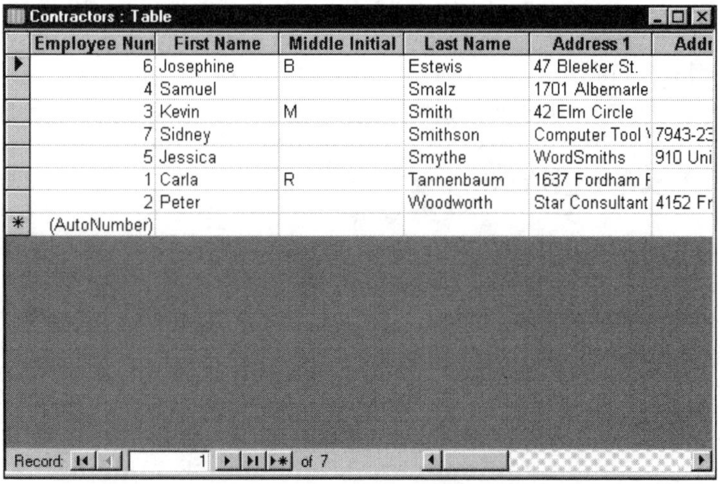

Employee Num	First Name	Middle Initial	Last Name	Address 1	Addr
6	Josephine	B	Estevis	47 Bleeker St.	
4	Samuel		Smalz	1701 Albemarle	
3	Kevin	M	Smith	42 Elm Circle	
7	Sidney		Smithson	Computer Tool \	7943-23
5	Jessica		Smythe	WordSmiths	910 Uni
1	Carla	R	Tannenbaum	1637 Fordham F	
2	Peter		Woodworth	Star Consultant	4152 Fr
(AutoNumber)					

Record: 1 of 7

FIGURE 3.9   A QUICK SORT BASED ON LAST NAME.

To do a quick sort, put the cursor in any record in the field you want the sort to be based on. Then do the following:

Click the **Sort Ascending** tool (or choose **Sort** and then **Ascending** from the Records menu) to sort the records in ascending order.

 Click the **Sort Down** tool (or choose **Sort** and then **Descending** from the Records menu) to sort the records in descending order.

The Sort Ascending tool has an A at its top and a Z at its bottom, while the Sort Descending tool has a Z at its top and an A at its bottom, indicating the order of the sort.

SHORTCUT

Another option is to right-click the field you want to use as the basis of the sort, and choose **Sort Ascending** or **Sort Descending** from its shortcut menu.

A sort is saved if it is in effect when you close the table, and remains in effect when you open the table again.

Changing the Format of the Datasheet

Often, you can view data more conveniently when you rearrange the table. Chapters 5 and 7 discuss forms, which are useful when you want to work with one record at a time, but simple changes in the table's format are more effective when you want to work with multiple records.

Working with Columns

The main limitation of Datasheet View is that you usually cannot see all the fields of a record. This can be a nuisance, for example, if you want to look at a list of names and phone numbers. The name fields may disappear beyond the left edge of the screen as you are scrolling right to see a telephone number. In addition, in Datasheet View, some columns are too narrow to display all the data they contain, while others are unnecessarily wide.

To resolve these problems, you can move or resize your table's columns. You must select columns before manipulating them in some of these ways.

SELECTING COLUMNS

Before you can move or resize your columns, you must select them. The way that you select columns is similar to the way you select fields.

To select a single column, simply click its field selector—the field name at the top of the column. When the pointer is on the field selector, it becomes a down arrow. You can then select the column by clicking on it and highlighting it, as shown in Figure 3.10.

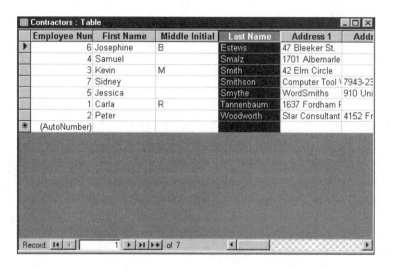

FIGURE 3.10 **THE LAST NAME COLUMN IS SELECTED.**

To select multiple columns, select a single column, hold down the **Shift** key, then select another column. The two columns you clicked and all the columns in between are highlighted, showing they are selected. You can also select multiple columns by clicking and dragging through the column selectors.

MOVING COLUMNS

Moving columns gives you one easy way to view names and phone numbers. You just have to move the phone number field left so it is next to the name fields.

You can move either one column or several adjacent columns. In either case, you must begin by selecting the column(s).

To move a single column, click and drag the column's field selector to move it. The pointer will be displayed with a small square at its base, as it is when you use the drag-and-drop feature of other Windows applications. Do not release the mouse button until the pointer is at the location where you want the column.

Access displays a heavy line to show that the column will be placed to the left of the column where the pointer is when you release the mouse button.

You move multiple columns just as you do single columns. Select a group of adjacent columns. Then click and drag the field selector of any of the selected columns to the new location.

RESIZING A COLUMN

Sometimes, you can view all the fields you want to see only if you make the columns smaller. It may be convenient, for example, to display just the first letter of first names. There are also times when you want to widen a column to see more of the data in a field than Access displays by default.

RESIZING USING THE MOUSE

It is easy to resize a column with the mouse. Just place the mouse pointer at the right edge of a field selector on the line that divides it from the next column. The pointer is displayed as a vertical bar with arrows pointing left and right. You can then click and drag the right edge of the column left to make the column narrower or right to make it wider.

RESIZING BY ENTERING COLUMN SIZE

You can also resize columns using the menu. Select a column, and then select **Column Width** from the Format menu to display the Column Width dialog box, shown in Figure 3.11. Enter the number of characters you want displayed in the field in the Column Width text box.

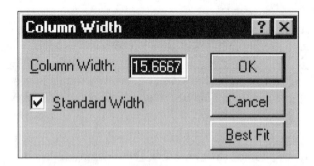

FIGURE 3.11   THE COLUMN WIDTH DIALOG BOX.

If you enter anything except the default width, the Standard Width checkbox is deselected. You can select it at any time to enter the default width in the Column Width text box.

If you select multiple columns before you select **Column Width**, they are all resized to the size you enter.

HIDING COLUMNS

Hiding columns you do not need is sometimes even more convenient than moving them. You can move through the datasheet without unnecessary fields getting in your way.

HIDING SELECTED COLUMNS

To hide columns, select the column or the group of adjacent columns you want to hide. Then choose **Hide Columns** from the Format menu. The selected columns will disappear.

THE UNHIDE COLUMNS DIALOG BOX

You can hide columns more selectively or you can make hidden columns reappear by choosing **Unhide Columns** from the Format menu to display the Unhide Columns dialog box, as shown in Figure 3.12.

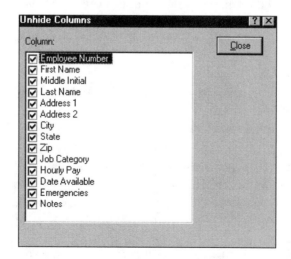

FIGURE 3.12   THE UNHIDE COLUMNS DIALOG BOX.

This dialog box lists the names of all of the fields in the table, with a checkmark to the left of the ones that are currently displayed. Select or deselect checkboxes to specify which you want displayed. When you have made all the changes you want, select the **Close** button.

Freezing Columns

Sometimes it is convenient to freeze columns so that they are always displayed, even as you scroll right to see additional fields. For example, you might want to display the First Name and Last Name fields permanently at the left edge of the table as you scroll right to see all the other data.

To freeze columns, select the column or the adjacent columns you want to freeze and choose **Freeze Columns** from the Format menu. The frozen columns are automatically moved to the far left of the table. They continue to be displayed even when you scroll through all the fields of the table.

To unfreeze columns, choose **Unfreeze All Columns** from the Format menu. When you do this, the columns that had been frozen are still displayed at the far left of the table. You can move them back to their original location using the techniques described in the section "Moving Columns" earlier in this chapter.

Other Format Changes

There are a few other methods of customizing the datasheet that you might sometimes find convenient, such as changing fonts, resizing rows, and hiding gridlines. They are particularly useful when you want to print the table.

Fonts and Styles

Choose **Font** from the Format menu to display the Font dialog box, shown in Figure 3.13. You can select the typeface, style, and size of the font used for all the data in the datasheet.

Select a font, such as **Arial** or **Times Roman**, from the Font list. The fonts you have available depend on the fonts you have installed under Windows. Use the Font Style list to specify whether the type should be regular, bold, italic, or bold italic. Select **Regular** to remove any effects. Select the **Underline** checkbox to underline the text, and use the color drop-down to change its color.

NOTE

Use the Size list to select the size of the font in points (the unit of measure used for type size, equal to 1/72 of an inch). Some fonts, such as TrueType fonts (displayed in the font list with a TT to their left), are scalable, and they are available in more sizes than can be displayed in the list. Type in a point size in the Size text box to use a size that is not listed.

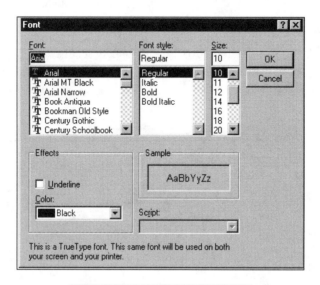

FIGURE 3.13   THE FONT DIALOG BOX.

RESIZING ROWS

You resize the height of rows in much the same way you resize a column. Move the pointer to the line between any two record selector buttons. The pointer becomes a horizontal line with arrows pointing up and down. Click and drag up to reduce the row height or drag down to increase the row height. The height of all rows will be changed. Another option is to select **Row Height** from the Format menu to display the Row Height dialog box shown in Figure 3.14. Enter the height in points in the Row Height text box.

FIGURE 3.14   THE ROW HEIGHT DIALOG BOX.

Select the **Standard Height** checkbox to automatically enter the height of the standard size in the Row Height text box. The standard size depends on the font you are using. After changing font size, you can select **Standard Size** to resize all rows to fit the new font, if they are not resized automatically.

FORMATTING CELLS

You can control the appearance of the datasheet's cells (the small areas that hold one field of one record) in a number of ways by choosing **Cells** from the Format menu to display the Cells Effects dialog box, shown in Figure 3.15.

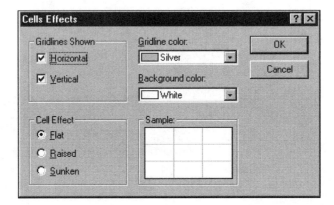

FIGURE 3.15   THE CELLS EFFECTS DIALOG BOX.

The checkboxes in the Gridlines Shown area let you remove or display the lines that separate rows and columns of the datasheet. The two drop-downs display color palettes that let you select the color of these gridlines and the color that fills the cell and acts as a background for its letters. The option buttons in the Cell Effect area let you give the cells a sunken or raised appearance, in addition to their usual flat appearance. The options you choose are illustrated in the Sample area.

Saving Datasheet Settings

Choose **Save** from the File menu to save changes to the table's layout. If you close the Table window without saving changes, Access displays the dialog box shown in Figure 3.16. Select **Yes** to save changes.

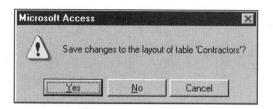

FIGURE 3.16   ACCESS PROMPTS YOU TO SAVE LAYOUT CHANGES.

These methods of saving changes are similar to the ways that you save your data in other Windows applications. As you know, data entered in Access is saved automatically as you move the highlight from record to record. In Access, you use these methods to save changes in the design of objects—in this case, changes in the layout of the table.

Resizing Columns in the Sample Table

You may have noticed that the width of your table makes it inconvenient to work with, since you must scroll back and forth to see different fields. Yet some of its columns are much wider than they need to be. You can make the table easier to use by narrowing these columns as follows:

1. If necessary, open the Contractors table. Place the mouse pointer on the right edge of the title of the Employee Number column, so it is displayed as a vertical line with arrows pointing left and right. Hold down the mouse button and drag left to narrow the column, until it is just wide enough to display the employee number.

2. Likewise, narrow the First Name column a bit. Click and drag the Middle Initial column so it is just large enough for a single letter, and narrow the remaining columns so they are just large enough for their data, as shown in Figure 3.17. Now you can see most of the fields for each record when you maximize the table window.

3. Choose **Save Layout** from the File menu to save these settings. In the future, when you open the table, it will have these column widths.

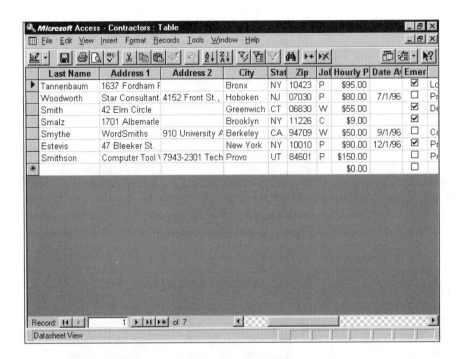

FIGURE 3.17   NARROWING THE COLUMNS.

Printing the Datasheet

The Report Wizard (covered in Chapter 5) lets you create sophisticated printed reports easily, but it is even easier to print the datasheet.

For many purposes, printing the datasheet is as useful as printing a report. For example, if you want to print out names and telephone numbers to call the people on your list, you can rearrange the columns, if necessary, so the telephone number column is next to the name columns.

The Print Dialog Box

Before you print a datasheet, select the rows that you want to print if you do not want to print the entire table. If you think it will make the table easier to read, you can also change the font and make other changes in the format of the datasheet. Then choose **Print** from the File menu to display the Print dialog box, shown in Figure 3.18.

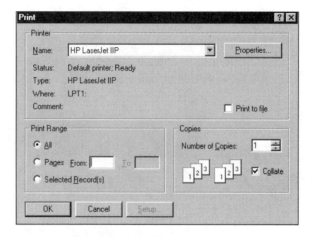

FIGURE 3.18 **THE PRINT DIALOG BOX.**

SHORTCUT

You can also click the **Print** tool to print the datasheet immediately, without displaying this dialog box. If necessary, use the **Name** drop-down to select which printer will be used to print the table. 🖶

The Print Range area lets you select how much of the table you want to print. You can print it all, print the rows of the table that are selected, or print only certain pages, beginning with the page number you enter in the From text box and continuing through the page number you enter in the To text box.

Use the Number of Copies spinner to indicate how many copies you want to print. The **Collate Copies** checkbox is selected by default, so that if you print more than one multipage datasheet, each copy of the datasheet is printed from beginning to end before the next one is printed. If you deselect this checkbox, all the copies of page one will be printed, then all the copies of page two, and so on.

If you select the **Print to File** checkbox, Access places the contents of the table and all the printer codes needed to print it in a disk file. The printer codes included in this file depend on the printer named at the top of the Print dialog box. If the **Print to File** box is checked, then after you select **OK**, Access displays the Print To File dialog box, shown in Figure 3.19, which lets you name the file. You can include a drive and path name in the file name. Anyone who has the proper printer can then print this file, even if they do not have Access.

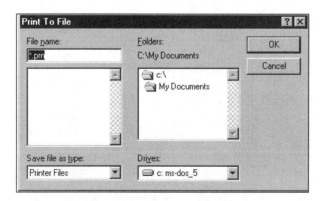

FIGURE 3.19   THE PRINT TO FILE DIALOG BOX.

Printer Properties

You can also select the **Properties** button of the Print dialog box to display the Printer Properties dialog box. This dialog box differs for different printers. For most printers, this dialog box can be used to control the following features of the document you are printing:

✳ **Paper Size:** This must be set to the size of the paper in the printer.

✳ **Orientation:** When you are printing database tables, it is sometimes useful to select **Landscape**, which prints across the longer dimension of the paper, so an entire record fits on one line, rather than the default **Portrait**, which prints across the narrower dimension of the paper.

✳ **Resolution:** On some printers, you can print a rough draft more quickly with lower resolution and print only the final draft in higher resolution. The options displayed here depend on the capabilities of your printer.

Most printers have other properties also, but these are some of the most useful common properties.

Print Preview

 You can also choose **Print Preview** from the File menu, or click the **Print Preview** tool to display the table in the Print Preview window, shown in

Figure 3.20. Print Preview lets you see exactly how the table will look when it is printed.

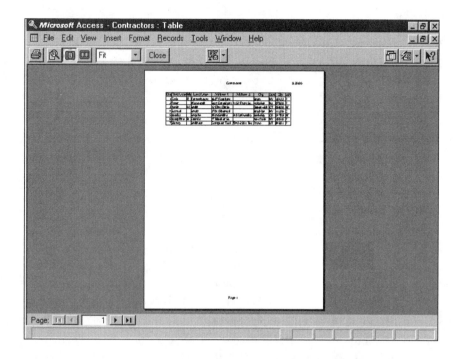

FIGURE 3.20 THE TABLE IN THE PRINT PREVIEW WINDOW.

 You can also display tables, queries, and reports in the Print Preview window by choosing **Print Preview** from the **File** menu or by clicking the **Print Preview** tool. Reports are displayed in Print Preview by default.

When the pointer is on the table in Print Preview, it is displayed as a magnifying glass. The report can be displayed in actual size or in a size small enough to see a full page in the window. It toggles between these two views when you click it.

 Clicking the **Zoom** tool has the same effect as clicking the page with the magnifying glass pointer, making it either actual size or small enough to view a full page.

Click the **One Page** or **Two Pages** tool to display the table so it is small enough to view the full page, with either one or two pages displayed.

Use the Zoom control drop-down to choose among a wider range of sizes, ranging from 200% to 10% of actual size.

Use the page controls at the bottom of the window to specify which pages are displayed. These work like the record controls and record indicator of the Datasheet, which were discussed earlier in this chapter.

Choose **Print** from the File menu or click the **Print** tool to display the Print dialog box and print the object displayed in the window.

Click the **Close** button of the toolbar to close the Print Preview window.

To Sum Up

In this chapter you learned to work with a table in Datasheet View. You began with the basics of data entry, including how to add and delete records, how to use the Access Editor to edit records, and how to move among the records of the table. Then you learned to use finds to search for specific records, and to use find and replace to change data quickly.

You learned to change the appearance of the datasheet in ways that make it easier to work with on the screen—by moving, hiding, resizing, and freezing its columns. You also learned how to change a datasheet's fonts to make it more attractive. And, finally, you leaned how to print a datasheet.

In Chapters 2 and 3, you learned all you need to know about tables. You can now proceed to Chapter 4, which describes another Access object, the query.

CHAPTER 4

Querying and Filtering Your Data

You have already learned how to use finds to locate a single record and to do Quick Sorts. In this chapter, you will learn to use filters and simple queries, called *Select Queries*, to isolate groups of records and determine their order in more sophisticated ways.

In this chapter you will learn about:

* the definition of a dynaset
* creating and saving a query
* specifying fields the query will display
* specifying the sort order of records the query will display
* entering criteria to specify the records the query will display
* using comparison operators in criteria to locate a range of values
* entering multiple criteria using a logical AND and a logical OR

107

✳ creating quick reports by designing a query and printing the dynaset

✳ using Filter By Selection to create a filter for a table

✳ using Filter By Form to create a filter for a table

✳ using Advanced Filter/Sorts

✳ saving a filter as a query

Queries

Queries are independent objects. Filters are not independent objects: they are attached to tables, forms, or reports. Yet you define filters in much the same way you define simple queries. In this chapter, you will learn about queries first, and then you can easily apply similar methods when you are working with filters.

Select queries let you specify which fields and records of a table are displayed. Access also lets you use queries in more powerful ways to join several tables in a relational database. These queries are discussed in Chapter 6 and advanced queries, such as Action Queries, which let you modify the data in tables, are covered in Chapter 10.

This chapter also describes sorts done through queries.

The Dynaset

The tab for Queries is to the right of the tab for Tables in the Database window. These two types of objects are fundamental to Access, because queries can often be used instead of tables. For example, a form or a report can be based on a table or on a query. Either the table or the query contains the set of fields and records displayed by the form or report.

A query, however, lets you enter criteria to specify which fields and records of a table are displayed and in what order they are displayed. You can create a query based on your Contractors table, for example, to display only the name and address fields of people from New York, with the records in alphabetical order by name.

A query displays a subset of all the fields and records in a table (or, when you work with relational databases, in multiple tables). Any changes you make in the data displayed by the query is also changed in the table. Because of this dynamic relationship between the query and the tables it is based on, the subset of data displayed by the query is called a *dynaset.*

The Query Window

Before looking at how to create and use a query, take a quick look at the Select Query window, shown in Figure 4.1, to get a general idea of its features.

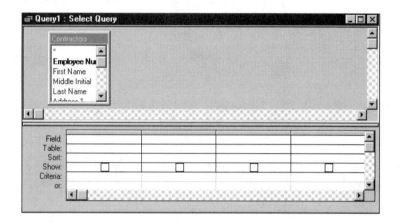

FIGURE 4.1   THE SELECT QUERY WINDOW.

THE FIELD LIST

As you can see, the panel in the top half of this window contains a list of all the fields in a table. You can see that the fields from our Contractors sample table are shown in Figure 4.1. When you work with relational databases, you can add multiple field lists here and then join them. When you are working with a single-table database, however, you should have only one field list here.

THE DESIGN GRID

The bottom half of the Select Query window includes what is called the Design grid, which has the following features:

✳   The first line lets you specify which fields are included in the dynaset that results from the query.

✳   The second line lets you specify which table the field is in and is useful if you are working with a relational database.

✳   The third line lets you specify which fields to sort the query on.

✳   The fourth line lets you specify which fields to display.

✳ The remaining lines let you enter criteria to determine which records are included in the dynaset.

This sort of query is called *Query By Example* (QBE) because the criteria consist of examples of the data you want to result from the query. For example, if the criterion **NY** is entered under the State field, only records with the value NY in that field will be included in the resulting dynaset.

You can select, move, and resize columns in this grid just as you do in a table.

✳ Move the pointer to the selector box above a column. It is displayed as a thick, black arrow pointing down. Then click and drag the column to move it.

✳ Move the pointer to the right edge of the selector box, and it is displayed as a vertical line with arrows pointing in both directions. You then can click and drag the line to resize the column.

Working with Simple Queries

You work with queries as you do with other objects:

✳ To create a new query, select the **Queries** tab in the Database window and then select the **New** button.

✳ To open an existing query in Datasheet View, select the **Queries** tab in the Database window, select the query name in the list box, and then select the **Open** button.

✳ To open an existing query in Design View, select the **Queries** tab in the Database window, select the query name in the list box, and then select the **Design** button.

Once a query is open, you can switch between Datasheet View and Design View by choosing **Query Design** or **Datasheet** from the View menu or by using the **View** tool on the toolbar. You also save and name queries as you do other objects, as described in the section "Creating New Objects" in Chapter 1.

Queries generate commands in Structured Query Language (SQL). You can view these commands at any time by choosing **SQL** from the View menu. SQL is useful for programmers but is not covered in this book.

When you create a query, Access displays the New Query dialog box, shown in Figure 4.2. You can choose to use one of the Query Wizards or you can select **New Query** to define the query in the Select Query window. Most of the Query Wizards let you create advanced queries, which will be discussed in Chapter 10. Here, we will look only at Select Queries.

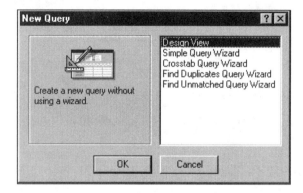

FIGURE 4.2   THE NEW QUERY DIALOG BOX.

Creating a New Query

If you select **New Query** in the New Query dialog box to define the query yourself rather than using a Wizard, Access begins by displaying the Show Table dialog box, shown in Figure 4.3. You can then select the field lists you need to add to the Select Query window.

You can also create a new query by selecting the table that you want it to be based on and selecting the **New Query** tool, which is on the New Object drop-down of the toolbar. Then, after you select **New Query** from the New Query dialog box, Access will bypass the Show Table dialog box and display the Query Design Window with the table that you selected included in it.

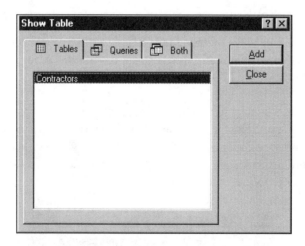

FIGURE 4.3 THE SHOW TABLE DIALOG BOX.

THE SHOW TABLE DIALOG BOX

To use the Show Table dialog box to select the tables or queries that will be the basis of the new query:

* Display a list of Tables, Queries, or both by clicking one of the tabs of this dialog box.

* Select a table or query name from the list and select the **Add** button, or double-click a table or query name.

A list of the fields for that table or query is placed in the Select Query window, and you can include any of these fields in the result of the query.

When you are working with a relational database, you can base queries on two or more tables. You can continue selecting tables and queries from this list until all you want are added to the Query window. When you are done, click the **Close** button to close this dialog box.

NOTE

With a simple database, you should add only one table to the Select Query window and then close the Show Table dialog box.

ADDING AND REMOVING TABLES

In the single-table queries you work with in this chapter, you should have no trouble adding the appropriate table or query when you first create the new query. However, when you begin working with more complex queries, you may sometimes find it useful to add or remove field lists as you work on the Query design.

You can change the tables or queries that are displayed in the Select Query window at any time:

 To add new tables or queries to the window, choose **Show Table** from the Query menu or click the **Show Table** tool to display the Show Table dialog box. Use it to add existing tables or queries to the query window, just as you do when you are first creating the query.

✳ To remove a table or query from the Select Query window, first select it by clicking on one of its fields to highlight it. Then choose **Remove Table** from the Query menu or press **Delete**.

WARNING
When you remove a table or query from the Select Query window, any of its fields that you added to the Design Grid are also removed. This can result in the loss of a considerable amount of work. As a precaution, save the query before removing the table. Then, if removing the table has unanticipated effects, you can close the query window without saving that change.

Selecting Fields to View

You can add a field from the field list to the Design grid so that it is included in the result of the query in any of the following ways:

✳ Click the field name in the field list, and while holding down the mouse button, drag the field name to one of the Field cells in the Design grid. If there is already a field name in the cell, the new one replaces it, and moves existing fields to the right.

✳ Click a field cell in the Design grid to display a drop-down list, of the fields in all the field lists in the Select Query window. Select a field from this list to place it in that cell.

✳ Click a field cell in the Design grid. Then type in a field name.

ADDING MULTIPLE FIELDS

There may be times when you want to include all the fields in the result of the query; for example, you may want the query to isolate specific records but you want all the fields of those records. For this reason, Access gives you an easy way to place all the fields in the Design grid.

First, select all the fields in the field list. The easiest way to do this is to double-click the field list's title bar. Then, click and drag any of the fields from the field list to the first field cell. All of the fields will be placed in field cells.

You can also include a subset of all the fields from the field list. First, select the fields you want in the field list. Clicking a field generally selects it and deselects other fields, but you can select multiple fields in two ways:

✳ Hold down the **Ctrl** key when you click a field to select it without deselecting other fields.

✳ Click one field, then hold down the **Shift** key and click a second field. All the fields between the first and last fields will be selected. This method is a quick way of selecting fields that are adjacent to each other in the field list.

Once you have selected all the fields you want, click and drag any of them to one of the field cells, and they will all be placed in field cells, beginning with the cell that you dragged to.

ADDING ALL FIELDS: THE ASTERISK

Field lists in the Select Query window always contain an asterisk, which represents all fields. The asterisk is always at the top of the field list.

If you click and drag the asterisk to a field cell, the QBE window displays the table name followed by an asterisk in that cell, as shown in Figure 4.4. You can also select the table name followed by a period, then the asterisk from the field cell's drop-down list, or just type it in the field cell.

N O T E

When you run the query, all fields from that table will be included in the resulting dynaset.

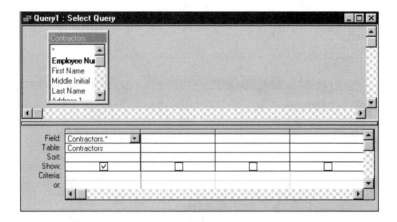

FIGURE 4.4   USING THE ASTERISK TO INCLUDE ALL FIELDS.

Using the asterisk is different in a couple of ways from the method of including all fields discussed in the previous section. If you use the asterisk, all fields will be included in the dynaset even if you change the structure of the table to add new fields. If you add individual field names, on the other hand, then you must manually add new fields if you modify the structure of the table.

The asterisk makes your work easier in this way, but it does make it a bit more difficult to sort or enter criteria for the fields, as you will see later in this chapter.

Generally, adding individual field names is the easiest way to work with a single table. The asterisk is most useful when including all fields from additional tables in a relational database.

N O T E

INSERTING, DELETING, OR MOVING FIELDS AND COLUMNS

The fields in the dynaset of a Query result are displayed in the order they appear in the Design grid.

You can insert a field in any location in any Field cell in the grid simply by clicking and dragging it from the field list to the location you want. The field already in that location and all the fields to its right will move right.

You can also manipulate fields after adding them to the Design grid just as you manipulate fields in tables. Click and drag the border between the field selector box above the Field name cell to resize the columns.

Click the **Field Selector** box to select a column, as shown in Figure 4.5. Once you have selected a column, you can move it by clicking and dragging the field selector right or left.

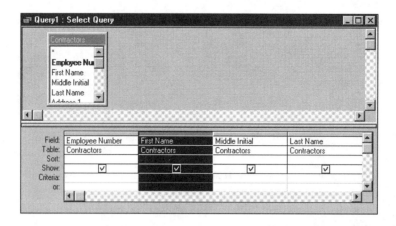

FIGURE 4.5   SELECTING A FIELD IN THE DESIGN GRID.

You can delete the selected column by choosing **Delete** from the Edit menu or by pressing the **Delete** key. You can also place the cursor in the column and choose **Delete Column** from the Edit menu.

To insert a new column or row, choose **Insert Column** or **Insert Row** from the Edit menu. You can also delete a row by choosing **Delete Row** from the Edit menu.

Specifying Sort Order

Queries let you specify the order in which the records are displayed in the dynaset.

To sort records based on a single field—for example, to sort records in Zip Code order—click the **Sort** cell under that field. Then click the Sort drop-down list to display these options:

✷ **Ascending** sorts records from the lowest to the highest value in the field. In text fields, sorts are in normal alphabetical order; in number fields sorts are from the smallest to the largest number; in date fields, sorts are from the earliest to the latest date.

* **Descending** sorts records from highest to lowest value.

* **(not sorted)** does not sort fields. This is the default. Select it if you no longer want to sort on a field you sorted on previously.

Access displays the word **Ascending** or **Descending** in the cell if the field is used in a sort and leaves it empty if it is not used in a sort.

SHORTCUT

You can speed up a sort you use frequently by creating an index based on the sort field or fields. Indexes are discussed in Chapter 12.

SORTS ON MULTIPLE FIELDS

You may need to base a sort on more than one field. For example, if you want to alphabetize records by name, you need to sort on both the last name and the first name fields to make sure that Aaron Jones comes before Zazu Jones. To do this, simply select **Ascending** in the Sort cell of both the Last Name and the First Name fields.

When you sort on multiple fields in this way, Access uses the leftmost field as the basis of the sort and uses fields to its right as tie-breakers when values in the leftmost field are the same. Thus, to sort by name, you must arrange the fields so the last name is to the left of the first name.

You can also combine ascending and descending sorts. For example, if you want the records sorted by state in descending order from Wyoming to Alaska, and the records within each state sorted alphabetically by name, make State the leftmost field and select **Descending** in its Sort cell. Make Last Name and First Name the next two fields and select **Ascending** in their Sort cells.

Hiding Fields

The **Show** checkbox is useful if you use the asterisk to include all the fields in a table. When you do this, you must also include a field individually if you want to enter criterion for it or if you want to sort on it. Add it in the way discussed earlier in this chapter.

When you run the query, this field would normally be displayed twice in the dynaset, once because of the asterisk and once because it is included in a column of its own. To avoid this repetition, click the **Show** checkbox in the field's own column and the check is no longer displayed.

N O T E

Except for this special case, you generally want to show all the fields you add to the Design grid, so the **Show** checkbox is automatically checked when you add a field to the grid.

Entering Criteria

You can enter a simple criterion (a value for a single field to match) in the following ways:

✳ **Number, Currency, or AutoNumber fields**—enter a number without currency signs or digit separators. For example, enter **3000** rather than 3,000.

✳ **Text fields**—enter the value you want to search for. When you leave the cell, Access automatically puts quotation marks ("") delimiters around it. For example, if you type **NY** as the criterion for the State field, Access will display it as **"NY"**, as shown in Figure 4.6. You can also include the quotation marks when you enter the text. These queries are not sensitive to capitalization. If you enter the criterion **"NY"** the query will also find any states that were entered in lowercase as **ny**.

✳ **Date fields**—enter the value you want to search for. When you leave the cell, Access automatically puts pound sign (#) delimiters around it. You can enter dates in number or text form, but the month, day, and year should be in the same order defined in the Windows International Panel. In the United States, for example, you can enter **1/1/96**, **Jan 1 96**, **1-Jan-96**, or any other valid American date order. Access will display any of these as #1/1/96#.

✳ **Yes/No fields**—enter the criterion **Yes**, **True**, **On**, or **1** to search for Yes. Enter **No**, **False**, **Off**, or **0** to search for No.

Later in this chapter, you will learn about complex criteria you can use in queries.

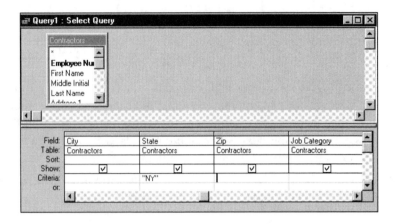

FIGURE 4.6   ACCESS AUTOMATICALLY ADDS DELIMITERS.

Running the Query

 After you have finished filling out the Design grid, you must run the query to produce its dynaset. You can do this by selecting **Run** from the Query menu or clicking the **Run** tool, which has an exclamation point on it.

You can also run the query by switching to Datasheet View. Either choose **Datasheet** from the View menu or click the **Datasheet** tool.

After processing the query, Access displays a datasheet with the fields, records, and sort order that you specified in the query.

The Quickest Report: Printing the Dynaset

In Chapters 5 and 9, you will learn to create presentation quality reports. However, if you need to print a report for your own use, the quickest way is by doing a query and printing the dynaset.

After running the query and displaying it in Datasheet View, you can manipulate the datasheet as you do a table in Datasheet View. You can use the Format menu to change font, row height, column width, and to hide, show, freeze, and unfreeze columns, using the same methods that you learned in Chapter 3.

You can also print the dynaset by choosing **Print** from the File menu. Use the Print and Print Setup dialog boxes exactly as you do when you are printing a table, as described in Chapter 3.

A Sample Query Using the Query Designer

In the rest of this chapter, we'll look at the more complex criteria you can enter to determine which records are displayed in the query.

First, though, you should get a bit of hands-on experience by creating sample queries based on simple criteria. The simplest criteria, as you learned at the beginning of this chapter, are examples of the value that you want in that field in the dynaset. For example, to display all the records of people from New York State, enter **NY** in the Criteria cell of the State field.

Try creating a sample query that displays names and addresses of contractors who live in New York State, sorted alphabetically by name.

1. Select the **Queries** tab on the Database window, and then select the **New** button. When Access displays the New Query dialog box, select **Design view** and click **OK**.

2. Access opens the Select Query window and displays the Show Table dialog box, with **Contractors** already selected. Click the **Add** button. A field list for the Contractors table is added to the Select Query window, as shown in Figure 4.7. Select the **Close** button of the Show Table dialog box.

3. Double-click the title bar of the Contractors field list to select all the fields. Click and drag any of the selected fields to the first Field cell in the Design grid to add all the fields to it.

4. Scroll right to view the Notes field, click the selector box above this column to select it, and press the **Delete** key to delete it. In the same way, delete the Emergencies column. Then click and drag over the selector boxes of the Hourly Pay and Job Category columns to select them both, and press **Delete** to delete both. Finally, press **Home** to scroll left and then select and delete the Employee Number column.

5. To sort alphabetically by name, you must make Last Name the first column of the query. Click the selector box of the **Last Name** column and release the mouse button. Now that the column is selected, click the selection box again, hold down the mouse button, and drag left to make it the first column.

6. Click the **Sort** box of the Last Name field, and use its drop-down list to select **Ascending**. Likewise, select **Ascending** for the First Name and Middle Initial fields.

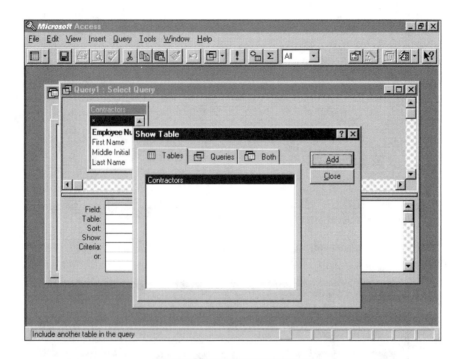

FIGURE 4.7   ADDING THE TABLE.

7. Scroll right so you can see the State field, and in its first Criteria cell, type **NY**. Click another field, so you can see that Access adds the quotation mark delimiters around this criterion.

8. Choose **Save** from the File menu. Access displays the Save As dialog box. As the Query Name, enter **Address List of Contractors from New York**.

9. If you want, you can narrow some of the columns to make the Design grid easier to see and to work with in the future. Do it as you did with the table in the exercise in Chapter 3. Click and drag the right edge of a column's selector box to narrow it. The query design with narrowed columns is shown in Figure 4.8.

10. Click the **View** tool or the **Run Query** tool, and after a moment, Access displays the results of this query, as shown in Figure 4.9. Close the Query window when you are done looking at it.

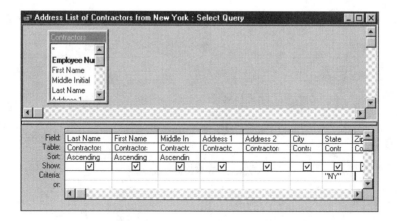

FIGURE 4.8 THE FINAL QUERY DESIGN.

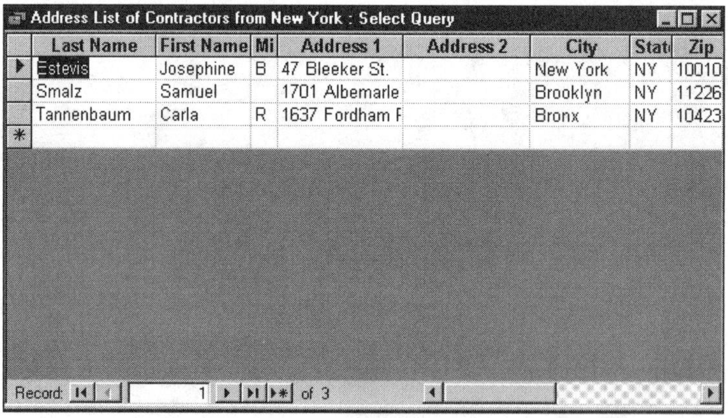

FIGURE 4.9 THE RESULT OF THE QUERY.

As you can see, only the name and address fields are displayed, all the state fields have the value NY, and the records are alphabetized by name.

The Query Wizard

The Wizard used to create a simple query is very easy to use but is not as powerful as Design View. As long as you are working with a single table, it simply lets you choose which fields are included in the result.

NOTE

If you do not know the basics techniques used to work with a Wizard, see the section on Wizards in Chapter 1.

Choose **Simple Query Wizard** from the New Query dialog box to display this Wizard.

The first step of the Simple Query Wizard, shown in Figure 4.10, lets you choose which fields are included in the result. Simply move the fields that you want to include from the Available Fields list of the Selected Fields list. Use this field picker like the field picker in the Table Wizard, which was described in Chapter 2.

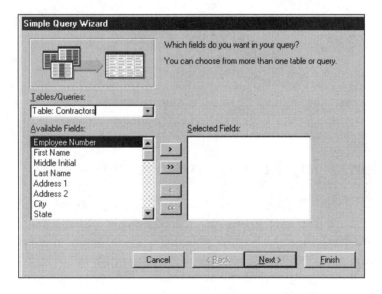

FIGURE 4.10   CHOOSING THE FIELDS TO INCLUDE.

Use the drop-down to select the table or query that this query is based on. You can use multiple tables or queries if you are working with a relational database, described in Chapter 2, but you should not do so at this point.

The next step of this Wizard, shown in Figure 4.11, lets you create the Query. The two radio buttons let you display the Query in Datasheet View to view information in it, or in Design View to modify its design.

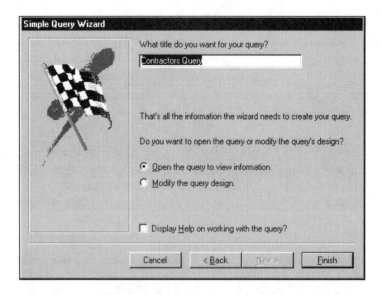

FIGURE 4.11   CREATING THE QUERY.

Because it is so easy to create a query in Design View that specifies which fields are created, there is rarely occasion to use this Wizard.

Working with More Complex Queries

Now that you have looked at all of the basics of creating a query with simple criteria, you can look at more complex criteria that can add more power to your query. There are two major ways in which you can use criteria more powerfully:

✳ You can use a criterion based on an expression (a special type of formula) rather than on a simple value such as NY. You can use expressions to find values greater or less than the value you specify, for example, and you can use them to do queries based on the current date rather than entering a specific date.

✳ You can use multiple criteria for a single query. Rather than simply finding records in the state of New York, for example, you can find records for New York and New Jersey, or you can find only the people in New York who are programmers.

Because you have learned how to use the Select Query window, the examples that follow show only the design of the query, without step-by-step instructions on how to create each query.

You should have no trouble creating and running the following query designs on your own, and you should do so, at least for some of the queries, to become more familiar with how queries work.

Expressions in Queries

Expressions are a complex topic discussed at length in Chapter 8. In this chapter, we look at a few features of Access expressions that are useful in queries. Though Access includes an Expression Builder which helps you to create complex expressions, the expressions you need for most queries are so simple that it is easier to type them in than to use the Expression Builder. For this reason, the Expression Builder is also described in Chapter 8.

LITERALS

So far, you have used only the simple criterion "NY" in queries. This sort of criterion is called a *literal*, because it is the actual, literal value that you are searching for.

You have already seen that:

* Text literals must be surrounded by the " (quotation marks) delimiter.
* Date literals must be surrounded by the # (pound sign) delimiter.
* Number literals do not need delimiters and should not include the currency sign or number separators.

In queries, Access automatically adds necessary delimiters to literals.

CONSTANTS

Access also has a few special literals called *constants*, which are often useful in queries. Do not use delimiters for constants.

You have already looked at Yes, True, On, No, False, and Off, which are used as criteria in Yes/No fields. For example, to find all contractors who are available for emergencies, use the query shown in Figure 4.12.

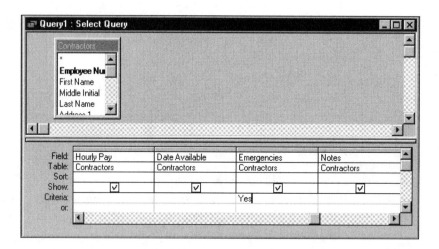

FIGURE 4.12   A QUERY FOR A LOGICAL FIELD.

FINDING EMPTY FIELDS

In addition, Access uses the constant Null for empty fields. You can enter it as a criterion for a field to find all records that have nothing entered in that field.

In your sample database, for example, you do not enter a value in the Date Available field unless contractors tell you they are not available. You can find all the contractors who have never said they are unavailable by using the query shown in Figure 4.13. Access automatically adds the operator Is when you use the criterion Null. Note that this query will not find contractors who were unavailable previously and now are available. To do that, you would have to use a query with a logical OR, which is discussed later in this chapter.

OPERATORS

Apart from literals, you also need to use operators in many queries. Operators let you search for more than a single value.

COMPARISON

It is most common to use a simple literal criterion such as "NY" when you are search a text field. When you are searching fields of other data types, you often want to find a range of values rather than an exact match. To do this, you use the comparison operators shown in Table 4.1.

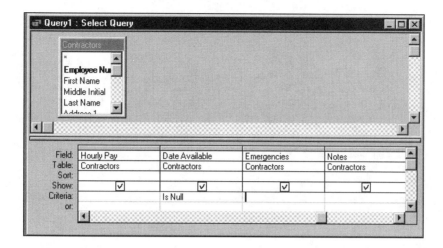

FIGURE 4.13 **A QUERY TO FIND AN EMPTY FIELD.**

TABLE 4.1 **THE COMPARISON OPERATORS.**

Operator	Meaning
=	Is equal to
>	Is greater than
>=	Is greater than or equal to
<	Is less than
<=	Is less than or equal to
<>	Is not equal to

You are probably familiar with these operators from mathematics, but you should bear in mind that in Access, they can be used with text and dates as well as with numbers.

For example, to display records for all the contractors who were not available previously and will be available by the third quarter of 1996, you can use the query shown in Figure 4.14. The criterion <#10/1/96# isolates records with an available date that is earlier than October 1, 1996, but as you can see in Figure 4.15, it does not include records that do not have a value entered in this field. To display all contractors who are available at that time, you would have to use a logical OR, discussed later in this chapter.

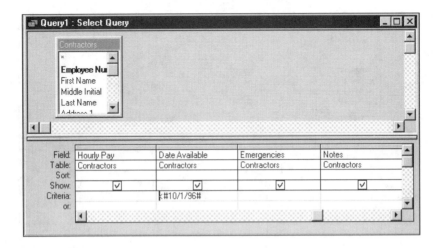

FIGURE 4.14   USING A COMPARISON OPERATOR IN A DATE FIELD.

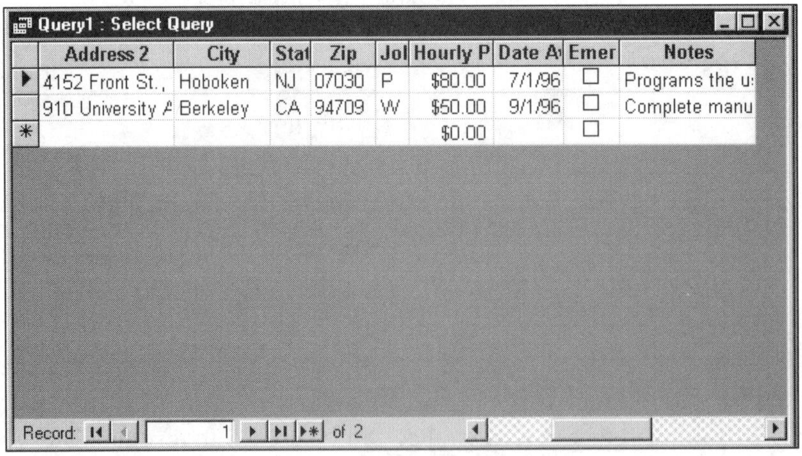

FIGURE 4.15   THE RESULT OF THE QUERY.

It is often useful to use the <> (is not equal to) operator with text values. For example, you can use this operator to find all contractors who do not live in New York State, as shown in Figure 4.16.

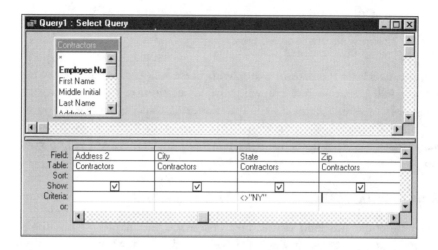

FIGURE 4.16 USING A COMPARISON OPERATOR IN A TEXT FIELD.

You can omit the = operator. The criterion **"NY"** is exactly equivalent to the criterion **="NY"**. You can also omit the delimiters around the literal in any of these queries. Access adds them just as it does when only the literal is used as a criterion.

BETWEEN...AND OPERATOR

Access has another operator it classifies as miscellaneous rather than comparison, but it is a very useful addition to the comparison operators.

You can use the Between...And operator to find a range of values. For example, to find the records for all contractors who become available during the third quarter of 1996, you can use the criterion Between #10/1/94# And #12/31/94#.

This operator finds a range that includes the two values you entered in it. In the example, it would include records with the dates 10/1/96 and 12/31/96 and all those records with dates in between.

As you will learn in the section "Logical AND" later in this chapter, you can create an equivalent query using the comparison operator: >= #10/1/94# and <= #12/31/94#. However, Between...And is usually easier to use.

WILDCARDS: THE LIKE OPERATOR

Two wildcard characters you use with Searches (Finds) can also be used with constant values in queries:

✳   * represents any group of characters

✳   ? represents any single character

You must include the Like operator with these wildcard characters. When you enter a value that includes a wildcard in a criterion cell, however, Access automatically adds Like, just as it automatically adds delimiters. If you want to find all last names beginning with A, you can enter the criterion **A*** in the Last Name field. Access automatically displays this as `Like "A*"` when you leave the cell.

Searching for Part of a Field's Value

Remember that the Find dialog box, discussed in Chapter 3, has the search options Start of Field, Any Part of a Field, and Match Whole Field. In queries, you can use the * (asterisk) wildcard as the equivalent of these options. To match the start of a field, add the * after the criterion, and to match any part of a field, include the * before and after the criterion.

For example, to find everyone in a table who lives on Main St., you can enter the criterion ***Main*** in the Address field. As always, Access adds the Like operator and delimiters.

Querying Memo Fields

NOTE

You almost always must use the * operator in order to query memo fields.

To find all contractors who program the user interface, use the query shown in Figure 4.17. Use the criterion ***interface*** to isolate all records that have the word "interface" anywhere in the memo field. As always, Access adds the Like operator and delimiters.

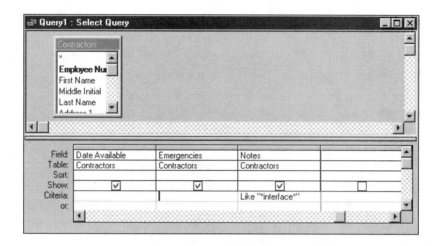

FIGURE 4.17   QUERYING A MEMO FIELD.

ARITHMETIC CALCULATIONS

Expressions can also include calculations using arithmetic operators. Table 4.2 includes the most useful of these operators, which are similar to symbols used in arithmetic and other computer programs.

TABLE 4.2   THE ARITHMETIC OPERATORS.

Operator	Meaning
+	Addition
–	Subtraction
*	Multiplication
/	Division

The addition and subtraction operators can be used to perform calculations on dates. Numbers used in date calculations refer to the number of days added to or subtracted from a date.

FUNCTIONS

Access functions are discussed in Chapter 8. In this chapter, we will look at just one function that is particularly useful in queries: the function Date( ) returns the system date of your computer, which is the current date if your computer's clock/calendar is working properly.

Like all functions, `Date( )` must include the open and close parentheses after it to show Access that it is a function and not a text literal.

This function is invaluable in queries used to identify records with time limits that have passed. For example, Figure 4.18 shows a query to identify contractors who have become available as of the current date. Using the `Date( )` function, which automatically represents the current date, is obviously much easier than reentering the current date each time you run the query.

NOTE

As mentioned earlier, this sort of query finds only records that have had a value entered in the field. To find all available contractors, you must include a second criterion to include those who have never had an entry in this field, as you will learn to do in the upcoming section "Using Multiple Criterion."

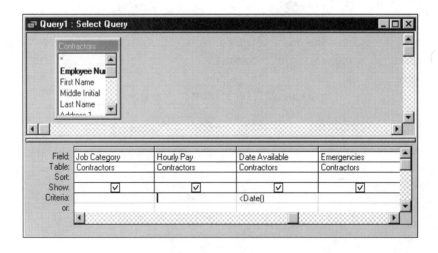

FIGURE 4.18   A QUERY USING THE `Date( )` FUNCTION.

You can also do calculations using the `Date( )` function, as you can with other date values. For example, if you changed the criterion in the previous query to ≤ `Date( ) + 30` instead of < `Date( )`, you would find all contractors who had already become available or would become available in the next 30 days.

The query in Figure 4.19 is even more precise. You can enter the criterion **Between Date( ) And Date( ) + 6** to isolate the records of contractors who are becoming available today or in the next six days. You could use this query to do a regular weekly mailing to all the contractors you expect to become available in the coming week.

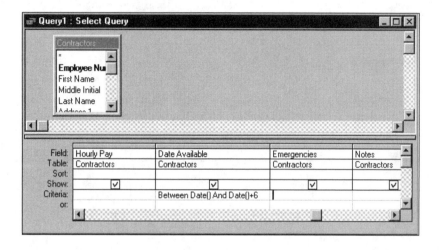

FIGURE 4.19 **A QUERY USING DATE ARITHMETIC.**

OBJECT NAMES

Access expressions can also include object names, such as names of fields and tables. For example, you can use field names for queries of relational databases where you want to compare the value in a field of one table with a value in another.

Using Multiple Criteria

Now that you have looked at how to use expressions to enter more powerful criteria in a single cell of the Design grid, you should learn how to enter criteria in multiple cells.

There are two ways that multiple criteria may be used:

✳ Logical AND includes the record in the dynaset only if all the criteria are true.

✳ Logical OR includes the record if any one of the criteria is true.

Notice that AND and OR are used in a more precise sense here than they are in ordinary conversation. Ordinarily, for example, you could say you are looking for people from New York or New Jersey or just as easily say that you are looking for people from New York and New Jersey.

However, you must use a logical OR to find records from either state. The record qualifies if it has NY or NJ in the State field. If you used a logical AND, a record would qualify only if it had both NY and NJ in the State field, which is impossible.

Logical AND is exclusive. For each new criterion you add, there will be fewer records that match all the criteria. Logical OR is inclusive. For each new criterion you add, there will be more records that match at least one criterion.

LOGICAL AND

To search for records with values in more than one field, simply enter all the criteria under the appropriate fields on the Criteria line. Access considers this a logical AND, and it finds only those records that meet all the criteria.

For example, to find records of people who live in New York and who are also programmers, use the query shown in Figure 4.20. Access isolates only those records that meet both criteria.

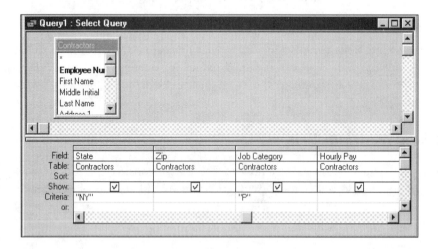

FIGURE 4.20   A QUERY USING A LOGICAL AND.

LOGICAL OR

To search for records that have several values in a field, list the first value in the criteria field, and each additional value in an OR field.

For example, you can find all of the contractors who are currently available by using the query shown in Figure 4.21. Under the Date Available field, type **Null** in the Criteria field and **< Date ( )** in the or field. This query isolates records that have no entry in the Date Available field or an entry that is earlier than the current date.

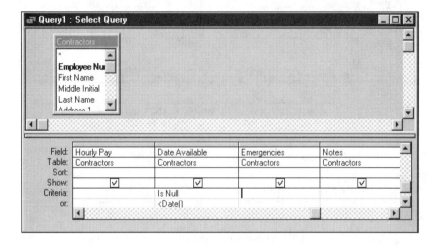

FIGURE 4.21   A QUERY USING A LOGICAL OR.

COMBINING AND WITH OR

You can combine logical AND with logical OR by entering several rows of criteria, each with criteria entered under several fields.

For example, Figure 4.22 shows a query to find all the people who are currently available, are programmers, and are available in an emergency. In this sort of query, Access reads each row and finds only the records that match all the criteria on the row. Thus, the query finds the records that match all the criteria in any row.

THE LOGICAL OPERATORS

You can create most queries you want by entering criteria in the Design grid as described above. However, there are cases where it is easier or more powerful to use logical operators, which are listed in Table 4.3.

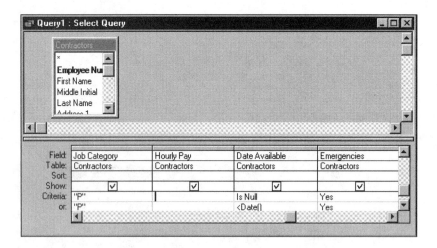

FIGURE 4.22   A QUERY COMBINING AND WITH OR.

TABLE 4.3   THE LOGICAL OPERATORS.

Operator	Meaning
And	Both criteria must be true to match
Or	Either criterion must be true to match
Xor	One of the criteria but not both must be true to match
Not	The criterion must be untrue to match

The Xor operator is used in programming and advanced expressions.

The Not operator reverses the expression that follows it. If an expression is true but is preceded by Not, it matches all records where the expression is false. If an expression is false and is preceded by Not, it matches all records where the expression is true. For example, `Not Between Date( ) and Date( ) + 6` would match all dates that are not in the next week.

THE AND OPERATOR

You must use the And operator if you want to enter multiple criteria for a single field.

This can be used to isolate a range of values, in the same way that the `Between...And` operator does. For example, the query in Figure 4.23 finds contractors who become available in the week beginning today. The value in the Date Available field must match both criteria. It must be greater than or equal to (>=) the current date and less than or equal to (<=) date( ) + 6. This is equivalent to the criterion `Between Date( ) And Date( ) + 6`, which you learned about earlier.

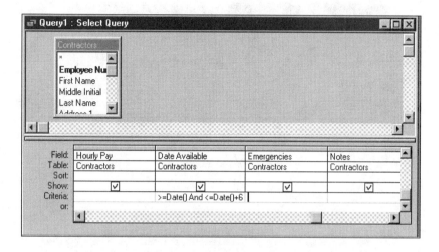

FIGURE 4.23 USING THE AND OPERATOR TO FIND A RANGE OF VALUES.

You could not enter this query by using different cells of the Design grid to represent the logical AND. It requires the And operator.

Use the logical And operator with comparison operators to find a range of values. Do not use the And operator with two literals. For example, you will not find any records if you use the criterion `NY And NJ` in the State field because no records have both NY and NJ entered in that field.

THE OR OPERATOR

The Or operator is used as a convenience. If you are combining logical AND with logical OR, it is easier to use the Or operator than it is to rewrite all the criteria for several fields.

For example, Figure 4.24 shows two ways of finding all the people who live in New York, New Jersey or Connecticut and are programmers.

SHORTCUT

In a query like this, which combines many conditions, it is easier to use the Or operator than to enter all the data in each row.

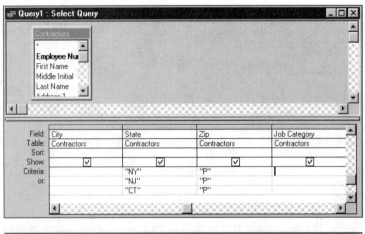

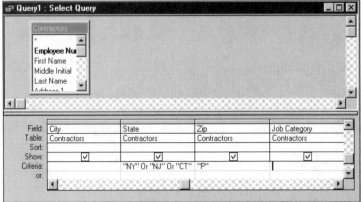

FIGURE 4.24   THE OR OPERATOR IS EASIER TO USE THAN MULTIPLE ROWS.

Filters

Queries are independent objects, listed in the Database window along with tables and other objects.

There are times when it is preferable to incorporate the features of a query into an existing object rather than creating a query as a new, separate object. By using a filter, you can incorporate features of a query into a table or form, without creating a separate query object.

Because filters do not have separate names, a table or form can have only one filter associated with it. If you create a new filter, it will replace the filter that already exists. However, you can save a filter permanently by saving it as a query, and as you will see, you can also create a filter based on an existing query.

 Whenever a table or form's filter is in effect, the Apply Filter button appears to be depressed. You can apply the filter to display only some records or remove the filter to display all records by clicking this button repeatedly.

 If you have used a filter before doing a find, Access will search through only the records that are still displayed. If Access cannot find a record you know you entered, it is probably because you have used a filter.

N O T E

Types of Filters

There are three types of filter:

✳ **Filter by Selection**: lets you specify which records are displayed by highlighting data in the table in Datasheet View.

✳ **Filter by Form**: lets you specify which records are displayed by filling out a form which is similar to the table in Datasheet View.

✳ **Advanced Filter/Sort**: lets you specify which records are displayed and the order in which they are displayed by using the Advanced Filter/Sort Window, which is like the Query Window.

All of these types of filters can be created either for tables or for Forms, which are covered in Chapter 5 and Chapter 7.

 You can always display a table's filter in either of the last two ways listed above, by choosing **Filter by Form** or **Advanced Filter/Sort** from the Filter menu. The same criteria you have entered with be displayed in the Filter by Form or in the advanced Filter window.

N O T E

Using Filter by Selection

To create a Filter by Selection, display the table or form window you want it to be based on, and highlight the value in any of the fields you want to find. Then choose **Filter** from the Records menu and **Filter by Selection** from the submenu, or click the **Filter by Selection** tool.

You can also just right-click a field to select its entire contents and display its shortcut menu. Then select **Filter by Selection** from the shortcut menu.

For example, to display only records from California, all you need to do is to highlight **CA** in the state field of one of the records in the datasheet, and click the **Filter by Selection** tool.

The value you highlight can be all or part of the contents of a field. For example, to find every record with a company name that includes the word *Computer*, highlight just that word in the Address 1 field of a record, and click the **Filter by Selection** tool.

FILTER EXCLUDING SELECTION

You can also display all records except those that include the selected value. Select the value you want to exclude, and then right-click the table to display its shortcut menu and select **Filter Excluding Selection**.

If you want to select the entire value in a field, simply right-click it to select it and display the shortcut menu in one step.

For example, to display all records except those from New York State, right-click the state field in a record from that state to select NY and display the shortcut menu; then select **Filter Excluding Selection**.

FILTER BY SELECTION WITH MULTIPLE CRITERIA

After using Filter by Selection or Filter Excluding Selection, you can narrow down which records are displayed even further by using these methods again on the resulting records that are displayed. For example, after displaying only records from California, you can highlight **P** in the Job Category field of one of the records that is displayed and click the **Filter by Selection** tool again; Access will display only the records of programmers from California.

Notice that, if you use Filter by Selection and Filter Excluding Selection repeatedly, the criteria are in a logical AND relationship: all the criteria must be satisfied for the record to be displayed.

Using Filter by Form

 To create a Filter by Form, display the table or form window you want it to be based on. Then choose **Filter** from the Records menu and **Filter by Form** from the submenu, or click the **Filter by Form** tool.

Access displays the Filter by Form Window, shown in Figure 4.25. As you can see, this window includes one record of the table, laid out exactly as it is in Datasheet view. Simply type the values you want to find in the appropriate fields of the record, or use the drop-down in each field to select the value you want from a list of all the values that have been entered in the field. Access automatically adds delimiters to the value you enter, as it does when you create queries.

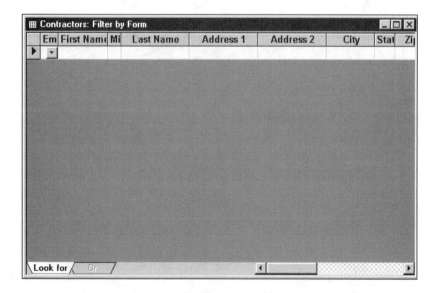

FIGURE 4.25   THE FILTER BY FORM WINDOW.

If you enter values in more than one field, they will be in a logical AND relationship. For example, if you enter **CA** in the State field and **P** in the Job Category field, the result will have only records of people who are both from California and are programmers.

To enter criteria in an OR relationship, click the **Or** tab at the bottom of this window to display a new sample record, and fill out criteria in it. Whenever you make an entry in an Or tab Access adds a new one, so you can add multiple criteria all in an Or relationship. Using multiple Or tabs to enter criteria is just like entering criteria on multiple lines of the Design grid of a query form.

When you have finished filling out the form, choose **Apply Filter/Sort** from the Filter menu or click the **Apply Filter** tool to return to the table, with only the records that you specified displayed. You can also click on the Filter window with the right mouse button to display a shortcut menu from which you can select **Apply Filter**.

Using Advanced Filter/Sorts

You can also create a filter using methods like those you use to create a query. Display the table (or form) it applies to and choose **Filter** from the Records menu and **Advanced Filter/Sort** from the submenu to display the Filter window shown in Figure 4.26.

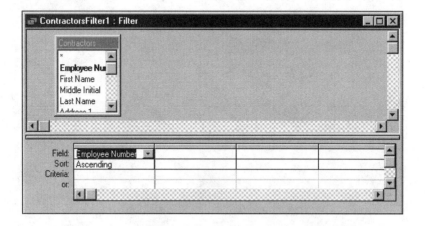

FIGURE 4.26 THE FILTER WINDOW.

As you can see, the Filter window is almost identical to the Select Query window. It automatically includes a field list with the fields of the underlying table or query. You can specify the fields to sort on, and enter criteria to determine which records are displayed just as you do when you are designing a query.

Unlike a Query, however, a filter displays all the fields of the table and only filters records. It does not have a Show row in its Design Grid, because it shows all the fields. It does not have a Table row, because all its fields come from the underlying table.

After you have designed the filter, you must apply it by choosing **Apply Filter/Sort** from the Filter menu or clicking the **Apply Filter** tool. You can also click on the Filter window with the right mouse button to display a shortcut menu from which you can select **Apply Filter/Sort**. A filter is not applied automatically when you close the Filter window.

Displaying All Records and Reusing the Filter

 You can remove any of these types of filter by selecting **Remove Filter/Sort** from the Records menu or from the Table's shortcut menu, or by clicking the **Apply Filter** button again. This button appears to be depressed when the filter is in effect, and when you click it to remove the filter, it appears to be raised again.

This option restores the original order of the records and displays all records and fields. The filter is still available and can be used at any time in any of the following ways:

✳ Clicking the **Apply Filter** tool.

✳ Choosing **Apply Filter** from the Records menu.

✳ Right-clicking the table and choosing **Apply Filter** from its shortcut menu.

Working with Filters

A filter is a feature of the design of the table or form that it is part of. If you save changes in the design of the table or form, its filter is saved like all the other features of its design.

If the filter is in effect when you close the table, it will be in effect when you reopen the table. If it is not in effect when you close the table, you can use it after reopening the table in any of the usual ways.

Because you do not name a filter when you save it, there can be only one filter associated with a table at a time. If you create a new filter, it will replace an existing filter, unless you save the existing filter as a query, as described below.

MODIFYING THE DESIGN OF A FILTER

Whenever you choose **Filter** from the Records menu and **Filter by Form** and **Advanced Filter/Sort** from the submenu, Access displays the design of the current filter, if there is one, in the Filter by Form or the Filter window. Change its design using the same methods you used to create it.

SHORTCUT

If you are creating an advanced filter, it is sometimes easiest to begin by creating it using Filter by selection and then modifying it in this way to add advanced features.

SAVING A FILTER AS A QUERY

Because a table can have only one filter, which is lost if you create a new one, you can save a filter permanently as a query if you think it will be useful in the future.

To save it, choose **Save As Query** from the File menu. Alternatively, click on the Filter window with the right mouse button to display the shortcut menu, and choose **Save As Query**. Access displays the Save As Query dialog box shown in Figure 4.27. Enter the name for the query. This new query will be displayed in the Database window and can be used like any other.

FIGURE 4.27   THE SAVE AS QUERY DIALOG BOX.

USING A QUERY AS A FILTER

Rather than designing a filter from scratch, you can use an existing query as a filter. The query must be a Select Query based solely on the table or query you want to apply it to as a filter.

Click on the Filter window with the right mouse button to display the shortcut menu, and choose **Load from Query**. Access displays the Applicable Filter dialog box shown in Figure 4.28, with a list of queries that can be applied as filters to this object.

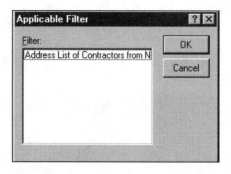

FIGURE 4.28   THE APPLICABLE FILTER DIALOG BOX.

Select a query from this list and select **OK**. The Filter window is automatically filled in with the same definition as that Query window. Then you can apply the query in the usual way.

A Sample Filter

Now, try using all of these methods of working with filters to create a complex filter and save it as a query.

1. If necessary, open the Contractors table. Scroll right so you can see the State field. Right-click one of the State fields that has NY in it to select this value and display the shortcut menu, as shown in Figure 4.29, and then choose **Filter by Selection**. Only records from New York are displayed, as shown in Figure 4.30. Notice that the Apply Filter tool appears to be depressed.

2. Now, scroll right to view the Job Category field. Select **P** in one of the fields, and click the **Filter by Selection** tool to display only records for programmers from New York State.

3. Next, click the **Filter by Form** tool to display the Form shown in Figure 4.31. Resize the State and Job Category columsn, so you can see that the criteria you selected are already in this form.

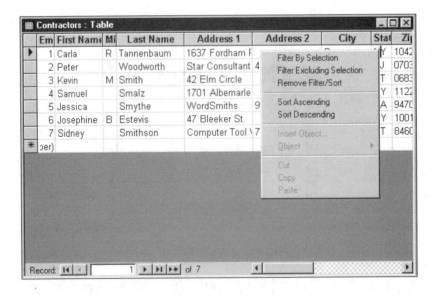

FIGURE 4.29 **CREATING A FILTER BY SELECTION.**

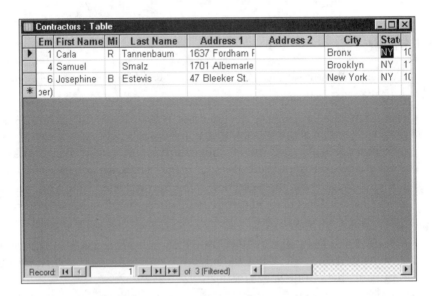

FIGURE 4.30 **THE TABLE WITH THIS FILTER IN EFFECT.**

4. Click the **Or** tab. Use the drop-downs to select **P** in the Job Category field and **NJ** in the State field. Click the next **Or** tab and select **CT** in the

State field and **P** in the Job Category field, as shown in Figure 4.32. Then click the **Apply Filter** tool to display the table. Scroll right so you can see that all the records are programmers and live in New York, New Jersey, or Connecticut, as shown in Figure 4.33.

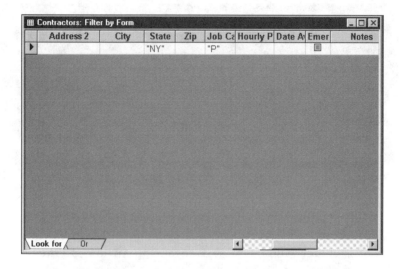

FIGURE 4.31 **A FORM WITH THE CRITERIA FOR THIS FILTER.**

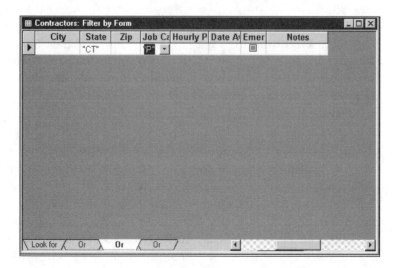

FIGURE 4.32 **USING THE FORM TO ADD MORE CRITERIA.**

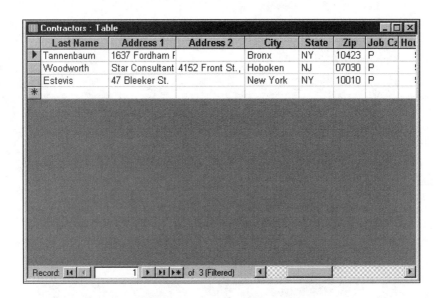

FIGURE 4.33   THE TABLE WITH THIS FILTER IN EFFECT.

5. Choose **Filter** from the Records menu and **Advanced Filter/Sort** from the submenu to display a Filter window (similar to a query window) with the criteria for this filter entered in it. Drag the bottom of the window downward so you can see all its rows. Drag the Last Name, First Name and Middle Initial fields from the Fields list to the Design Grid and select **Ascending** from the drop-downs in all of their Sort cells, as shown in Figure 4.34. (The columns in the illustration have been resized so you can see them all.) Click the **Apply Filter** tool to display the table and note that the records are in alphabetical order by name, as shown in Figure 4.35.

6. Finally, since this is a specialized filter that you will only want to use on occasion, you should save it as a query. Choose **Filter** from the Records menu and **Advanced Filter/Sort** from the submenu to display the filter form again. Right-click it and select **Save As Query** from its shortcut menu. In the Save As Query dialog box, enter **NY, NJ and CT Programmers** and click **OK**. Then close the Filter window to display the table window, and click the **Apply Filter** tool to display all records. Notice that the records are still in alphabetical order: the sort order of the Filter/Sort is still in effect, even though you have removed the filter.

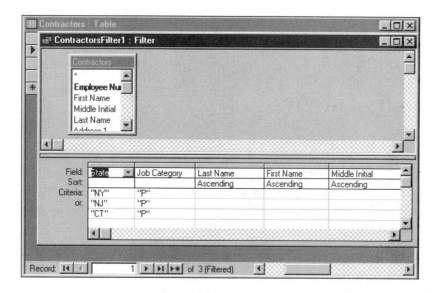

FIGURE 4.34 SPECIFYING THE SORT ORDER.

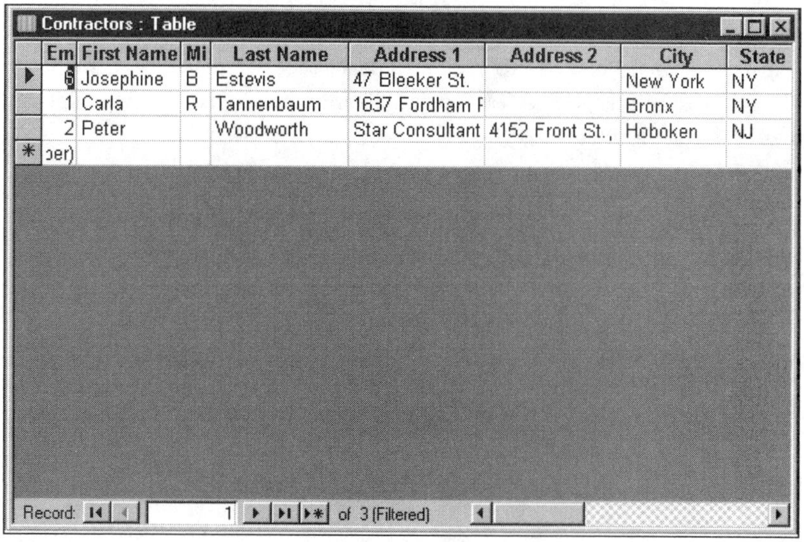

FIGURE 4.35 THE TABLE WITH THIS FILTER/SORT IN EFFECT.

You see that you can start with a simple filter and gradually add extra features to it to make it more complex. Because you saved this filter as a query, you can create a new filter without losing all the work you put into designing it.

A Note on Indexes

In some cases, it is useful to index a table to speed up a query or sort, particularly when you are working with large amounts of data. In order to know when to create an index, however, you must have a basic understanding of how they work, as well as learning the mechanics of creating them in Access. Because they are not absolutely necessary to using Access, they are not included in Part I of this book, which is designed to get you up and running as quickly as possible. Instead, they are covered in Chapter 12.

To Sum Up

In this chapter, you learned to use Select Queries. These are the most important type of query in Access because they can be used instead of tables as the basis of reports or forms.

The result of a Select Query is a dynaset. The fields and records that you specify are a dynamic subset of the table, and changes you make in them are also made in the original table.

You learned to use the Query window in Design View to specify which fields are included in the dynaset, and to use the column of the Design grid under each field to specify whether that field should be displayed or used as the basis of sort order. You also learned to enter simple or complex criteria under the fields in the Design grid to include only fields that have certain values in those fields in the dynaset.

Finally, you learned about Filters, which use the same concepts as Select Queries but can also be created in easier ways.

In the next chapter, you learn to create forms and reports.

CHAPTER 5

Fast Forms, Reports, and Mailing Labels

In Chapters 1 through 4, you learned to design tables, add and edit data, and use queries to define what data is displayed. In this chapter you learn to use forms and reports to specify how data is displayed.

When you design a form or report, you control how your data is laid out. Forms are used primarily to display and edit data on the screen, and reports are designed primarily to be printed. In this chapter, you learn to:

 ❋ Create AutoForms
 ❋ Create single-column forms
 ❋ Create tabular forms
 ❋ Create single-column reports
 ❋ Create tabular reports
 ❋ Create mailing labels
 ❋ Work with forms and reports from the Database Window

Like other database management programs, Access includes windows that let you design custom forms and reports. You can control the exact location of fields and add the text and graphic enhancements you want in the design. Access also includes Form and Report Wizards, which let you fill out dialog boxes and then do the work of designing a form or report for you.

These wizards are sophisticated enough that many users can get by without designing custom forms or reports. For this reason, custom forms and reports are covered in Chapters 7 and 9 in Part II of this book. Part I is meant to let you work with Access as easily as possible, so this chapter covers Access' AutoForms and AutoReports and its Form Wizards and Report Wizards, which you can learn about almost effortlessly.

Using Forms

As you know, you can view and enter data directly in Access tables. However, this is sometimes inconvenient because you usually cannot see all the fields of a record at the same time.

Forms let you redesign the display to make it easier to view on the screen. Though you can print forms—they sometimes are a valuable addition to your printed reports—they are meant primarily to be viewed on the screen.

The easiest form to use is the AutoForm, which you can create by clicking a single button. The Form Wizards let you create more sophisticated forms very easily, including bar graphs, pie charts, and other graphics.

AutoForms

The AutoForm, shown in Figure 5.1, displays the fields of each record one above another, rather than side by side, as they are displayed in the Datasheet View of a table or query. If there are too many fields to fit into one column, it creates a second column, if possible, as it does for the Notes field in the illustration. The AutoForm lets you see all or most of the fields of a record displayed on the screen, though it does not let you view multiple records at the same time.

NOTE

Though this is the default type of AutoForm, you will see in a moment that you can also use the New Form dialog box to Create Tabular and Datasheet AutoForms.

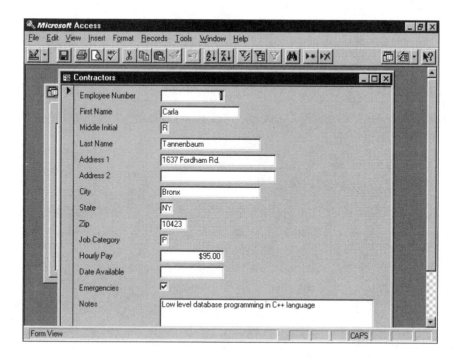

FIGURE 5.1   THE AUTOFORM FOR THE CONTRACTORS TABLE.

To create an AutoForm, simply select the table or query in the Database window that you want it to be based on and use the New Object tool drop-down to select the **AutoForm** tool. Access automatically gives the AutoForm the name of the table they are based on, with a number added if necessary to distinguish it from other forms. You can rename it, as you learned in Chapter 1, by selecting the name in the Database Window and then either clicking the name again or choosing **Rename** from the Edit menu. Alternatively, right-click the form's name and choose **Rename** from its shortcut menu.

You should create an AutoForm, so you have it to look at while you read about the features of the Form window in the next section:

1. If necessary, open the Database window or click the **Tables** tab. Select the **Contractors** table in the Tables list.

2. Click the **AutoForm** tool, or use the New Object tool drop-down to select it if necessary. After taking a moment to generate it, Access displays the AutoForm for this table.

3. Close the form when you are done looking at it. When Access prompts you to save the changes, select **Yes**, and in the Save As dialog box, click **OK** to enter the name **Contractors**.

Notice that the AutoForm automatically creates a data entry area for the Notes field or other memo fields. This area has a scroll bar added to it if there is too much data in a record to display in this area.

Creating and Using Forms

Apart from AutoForms, you create and work with forms in the same way you do other objects. First, click the **Forms** tab of the Database window to display the Forms list, and then use the Database window's buttons:

❋ To create a new form, click the **New** button.

❋ To use an existing form, select it and click the **Open** button.

❋ To change the design of a form (using the methods described in Chapter 7), select it and click the **Design** button.

When you create a new form in this way, Access displays the New Form dialog box, shown in Figure 5.2.

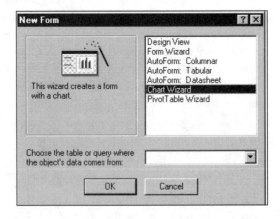

FIGURE 5.2   THE NEW FORM DIALOG BOX.

First you must use the drop-down list in this dialog box to select the table or query that the form is based on. Then select **Design View** to create a custom form from scratch (using the methods described in Chapter 7), or select the **Form Wizards** button to have Access design the form for you.

As with other objects, you can also create a form by selecting a table or query in the Database window and selecting the **New Form** tool (or choosing **New** and then **Form** from the File menu). Access displays the New Form dialog box with that table or query already entered in its drop-down list.

The New Form dialog box gives you the following options:

✳ **Design View**: create a Form from scratch, using the methods covered in Chapter 7.

✳ **Form Wizard**: create a Form using the Form Wizard, discussed later in this Chapter.

✳ **AutoForm Columnar**: create an AutoForm like the one described above, with the fields one above another.

✳ **AutoForm Tabular**: create an AutoForm with the fields arranged across the table, like the one shown in Figure 5.3. This form lets you view a few records at the same time, and you can use its scroll bar to scroll through the table.

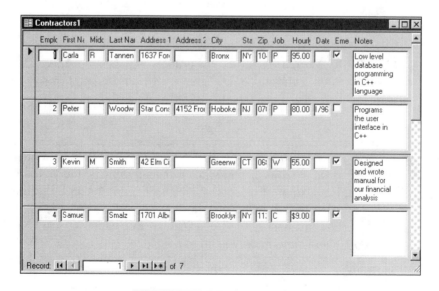

FIGURE 5.3 A TABULAR AUTOFORM.

✴ **AutoForm Datasheet**: create an AutoForm that resembles a datasheet, like the one shown in Figure 5.4.

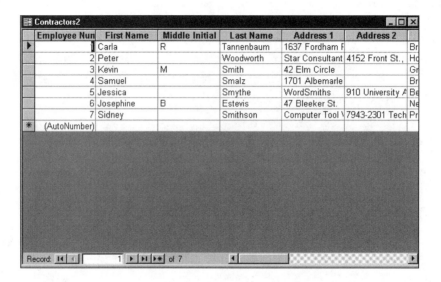

Employee Num	First Name	Middle Initial	Last Name	Address 1	Address 2	
1	Carla	R	Tannenbaum	1637 Fordham F		Br
2	Peter		Woodworth	Star Consultant	4152 Front St.,	Ho
3	Kevin	M	Smith	42 Elm Circle		Gr
4	Samuel		Smalz	1701 Albemarle		Br
5	Jessica		Smythe	WordSmiths	910 University A	Be
6	Josephine	B	Estevis	47 Bleeker St.		Ne
7	Sidney		Smithson	Computer Tool V	7943-2301 Tech	Pr
(AutoNumber)						

FIGURE 5.4   A DATASHEET AUTOFORM.

✴ **Chart Wizard**: create a graph, using the Chart Wizard.

✴ **PivotTable Wizard**: create a PivotTable, which summarizes data in cross-tabulated form and is available in a number of Microsoft products.

It is important to remember that a form can be based on a query as well as on a table. If you want to specify which records are displayed in a form or to specify their sort order, begin by creating a query that includes the appropriate records, using the methods described in Chapter 4. As you learned in Chapter 4, you can also add a filter to a form, as you do to a table.

The Form Wizard

Like other wizards, the Form Wizard is a series of dialog boxes which let you enter information used to generate your form. If you do not know the basic techniques of using wizards, such as how to move from one dialog box to the next, see the section on Wizards in Chapter 1.

The Wizard lets you choose among the same basic layouts that are available for AutoForms, but it also lets you specify the fields included, the style, and the title of the form.

CHOOSING THE FIELDS

The first step of the Form Wizard, shown in Figure 5.5, lets you choose which fields of the underlying Table or Query will be displayed in the Form. It is used like other field pickers, as described in Chapter 2.

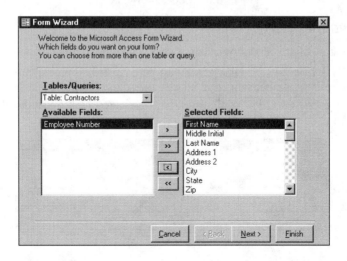

FIGURE 5.5 **CHOOSING THE FIELDS TO INCLUDE IN THE FORM.**

CHOOSING THE LAYOUT

The second step of the Form Wizard, shown in Figure 5.6, lets you choose how the fields are laid out. As you can see, you can lay them out in columnar, tabular, and datasheet arrangement, the same choices available when you create AutoForms. The layout that you select is illustrated to the right.

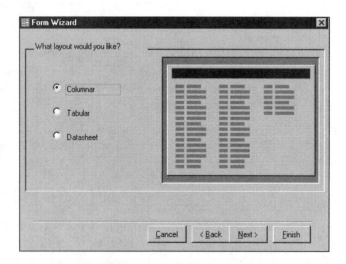

FIGURE 5.6 CHOOSING THE LAYOUT.

CHOOSING THE STYLE

The third step of the Form Wizard, shown in Figure 5.7, lets you choose the style of the form. The Wizard lets you choose from a wide variety of styles, which control the appearance of labels and data in the form. As you scroll through the options in the list, the one that is selected is illustrated to the right.

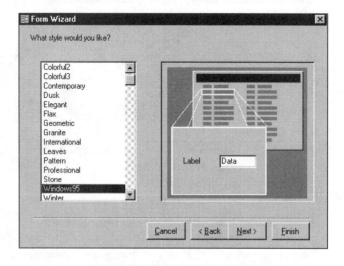

FIGURE 5.7 CHOOSING THE STYLE.

CREATING THE FORM

The final step of the Form Wizard, shown in Figure 5.8, lets you specify the title and create the form and is similar to the final step of other wizards.

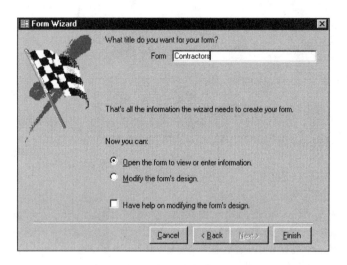

FIGURE 5.8   CREATING THE FORM.

Enter a title in the text box. This title will be used as the name of the form, as well as being used as a title for the form that is displayed in its title bar.

By default, the radio button is selected that displays the form with data after it is created. If you select the **Modify the form's design** radio button, the form will be displayed in Design View when you click the **Finish** button to create it, so that you can customize its design. It is common to begin creating custom forms and reports by using a wizard, and then make further changes to them in Design View. You will learn to modify a form's design in Chapter 7.

Working with Data in the Form Window

Given what you already know about working with the table and Query windows, it should be very easy for you to see how to work with the Form window after you are done creating a form.

SWITCHING VIEWS

Notice that the toolbar's View tool drop-down, shown in Figure 5.9, now includes a Datasheet tool in addition to the usual Design View and Datasheet View tools that you are familiar with from working with the Table window.

FIGURE 5.9   THE VIEW TOOL DROP-DOWN FOR FORMS.

✳ Click the **Design View** tool (or choose **Form Design** from the View menu) to work with the Form window in Design View so you can move objects, add graphics, and so on. It should not be confused with the Design View tool for the Table window, which lets you change the definitions and properties of fields. Chapter 7 covers Design View for forms.

✳ Click the **Form View** tool (or choose **Form** from the View menu) to switch back to Form View.

✳ Click the **Datasheet View** tool (or choose **Datasheet** from the View menu) to display the form as a table, as shown in Figure 5.10.

SHORTCUT

It is often easiest to work with most simple, single-table databases by creating an AutoForm and using it as the main object you work with. Then you can use these tools to toggle easily from Form View to Table View, and it is usually most convenient to be able to work with both of these at different times.

PRINTING THE FORM

To print the form, simply click the **Print** tool or choose **Print** from the File menu. Access displays the Print dialog box, as it does when you print a table or a query. Before printing the form, you may want to click the **Print Preview** tool or choose **Print Preview** from the File menu to display the form in the Print Preview window.

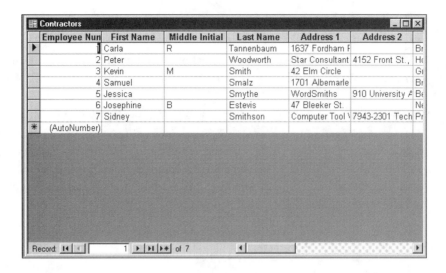

Contractors						
Employee Num	First Name	Middle Initial	Last Name	Address 1	Address 2	
1	Carla	R	Tannenbaum	1637 Fordham F		Br
2	Peter		Woodworth	Star Consultant	4152 Front St.,	H(
3	Kevin	M	Smith	42 Elm Circle		G(
4	Samuel		Smalz	1701 Albemarle		Br
5	Jessica		Smythe	WordSmiths	910 University A	Bf
6	Josephine	B	Estevis	47 Bleeker St.		N(
7	Sidney		Smithson	Computer Tool \	7943-2301 Tech	Pr
(AutoNumber)						

Record: 1 of 7

FIGURE 5.10   A FORM IN DATASHEET VIEW.

OTHER FEATURES OF THE FORM WINDOW

Other features of the Form window are the same as those of the Table window. The most important are listed below:

 Click the **Save** tool (or choose **Save** from the File menu) to save changes on a record while you are still working on it, rather than waiting for Access to save the changes automatically when you switch records.

 Click one of the two **Quick Sort** tools (or choose **Quick Sort** from the Records menu) to do a quick sort of the records. You use filters with forms just as you do with tables, as described in Chapter 4.

 Click the **Filter by Selection** or **Filter by Form** tool (or choose **Filter** from the Records menu and **Filter by Form**, **Filter by Selection**, or **Advanced Filter/Sort** to create a filter. Click the **Apply Filter** tool or choose **Apply Filter/Sort** from the Records menu to add a filter. Choose **Remove Filter/Sort** from the Records menu to remove the filter and show all records.

 Click the **Find** tool or choose **Find** from the Edit menu to use the Find dialog box to search for a record on the basis of its content. You use both **Find** and **Find and Replace** with forms just as you do with tables, as described in Chapter 3.

Click the **New Record** tool (or choose **GoTo** and then **New** from the Edit menu) to add a new record.

 Click the **Delete Record** tool (or choose **Delete Record** from the Edit menu) to delete the current record.

As you can see, you work with data in forms just as you do in tables.

You also navigate among records when you are using a form just as you do when you are using a table. Use the record indicator and arrow tools at the bottom of the window (or the equivalent GoTo commands in the Edit menu) to move to the first record, previous record, next record, last record, or a record whose number you enter.

Creating a Sample Form

To get a feel for the Form Wizards, you should try creating a simple but useful sample form, which includes all the fields of the Contractor table except for the Employee Number and Notes fields. Because the employee number is in a counter field, which is entered automatically, and the Notes field may contain confidential information, you might want to let people who routinely enter and look up data use this form.

1. If necessary, close the AutoForm you created earlier or click the **Forms** tab to display the Form list in the Database window. With the Form list displayed, select the **New** button of the Database window.

2. In the New Form dialog box, use the **Choose the Table or Query** drop-down list to select **Contractors**, select **Form Wizard**, then click **OK**.

3. The first step lets you select the fields. Click the **>>** button to add all fields to the form. Then, with the **Notes** selected in the Selected fields list, click the **<** button to remove it from the form. Likewise, select the **Employee Number** field and click the **<** button to remove it from the form. Click the **Next>** button.

4. In the next step, keep the default Columnar layout. Click **Next>**. In the next step, keep the default Standard style (or select a different style, if you want to experiment), and click the **Next>** button.

5. In the next step, enter the title **Contractors Data Entry** and click the **Finish** button to create the form, shown in Figure 5.11. Try using this form, and then close the Form window when you are done.

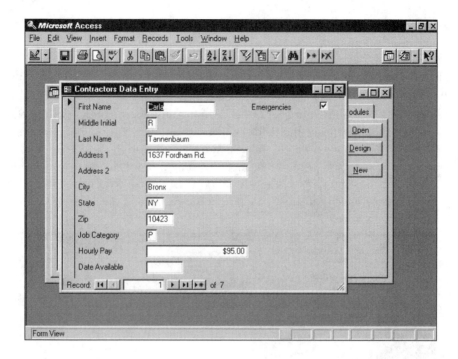

FIGURE 5.11   THE NEW FORM.

Leaving out two fields gives you a compact and easy-to-use form.

Using Reports

In Access, a report is any output designed specifically to be printed. The Report Wizard lets you create mailing labels as well as other types of printed reports.

Because a report is meant to be printed, Access displays it in the Print Preview window when you view it. You cannot edit data displayed in reports, as you can in tables, queries, and forms. The Print Preview window is the same as the window that is displayed when you are viewing a table, query or form in Datasheet View and you choose **Print Preview** from the File menu (or click the **Print Preview** tool).

AutoReports

You can create an AutoReport in the same way that you create an AutoForm. Select the table or query in the Database window that you want it to be based on and click the **AutoReport** tool.

As you can see in Figure 5.12, the default AutoReport simply lists the field names and the contents of the fields one above another. This layout is not generally useful for reports on tables, as it is not easy to read. It can be very useful, however, if you create a query that includes only a few fields you want to display and use it as the basis of the AutoReport. Of course, you can also use the query to specify which records to include in the report and their sort order.

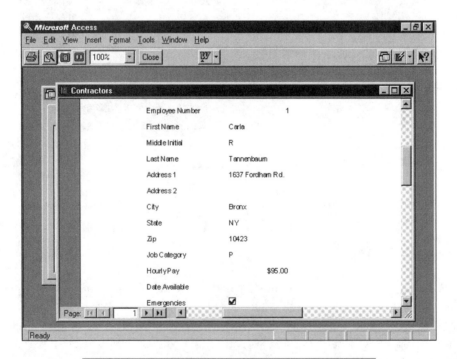

FIGURE 5.12   THE AUTOREPORT ON THE CONTRACTORS TABLE.

Creating and Using Reports

You create and use reports in the same way you do forms and other objects. Because they are meant to be printed, you view their contents in the Print Preview window rather than in Datasheet View.

After you click the **Reports** tab of the Database window to display the Report list, the Database window has the following buttons:

✳ **New**: creates a new report.

✳ **Preview**: opens an existing report and displays it in the Print Preview window.

✳ **Design**: lets you change the design of a report (using the methods described in Chapter 7).

Like forms, reports are named automatically, and you can rename them by editing their names in the Database window.

When you click the **New** button, Access displays the New Report dialog box, shown in Figure 5.13. As with forms, you use the drop-down list in this dialog box to select the table or query that the report is based on. Then choose one of the following options:

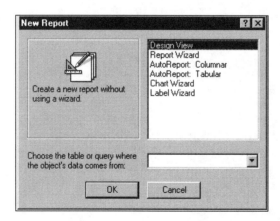

FIGURE 5.13   THE NEW REPORT DIALOG BOX.

✳ **Design View**: lets you create a custom report from scratch (using methods described in Chapter 7).

✳ **Report Wizard**: lets you use the Wizard to define the report, as described below.

✳ **AutoReport Columnar**: creates an AutoReport with the fields laid out one above another, like the one shown above.

✳ **AutoReport Tabular**: creates an AutoReport with the fields laid out one next to another. The tabular AutoReport is useful if it is based on a query that includes only a few fields, so they all fit in the width of the page.

✳ **Chart Wizard**: displays the Chart Wizard, which you can use to create a graph.

✳ **Label**: displays the Label Wizard, which you can use to create labels, as described later in this chapter.

SHORTCUT

As with forms, you can also create a report by selecting a table or query in the Database window and selecting the **New Report** tool to display the New Report dialog box with that table or query already entered in its drop-down list.

You can base a report on a query rather than on a table, in order to specify which records are displayed in it. Begin by creating a query that includes the appropriate records, using the methods described in Chapter 4. For example, you might want to create a report just for the hours worked by contractors who are programmers. You could begin by creating a query with "P" as the criterion in the Job Category column of the Design grid, and use this query as the basis of the report. You cannot add filters to reports, as you can to tables and forms.

The Report Wizard

When you select **Report Wizard** in the New Report dialog box, Access lets you use the Report Wizard to determine the fields included, the style, and the title of the form.

The Report Wizard is also powerful enough to create reports with records divided into groups based on the content of specific fields, with subtotals of numeric fields for each group, and with a final total of numeric fields for the entire table.

CHOOSING THE FIELDS

The first step of the Report Wizard, shown in Figure 5.14, lets you choose which fields of the underlying Table or Query will be displayed in the form.

When you are selecting fields, you should think about what type of layout you are going to create. If you are going to use a tabular layout, be sure the fields you select will fit in the width of a page.

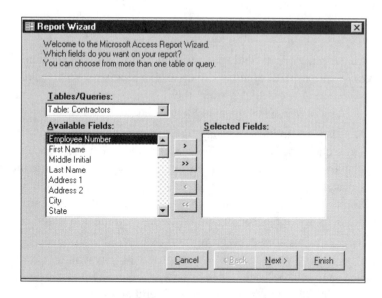

FIGURE 5.14 **CHOOSING THE FIELDS TO INCLUDE IN THE REPORT.**

GROUPED REPORTS

The next step, shown in Figure 5.15, lets you create grouped reports.

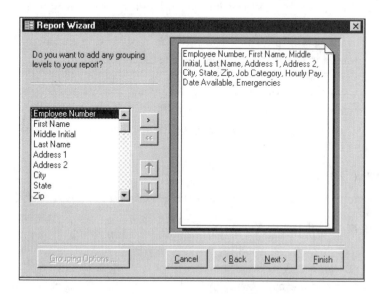

FIGURE 5.15 **CREATING A GROUPED REPORT.**

If you do not include fields to group on, the report will provide grand totals of all the numeric fields of the entire table or query it is based on.

You can select a single field to group on, and the report provides subtotals for that group and a grand total for the table. For example, you could produce a report on your contractors that groups them by job category; the report would provide totals for each job category and a grand total for all records.

You can also use multiple groups. For example, you can produce a report on contractors that groups them by state and within each state groups them by city, and within each city groups them by zip code. You can use up to four groupings nested within each other in this way. The report includes a grand total, subtotals, and sub-subtotals for all groups. This wizard automatically includes subtotals and totals for all numeric fields you include in the report.

Reports are always sorted by group. For example, if you group by state, the states will be listed alphabetically. If you group by city within each state, the cities of each state will be listed alphabetically. Click the up and down arrows in this step to specify that you want to sort in ascending or descending order.

NOTE When you are creating this sort of report, remember that all numeric fields you include, even employee number, will be totaled for each group and for the entire report, unless you choose them as the field to group by. Do not include numeric fields that you do not want totaled (such as the Hourly Pay field in the sample application), unless you plan to customize the report using the techniques covered in Chapter 9, "Designing Custom Reports."

Grouped reports are particularly useful when you are working with relational databases, where you have a second table with many records for each in the first table. Chapter 6 covers relational databases and includes an exercise where you create a grouped report.

CHOOSING THE LAYOUT

The next step of the Report Wizard lets you choose how the fields are laid out.

LAYOUTS FOR ORDINARY REPORTS

If you did not create a grouped report, this step is displayed as shown in Figure 5.16. As you can see, you have the choice of a Vertical layout (with fields one above another and the name of each field to its left) or of a Tabular layout (with fields one next to another, and the name of each field at the top of each page).

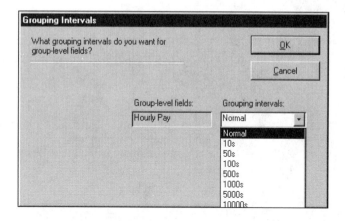

FIGURE 5.16   **CHOOSING THE LAYOUT FOR ORDINARY REPORTS.**

You also have the option of laying out the page in portrait orientation, so it is higher than wide, or in landscape orientation, so it is wider than high. Though portrait is the default, it is often better to use landscape orientation for a tabular report if it is necessary to fit more fields across the page.

The checkbox, which is selected by default, adjusts the width of fields so they all fit in the page. This feature is useful if the field widths are a bit too wide for the page, but some data will not be printed if they are much too wide for the page.

LAYOUTS FOR GROUPED REPORTS

If you created a grouped report, the layout step is displayed as shown in Figure 5.17. Fields are displayed in tabular layout (one next to another), and this step lets you specify how the group and subgroup headings are laid out. Select the radio buttons to display samples of the available layouts to the right.

As with ordinary reports, you have the option of laying out the page in portrait or landscape orientation, and you can deselect the checkbox if you do not want to adjust the width of fields so they all fit in the page.

GROUPING BY RANGE

After you select a grouping level, you can click the **Grouping Options** button in this step to display the Grouping Options dialog box, which lets you group by a range of values in a record, rather than by individual records. If you are using a date field as the basis of a grouping, for example, you might want a separate group for each different year or for each different month in that field, rather than a separate group for each record that has a different date in the field.

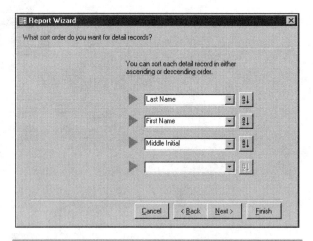

FIGURE 5.17   CHOOSING THE LAYOUT FOR GROUPED REPORTS.

The types of ranges that you can define differ for different data types. The grouping level dialog box includes the fields that are used at the basis of groupings with a drop-down to the right of each, which you can use to select the intervals that are appropriate for that data type.

The drop-down for the Date/Time fields, shown in Figure 5.18, includes a selection of ranges of dates and times—Year, Qtr, Month, Week, Day, Hour, and Minute.

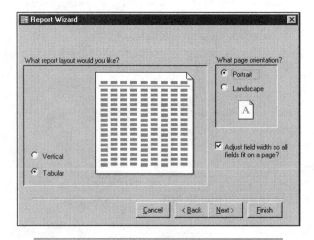

FIGURE 5.18   GROUPING DATE/TIME DATA BY RANGE.

The drop-down for text data, shown in Figure 5.19, lets you select how many characters you want to group on. For example, if you want to group records by the first letter of the last name, so all names beginning with A, B, and so on are listed together, you would select **Last Name** as the field to group on, and select **1st Character** as the grouping interval.

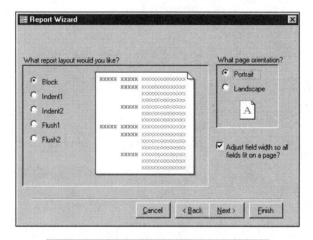

FIGURE 5.19   GROUPING TEXT DATA BY RANGE.

To group numeric data (including Number, Currency, or Counter fields) by a range of values, you use the drop-down list shown in Figure 5.20.

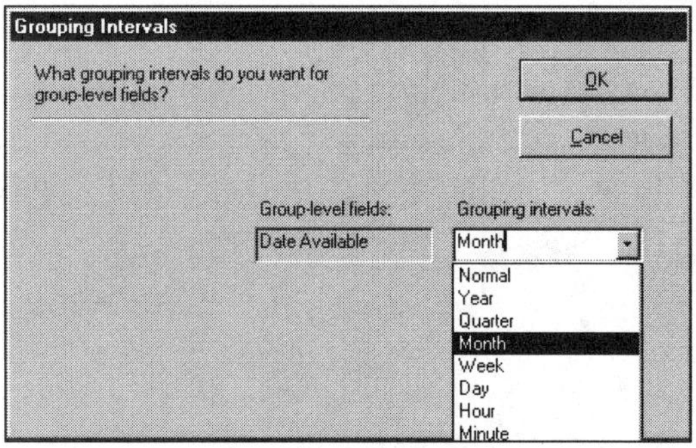

FIGURE 5.20   GROUPING NUMERIC DATA BY RANGE.

For example, you could group contractors by their hourly pay with $10 as the range of values, so contractors who earn less than $10 per hour are included in one group, contractors who earn $10 or more but less than $20 are included in a second group, and so on. To do this, select **Hourly Pay** as the field to group on, and select **10** as the grouping interval.

CHOOSING SORT ORDER

The next step, shown in Figure 5.21, lets you choose the sort order for the detail records in each group.

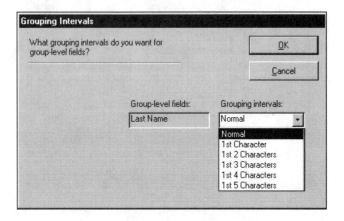

FIGURE 5.21 CHOOSING SORT ORDER.

Simply choose a field from the top drop-down to select the primary field that the sort order is based on. If you want, click the button to the right of the drop-down to toggle from ascending to descending sort.

You can choose fields from additional drop-downs to use them as tie-breakers. For example, if you want to sort by name, choose **Last Name** from the top drop-down, **First Name** from the next drop-down, and **Middle Initial** from the third drop-down.

This step only determines the sort order of the detail records within each group, not of the groups themselves.

N O T E

CHOOSING THE STYLE

The next step of the Report Wizard, shown in Figure 5.22, lets you choose the style of the report. Like the Form Wizard, this Wizard lets you choose from a wide variety of styles which control the appearance of data in the report. As you scroll through the options in the list, the one that is selected is illustrated to the right.

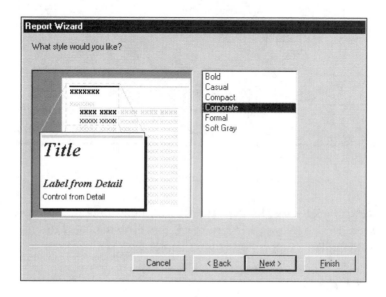

FIGURE 5.22   CHOOSING THE STYLE.

CREATING THE REPORT

The final step of the Report Wizard, shown in Figure 5.23, lets you specify the title and create the report and is similar to the final step of the Form Wizard and of other wizards.

The title you enter in the text box is displayed at the top of the report as a header.

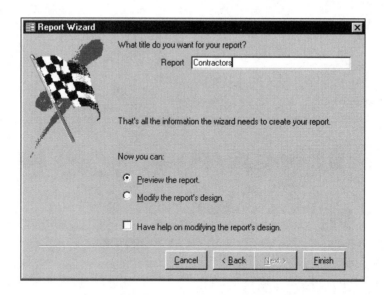

FIGURE 5.23   CREATING THE REPORT.

If you select the **Modify the report's design** radio button, the report will be displayed in Design View when you click the **Finish** button to create it. You will learn to modify a report's design in Chapter 9.

Mailing Labels

If you display the Reports tab and click the **New** button and then select **Label** in the New Report dialog box, Access lets you use the Label Wizard to specify the size of the label, lay out the fields on it, and specify the typeface and sort order of the labels. Use this Wizard to create mailing labels or other types of labels.

CHOOSING LABEL SIZE

The first step of the Wizard, shown in Figure 5.24, lets you specify the dimensions of the label form you are using. The list box lets you choose among standard label sizes, each identified by the following:

* **Avery number** is the product number on the package of Avery labels.
* **Dimensions** is the size of each individual label.
* **Number across** is the number of labels next to each other on a line.

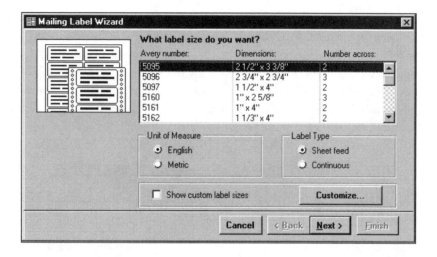

FIGURE 5.24   SPECIFYING THE DIMENSIONS AND TYPE OF LABEL FORM.

Avery is the most popular brand of label. Most users will simply be able to look at the number on their Avery label packages to see which number to choose. If you use another brand, however, you will almost certainly be able to find a label of the dimension and number across that you need.

The radio buttons below the list box offer the following options:

✳ **English**: dimensions are in inches.

✳ **Metric**: dimensions are in millimeters.

✳ **Sheet feed**: the labels are on forms that are fed into the printer one sheet at a time. This is generally used for laser printers.

✳ **Continuous feed**: the labels are on forms that are on a continuous strip. This is generally used for dot-matrix printers with tractor-feeds.

The items available in the list box change as you select different radio buttons, so it includes only the Avery labels that use that unit of measure and are that type.

CREATING CUSTOM LABEL SIZES

To customize the items in the list of standard labels in the first step of the Wizard, click **Customize** to display the New Label Size dialog box, shown in

Figure 5.25. To create a new label size, click the **New** button and use the New Label dialog box to define it. This dialog box works like the Edit Label dialog box, described below.

The New Label Size dialog box includes a list of all the user-defined labels you have created in the past. Select the radio buttons to include suggested labels in the list with the unit of measure and type you select. Select an item and click the **Delete** button to delete it from this list.

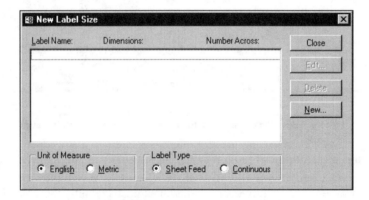

FIGURE 5.25   THE USER LABEL SIZES DIALOG BOX.

To edit the specifications of a suggested label in this list, select it and click the **Edit** button to display the Edit Mailing Label dialog box, shown in Figure 5.26. The options are as follows:

✳   Use the **Label Name** text box to edit the suggested name label specification.

✳   Use the radio buttons to specify the unit of measure and label type.

✳   Use the **Number Across** text box to specify how many labels fit across a page.

✳   Edit the dimensions in the text boxes on the illustration of the sample labels to indicate the height and width of each label, the right and left margin, the vertical and horizontal space between labels, and the distance of the text on the label from the label's top and left edge, as shown in the Figure 5.26.

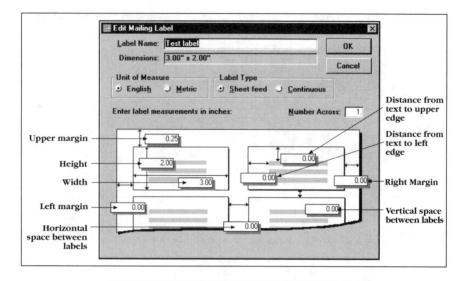

FIGURE 5.26 **THE EDIT MAILING LABEL DIALOG BOX.**

N O T E

After you have created custom label sizes, select the **Show custom label sizes** checkbox of the first step of the Wizard to display only these custom sizes in its list, or deselect this checkbox to display the standard label sizes in this list.

SPECIFYING THE TYPEFACE

Once you have chosen the label size you want, click **Next** to display the second step of the Wizard, shown in Figure 5.27, which lets you specify the typeface of the label.

The options included in two upper drop-downs, which let you choose font name and size, depend on the fonts that you have installed in Windows. The Font weight drop-down gives you a wide range of choices, such as Extra Light and Extra Bold; the checkboxes let you use all of these weights in italic or underlined. If you click the button to the right of the Color box, Access displays a color palette, so you can select the color of the font. The typeface you choose is displayed in the sample area to the left.

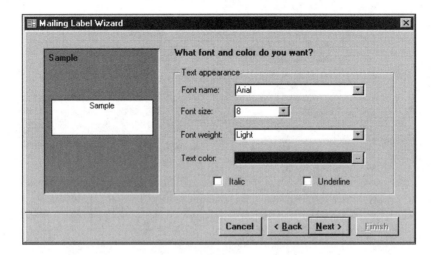

FIGURE 5.27 SELECTING THE TYPEFACE.

LAYING OUT THE LABEL

The next step of the Wizard is shown in Figure 5.28. Though it looks similar, this dialog box works differently than the field pickers that you looked at earlier, because it actually lets you lay out the label, rather than just specifying which fields it includes.

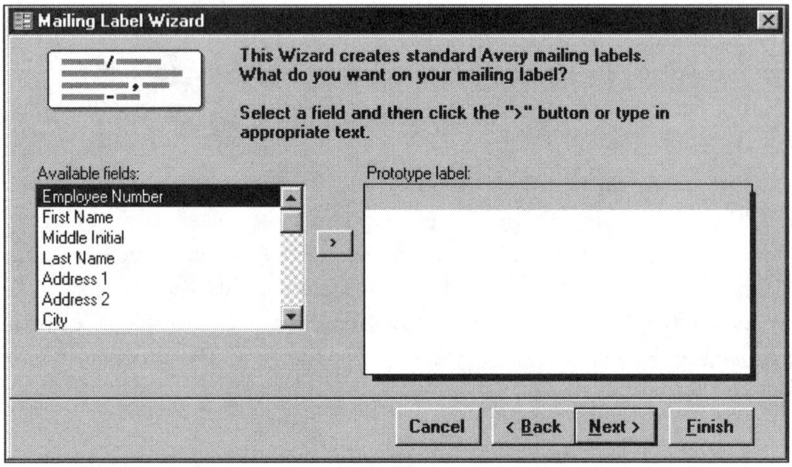

FIGURE 5.28 LAYING OUT MAILING LABELS.

You move individual fields to the Label appearance box in the usual way. Double-click a field in the Available fields box or click it and click the **>** button to move it to the Prototype label list box. Field names are enclosed in curly brackets to distinguish them from other text. You also remove it in the usual way.

In addition to adding fields, however, you can also type text directly into the Prototype label. For example, you must type a space after the First Name before adding the Middle Initial field.

To add a new line to the label and move the cursor to it, simply press the **Down Arrow** key or click a location on the Prototype label. You must actually place fields as you want them to appear on the label. Do not press **Enter** to move to a next line, as this will move you to the next step of the Wizard.

SPECIFYING SORT ORDER

The next step of the Wizard, shown in Figure 5.29, lets you select a field or fields to sort by—usually zip code or last and first name—and it is used like the sort step of other Wizards.

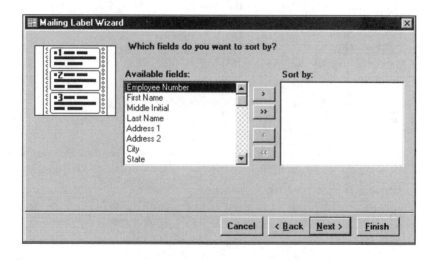

FIGURE 5.29   CHOOSING THE SORT ORDER.

CREATING THE LABELS

The final step simply lets you display the labels in the Print Preview window or in Design View (which will be covered in Chapter 9). Unlike other wizards, it does not let you enter a title, as this is not appropriate for mailing labels.

Creating Sample Mailing Labels

The Report Wizard should be very easy for you to use, particularly if you did the exercise earlier in this chapter using the single-column Form Wizard, which has dialog boxes similar to the Report Wizard. Chapter 6 has an exercise where you create a grouped report, which uses the more advanced features of this Wizard.

Here, you should try doing an exercise using the Mailing Label Wizard. This wizard works a bit differently than the others, and you will need it in most practical applications.

1. Begin with the Database window open and the Reports list displayed. Select the **New** button. When Access displays the New Report dialog box, use the drop-down list to select **Contractors** as the table that the report is based on, select **Label Wizard**, and click **OK**.

2. Access displays the first step of the Wizard. If you have label forms of your own that you want to print the labels on, select their Avery number. Otherwise, leave **Avery 5095** selected, a common size for two-column labels, and click **Next>**.

3. In the next step, leave the default font and color and click **Next>**. (You can try changing fonts if you want, but remember not to use a font size so large that the fields do not fit on a label.)

4. The next step lets you lay out the label. Double-click the **First Name** field to add it to the Prototype label box. Press the **Spacebar**. Double-click the **Middle Initial** field. Press the **Spacebar**, and double-click the **Last Name** field.

5. You have finished adding the first line of the label. Press the **Down Arrow** key to move to the next line. Then, in the Available fields list, double-click the **Address 1** field. Again, move to the next line, either by pressing the **Down Arrow** key or clicking it with the mouse, and then double-click the **Address 2** field.

6. One more line is needed in the label. Press the **Down Arrow** key. Then double-click the **City** field. Type a comma (**,**) and press the **Spacebar**. Double-click the **State** field. Press the **Spacebar**. Double-click the **Zip** field. You have added all the necessary fields and other characters to the label, as shown in Figure 5.30. Click the **Next>** button.

7. In the next dialog box, double-click the **Zip** field to add it to the Sort by box, assuming that you are doing a bulk mailing that you want sorted in zip code order. Click the **Next>** button.

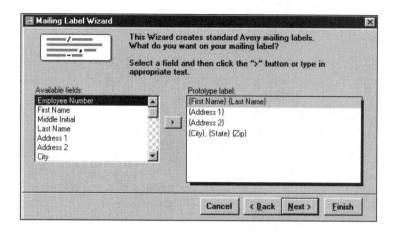

FIGURE 5.30 THE FIELDS NEEDED IN THE LABEL.

8. You have reached the final step of this wizard. Enter **5095 Mailing Labels** as the name for the report. (Of course, if you created different size labels, you should name them accordingly.) Click **Finish** to generate the labels and view them in the Print Preview window. When you are done looking at the labels, close the Preview window.

Notice that the labels, as shown in Figure 5.31, do not include a blank line when a record does not have an Address 2 field. Access automatically adjusts the spacing for either three- or four-line addresses.

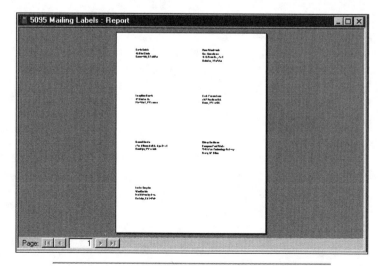

FIGURE 5.31 THE LABELS IN THE PRINT PREVIEW WINDOW.

To Sum Up

In this chapter, you learned to create AutoForms and to use the Form Wizards to create single-column forms and graphs. You also learned to use the Report Wizards to create reports and mailing labels. Part II of this book includes chapters on designing custom forms and reports, but many users will find that the wizards are powerful enough to create all the forms and reports they need.

Now you have learned about all the different objects that you need to know about to manage your own data. Chapter 6 teaches you how to use these objects when you are working with more complex data that requires you to use multi-table databases.

CHAPTER 6

Relational Databases

In this chapter, you'll learn to store more complex data in multiple tables that are related to each other with common key fields. This is called a *relational database*. First we discuss general database design, so you understand the types of relationships that can exist between tables. Then you'll learn the techniques used in Access to join the tables of a relational database and to work with their data. This chapter covers the following:

* The definition of a many-to-one relationship
* How the primary key and foreign key fields are used in the two tables in a many-to-one relationship
* When it is best to use a one-to-many rather than a many-to-one relationship
* What a many-to-many relationship is
* How to break down a many-to-many relationship into two many-to-one relationships
* How to create a default relationship in Access
* How to enforce referential integrity in Access

183

✳ When to use the three different join types available in Access

✳ How to create queries based on relational databases

✳ How to use the Report Wizard to create grouped reports on relational databases

✳ How to use the Main/Subform wizard to create a form that displays a one-to-many relationship

Database Design

Before you can do any hands-on work with a relational database in Access, you must have some basic understanding of database theory. Before you can do anything practical, you need to understand enough theory to know how to break up the data into different tables, which you then relate to each other using a common key field. In database terminology, this is called *normalizing data.*

This book does not cover the technical rules of normalization, which are discussed in textbooks on database theory. Instead, it gives you some simple common-sense guidelines, which are easy to apply once you understand why multi-table databases are sometimes necessary and once you understand the two basic types of relationships that require multi-table databases—the many-to-one and the many-to-many relationship.

Single-Table Databases

When you were first designing your sample Contractors table, you learned that you must be sure there is a one-to-one relationship between each field and the record.

In the sample table you have used so far, each record contains data on a contractor. When you designed it, you had to make sure that each field contained data that applied only once to each contractor. You saw that each contractor has one first name, one last name, one address, one wage rate, and one availability date. You assumed that everyone works as a programmer, a writer, or clerical help, but not as more than one of these. Therefore, this information was also in a one-to-one relationship with the record and could be kept in a single field. If some people did more than one of these jobs, you could have designed the table differently. Instead of one Job Category field, you could have created three Yes/No fields—one for Programmer, one for Writer, and one for Clerical—so that you could select more than one for some contractors.

One-to-One Relationships

It is possible to break up data like this into several tables and to relate them. You could conceivably keep each contractor's name and address in one table and the other information on this contractor in a second table. Both tables would have the Employee Number field as their primary key which would be used to relate them, so you could get all of the information on each contractor.

Though it is possible to create a database with this sort of one-to-one relationship between tables, it is usually easier and more effective to keep all the data in one table.

Access, like other database programs, makes it possible to join tables in a one-to-one relationship, but this is useful only in special cases. For example, you might use it to join two tables made to record data on your employees for two different applications, which you have some special reason for combining. (First, you would have to import or link the tables within a single application, using the methods covered in Chapter 12.)

NOTE

When you are designing an application, you should keep this sort of data in a single table.

Many-to-One Relationships

As you learned in Chapter 2, you need information on contractors for this application that cannot be stored in a single table. Billing data is a good example. Since each contractor sends a bill periodically—say, at the end of the month—you will get many bills for each contractor. Each time you get a bill, you will have to enter the billing date, the number of hours worked, and other billing data.

This billing data is in a many-to-one relationship with the records in your contractor file. You must record many bills for each contractor.

As you learned in Chapter 2, it is impossible to enter this data in the same table as the contractor's name and address. If you included fields for billing date and hours worked in the same record as the contractor's name and address, it would be easy to enter the date and hours of the first bill, but how would you enter the data on the second bill you got?

You might try adding a new contractor record to hold this data, but then you would have to reenter all the basic name and address data for a contractor each time you got a bill.

You might try adding new fields to the table called Billing Date 2, Hours Worked 2, Billing Date 3, Hours Worked 3, and so on, but then you would have an unwieldy table with many empty fields for contractors who work on fewer jobs. You also would have trouble producing reports summarizing billing data kept in fields with different names.

In this chapter, you learn the right way to record this data. You create a separate table for it, called the Billing table, which has fields for the employee number, the billing date, the hours worked, and so on. As you know, each record in the Contractor table also has an Employee Number field. You can see in Figure 6.1 how these key fields are used to relate the two tables in a many-to-one relationship.

Billing table			Contractors table		
EmpNo	**Bill Date**	**Hours**	**EmpNo**	**Name**	**etc.**
1	1/31/96	95.5 →	1	Carla Tannenbaum	...
1	2/28/96	32.0			
1	3/31/96	150.5			
3	3/31/96	28.5 →	3	Kevin Smith	...
4	2/28/96	162.5 →	4	Samuel Smalz	...
4	3/31/96	22.0			

FIGURE 6.1   A MANY-TO-ONE RELATIONSHIP.

The figure shows just a bit of the data that would actually be in the Billing table; the bills for Employee Number 1 to Employee Number 4 for the first three months of 1996. For the sake of simplicity, it does not show all the fields.

The arrows make it easy for you to see how Access can use the key field to look up the record in the Contractors table that goes with each record in the Billing table. The Billing table includes fields for Employee Number, Billing Date, and Hours Worked. By finding the record with the same employee number in the Contractors table, you know the name and address of the person who worked those hours.

USING KEY FIELDS

The key field is used differently in these two tables, and by looking carefully at how this relationship works, you can understand how the two different types of key fields work.

THE PRIMARY KEY

Now that you see how the Contractor table fits into a multi-table database, you can understand why its primary key, the Employee Number field, must be unique to each record.

If the Billing table has a record of January's bill for employee number 1, there must be only one record in the Contractor table with that Employee Number. If you were ready to pay that January bill and two records in the Contractor table had that same Employee Number, you would not know who to make out the check to.

NOTE

When you are joining two tables that are in a many-to-one relationship, the key field that you use in the table on the "one side" of the relationship must be the primary key of that table. It must be unique, so you can look up a record in that table. You need to find only one record in the table that has that value in the key field. There can only be one contractor who sends each bill. The Employee Number in the Contractor table is the primary key of this relation.

THE FOREIGN KEY

On the other hand, the Employee Number field in the Billing table is not the primary key for that table, and it is not unique in each record.

The key field used in the table that is on the "many side" of a many-to-one relationship cannot possibly be unique for each record. By definition, a one-to-many relationship can always have more than one record in this table with the same key as each record in the "one table" it is related to. There can be many bills from each contractor.

The Billing table can have its own primary key, called something like Bill Number, but it cannot use the Employee Number field as its primary key. The Employee Number field is the primary key of another table and is used to relate the Billing table to that other table. In Access, this is called a *foreign key*, to emphasize that it is a primary key of another table. The Employee Number in the Billing table is the foreign key of this relation.

VALID VALUES IN KEY FIELDS

The primary key and the foreign key have different criteria for their validity.

As you know, the primary key must be unique and must be entered in each record. When you designate a field as a primary key, Access automatically makes sure that the value you enter in that field meets these criteria.

NOTE

When you are using a field as a foreign key, the value must be present in the other table and must be entered in each record.

For example, if you enter 1 in the Employee Number field of the Billing table, there must also be a record with Employee Number 1 in the Contractors table. If you enter an employee number in the billing table that does not correspond to an Employee number in the Contractor table, or if you do not enter an employee number in the Billing table at all, then you will not be able to look up the name and address of the person to whom you send the check.

You can make Access check the validity of entries in a field that is a foreign key as it checks the validity of the primary key field. This is known as *checking for referential integrity*. In other words, Access checks to make sure that there is some record in the other table that the foreign key refers to.

ONE-TO-MANY RELATIONSHIPS

One other point that you should know about this sort of relational database is that sometimes it is most convenient to work with it as a one-to-many relationship rather than as a many-to-one relationship.

Rather than using the table on the "many side" as the main table of the database and looking up a record in the table on the "one side" that corresponds to each of its records, as shown earlier in Figure 6.1, you will sometimes find it easier to use the table on the "one side" as the main table of the database and look up a record in the table on the "many side" that corresponds to each of its records, as shown in Figure 6.2.

If you compare these two figures, you will see that you can use exactly the same tables in either a many-to-one or a one-to-many relationship, and that there is no difference in the use of the primary and foreign key fields in the two tables. There is one significant difference between the two types of relationship, however.

If you are working with a many-to-one relationship, you can find a single record in the table on the one side that matches each record in the table on the many side. You can find Name and Address fields in the Contractors table, for example, for each record in the Billing table. Thus, you can join the two tables into a single table, as shown in Figure 6.3.

Contractors table			Billing table		
EmpNo	**Name**	etc.	**EmpNo**	**Bill Date**	**Hours**
1	Carla Tannenbaum	... ⟶	1	1/31/96	95.5
			1	2/28/96	32.0
			1	3/31/96	150.5
3	Kevin Smith	... ⟶	3	3/31/96	28.5
4	Samuel Smalz	... ⟶	4	2/28/96	162.5
			4	3/31/96	22.0

FIGURE 6.2   A ONE-TO-MANY RELATIONSHIP.

Bill Date	**Hours**	**Name**	**etc.**
1/31/96	95.5	Carla Tannenbaum	...
2/28/96	32.0	Carla Tannenbaum	...
3/31/96	150.5	Carla Tannenbaum	...
3/31/96	28.5	Kevin Smith	...
2/28/96	162.5	Samuel Smalz	...
3/31/96	22.0	Samuel Smalz	...

FIGURE 6.3   JOINING TWO TABLES THAT ARE IN A MANY-TO-ONE RELATIONSHIP.

If you compare this joined table with Figure 6.2, you will see that creating the joined table is simply a matter of following the arrows from each record in the Billing table and filling in the blank spaces with the data from the Contractor table. Of course, the joined table has repetitious data, but you can fill in the extra data for each of its records.

In Access (as in some other database management programs), you can use a query to join two tables that are in a many-to-one relationship to produce a result like the one shown in Figure 6.3. The employee numbers do not have to be included, since you can see in the query's result which person each bill applies to. In fact, since you can arrange the fields in a query in any order, you can easily display names in the left columns and the billing data on the right.

On the other hand, if you are working with a one-to-many relationship, you cannot find a single record in the table on the many side that matches each record in the table on the one side. There are several records in the Billing table for each Name and Address field in the Contractors table. Thus, you cannot join the two tables in a table that looks like Figure 6.3. Instead, you must display one record from the Contractors table (or other table on the one side) with several records from the Billing table (or other table on the many side) below it.

In Access, you can display this sort of relationship by using the Form/Subform wizard, which was mentioned in Chapter 5. By now, you should see why it is that the form holds data from the Contractors table, and the subform has multiple lines to hold the corresponding records of the Billing table. This is what you need in a one-to-many relationship.

Later in this chapter, you learn how Access works with relational databases using both queries and the Form/SubForm wizard. They should be easy for you to understand now that you know the database theory behind them.

Many-to-Many Relationships

Not all applications are based on the sort of one-to-many relationship that you have looked at so far. Some are based on a many-to-many relationship.

Consider an example similar to the one you have been looking at so far. Imagine that you run a referral agency for contractors, matching them with employers and billing the employers for their work. This involves a many-to-many relationship, because each contractor can work for many different employers, and each employer can hire many different contractors over the course of the years. You need tables with data on each contractor and on each employer, but you cannot relate these to each other using the one-to-many and many-to-one relationships discussed previously.

It is easy to come up with other examples of many-to-many relationships. For example, students and classes in a school have this relationship. Each student can take many different classes, and each class can enroll many different students.

N O T E When two tables are in a many-to-many relationship, you must work with them by breaking down the relationship into two separate one-to-many relationships. This involves creating a third table that is in a one-to-many relationship with both of the original tables.

In the case of the contractor referral business, you would create a Billing table, such as the one shown in Figure 6.4. Like the previous example, this includes the work of employee numbers 1 to 4 during the first three months of 1996. As you can see, those four people happened to work for only two different employers during that time. Employer number 25 needed more people during the beginning of the period, and employer number 14 needed more toward the end of the period.

Billing table			
Employee No	**Employer No**	**Bill Date**	**Hours**
1	25	1/31/96	120.5
1	25	2/28/96	23.0
1	14	2/28/96	52.5
1	14	3/31/96	94.5
3	25	1/31/96	48.0
4	25	2/28/96	62.0
4	14	3/31/96	56.0

FIGURE 6.4   A THIRD TABLE TO LINK TWO TABLES IN A MANY-TO-MANY RELATIONSHIP.

This Billing table has two foreign keys. The Employee Number field is the primary key of the Contractor table, just as it was in the previous example. In addition, the Employer Number field is the primary key of a table that holds data on employers.

Notice that you can relate this Billing table to the Contractors table by using a one-to-many relationship (or a many-to-one relationship), just as you did in the previous example, as shown in Figure 6.5. You could find out how many hours each employee worked, exactly as you did in the previous example.

Contractors table			Billing table		
EmpNo	**Name**	**etc.**	**EmpNo**	**Bill Date**	**Hours**
1	Carla Tannenbaum	...	1	1/31/96	120.5
			1	2/28/96	23.0
			1	2/28/96	52.5
			1	3/31/96	94.5
3	Kevin Smith	...	3	1/31/96	48.0
4	Samuel Smalz	...	4	2/28/96	62.0
			4	3/31/96	56.0

FIGURE 6.5   ONE HALF OF THE MANY-TO-MANY RELATIONSHIP.

Looking at the data in the illustration, you can see that you could also add a bit of information on the employers they worked for, since each record in the

Billing table has a foreign key that refers to only one record in the Employer table. You could print a report to send out with employees' paychecks that not only lists the hours they worked each month, but also includes the name of the employer (or employers) they worked for. Looking at the illustration, you can see that you could look up one Employee Name for each Employee Number.

You could also use the same methods to join this Billing table with the Employer table, as shown in Figure 6.6. The Employer table would hold all the data on each employer, including the employer number and name, address, contact person, and so on. This table can be joined in a many-to-one or a one-to-many relationship with the Billing table, just as the Contractors table is.

Employer table			Billing table			
EmpNo	Name	etc.	Employer No	Employee No	Bill Date	Hours
14	ABC Inc.	… →14	1		2/28/96	52.5
		↘14	1		3/31/96	94.5
		↘14	4		3/31/96	56.0
25	XYZ Ltd.	… →25	1		1/31/96	120.5
		↘25	1		2/28/96	23.0
		↘25	3		1/31/96	48.0
		↘25	4		2/28/96	62.0

FIGURE 6.6 THE OTHER HALF OF THE MANY-TO-MANY RELATIONSHIP.

Looking at the illustration, you can see how easily you could use this one-to-many relationship to produce a list of the hours worked for each employer, so that you know how much to bill them. Because the records in the Billing table also have employee numbers, you could also pull in data from the Contractors table. For example, you could send a bill with the name of the employee next to the hours that person worked.

You can always treat a many-to-many relationship between two tables as two many-to-one relationships in this way. You just need to create a third table whose records include the primary key fields from the two other tables, plus any other data that is in a many-to-one relationship with those tables.

N O T E

Students and classes are in a many-to-many relationship with each other. If you had a table with students (each with a student number, name, and so on), and a table with classes (each with a class number, number of credits, room, days, and times in session, and so on), you could link them with a table of enrollments, each of which has the student number and the class number.

The Enrollments table is in a many-to-one relationship with the Students table. Each student has many enrollments, but each enrollment involves one student. Likewise, the table is in a many-to-one relationship with the Classes table. Each class has many enrollments, but each enrollment involves one class.

What other data would you need in the Enrollments table? It would also hold the student's grade for that class. The grade is in a many-to-one relationship with classes and students. Each student gets many grades, and each class has many grades for its students. Grade is in a one-to-one relationship with the Enrollments table. There is one grade given out for each enrollment of a student in a class.

More Complex Relationships

There are also more complex databases that must be broken down into more than three tables. Like many-to-many databases, however, these can all be broken down into a number of one-to-many relationships.

An example is a database recording sales. Each salesperson deals with many customers, and each customer deals with many salespeople. This many-to-many relationship can be broken down into two one-to-many relationships, like the one above. You need a Salesperson table with Employee Number as its key field, a Customers table, with Customer Number as its key field, and an Invoice table with fields Employee Number, Customer Number, Date and other information about each sale. The Invoice table would also have an Invoice Number field as its own primary key. With these three tables, you could easily print out a list of when each customer made purchases and when each salesperson made sales, just as you would with the Contractor and Employer database previously described.

However, you also need to record all the products sold in each sale, how many of each is sold, the price of each, and so on. Any number of products could be sold in each sale, so products are in a many-to-one relationship with invoices. The usual way to handle this relationship is to create a separate Invoice Line table, which includes fields for the invoice number, the price of each product, the quantity sold of the products, and other data. Use the Invoice Number field to join the Invoice Line table with the Invoice table. You could print out the heading of the Invoice, which includes:

✳ **The date** from the Invoice table.

✳ **The customer's name**, which you find by looking in the Customer table for the record whose primary key is the same as the customer number in the Invoice table. This is a typical many-to-one relationship, as there are many invoices for each customer.

✳ **The salesperson's name**, which you find by looking in the Employee table for the record whose primary key is the same as the employee number in the Invoice table. This is also a typical many-to-one relationship, as there are many invoices for each salesperson.

Under this heading, you could print all the lines of the invoice, which you find by looking in the Invoice Line table for all the records that have this invoice number as their foreign key. This is a typical one-to-many relationship, as there are many invoice lines for each invoice.

You would also want to include the product's name in each line of the invoice. You would probably have a Product table, with product number, product name, product cost, and other data on each product. If you include the product number as a foreign key in each invoice, you can pull in the product name from the Product table. This is a typical many-to-one relationship, as there can be many invoice lines that include each product.

As you can see, this example includes many different types of data stored in many tables that must be related to one another. However, it is finally broken down into a number of typical one-to-many and many-to-one relationships.

However complex the database, you can always break it down in this way into a number of many-to-one relationships.

Normalization Made Easy

The technical rules of data normalization, which are covered in more advanced textbooks on database theory, are useful in complex cases, but in most cases you can do just as well by using the common-sense rules you learned in this chapter:

✳ Be sure there is a one-to-one relationship between each table and all of the fields in it. The entity represented by each record in the table should have the data in each field recorded for it only once. For example, an employee has only one address and one zip code, so these fields can go in the Employee table, but an employee sends many bills, so these cannot go into the Employee table.

✴ If there is a one-to-many relationship between the table and some data, put this data into a second table, which includes the primary key of the first table as its foreign key. For example, to record the employee's bills, create a Billing table that includes the Employee Number field as a foreign key.

✴ Break up a many-to-many relationship between two tables into two many-to-one relationships by creating a third table that includes the primary keys of both original tables as its foreign keys. For example, if each employee bills many customers and each customer pays many employees, then the Employee table and the Customer table are in a many-to-many relationship, and you need a Billing table with both the Employee Number and Customer Number fields as foreign keys.

N O T E

If you keep looking for one-to-many and many-to-many relationships where you must break the data down into separate tables, and if you use common sense, you can generally normalize even complex data.

Since the data is always normalized into a series of tables with many-to-one relationships, you can work with even complex data using the techniques you'll learn in the following examples, where you use Access to create many-to-one and one-to-many relationships.

Relational Databases in Access

Access gives you a number of ways of defining relationships. For example, you can use the Query window to define a relationship among tables that is used as the basis of that single query.

In general, however, you should begin by using the Relationship window to define the relationship among tables that are the fundamental to your database, such as the relationship between the Employee table and the Billing table in your sample application, so they are used as the default relationship when you work with the tables.

Creating a Default Relationship

To create a default relationship, open the database and select **Relationships** from the Tools menu. The first time you do this, Access displays the Show Table dialog box, shown in Figure 6.7, which lets you choose the tables or queries that you want to include in the Relationships window. Double-click a table or select a table and click the **Add** button to add it to the window.

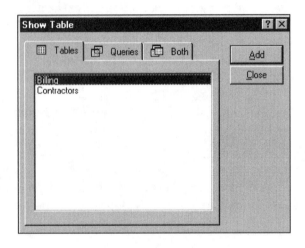

FIGURE 6.7   ADDING THE TABLES.

When you are done, close the Show Table dialog box to display the field lists for the tables, as shown in Figure 6.8. Notice that name of the field that is the primary key for each table is displayed in darker type.

WORKING WITH THE TABLES

At any later time, you can add new tables to the Relationship window by choosing **Show Table** from the Relationships menu, or clicking the **Show Table** tool to display and use the Show Table dialog box again.

You can remove a table from the Relationships window by selecting it and pressing **Delete** or choosing **Hide table** from the Relationships menu.

You can move a table simply by clicking and dragging its title bar. It is sometimes convenient to move tables in complex databases to make it easier to see the connections between them.

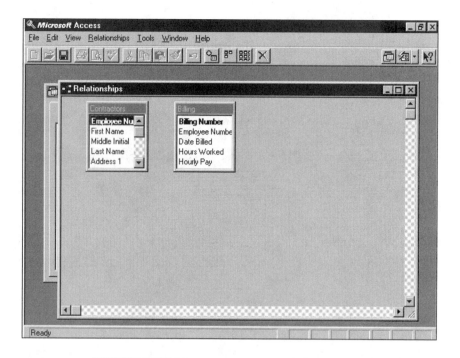

FIGURE 6.8   FIELD LISTS IN THE RELATIONSHIPS WINDOW.

CREATING THE RELATIONSHIP

To create the relationship, click and drag from one of the fields that it is based on to the other. For example, in the sample application, you would click and drag the Employee Number field of the Contractor table to the Employee Number field of the Billing table.

N O T E

You should begin dragging from the field that is the primary key of the table on the "one side" of the relationship. In the sample application, you should be sure to drag the Employee Number field from the Contractors table to the Billing table. The table that you begin dragging from is called the *primary table* of that relationship. As you will see, you must use the "one table" as the primary table in order to enforce referential integrity.

When tables are joined in this way, Access displays a line connecting the fields that the join is based on, as shown in Figure 6.9. Notice the number 1 near the Contractors table, and the symbol ∞ near the Billing table, indicating that this is a one-to-many relationship. There can be an indefinite number of Billing records associated with each Contractors record. This is sometimes called *Graphical System Relationships*, since it displays the relationship graphically.

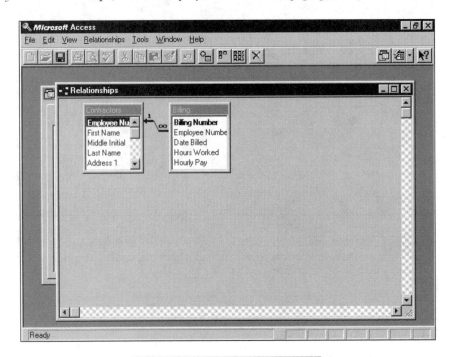

FIGURE 6.9   ACCESS DISPLAYS THE JOIN.

Defining the Relationship

When you first create a relationship in this way, Access displays the Relationships dialog box shown in Figure 6.10.

If you want to change the definition of the relationship, you can display this dialog box at any time by double-clicking the line that represents the relationship, or by clicking the line to select it and choosing **Edit Relationship** from the Relationships menu.

The primary table or query of the relationship is listed on the left, and the table or query that is related to it is listed on the right.

Enforce Referential Integrity

As explained earlier, in one-to-many relationships, the primary key in the "one table" has to be unique in each record, and the foreign key in each record of the "many table" has to be present as the primary key in one of the records of the "one table."

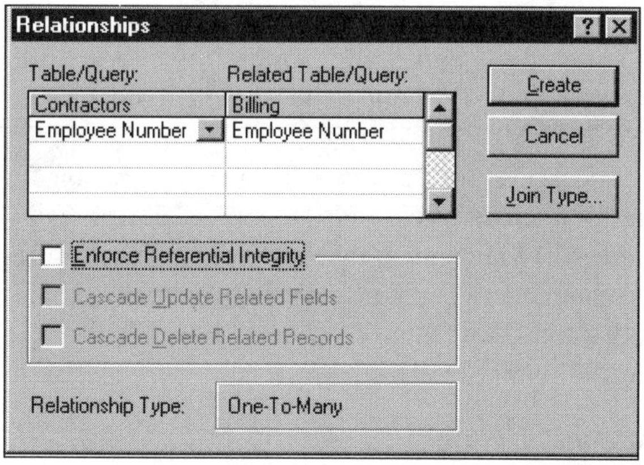

FIGURE 6.10 **THE RELATIONSHIPS DIALOG BOX.**

For example, the Employee Number field had to be unique in each record in the Contractor table, and each record of the Billing table had to have an Employee Number field that was present in some record of the Contractor table, so you could find the name of the person who worked those hours.

A record in the "many table" whose foreign key does not refer to any record in the "one table" is sometimes called an *orphan record*. If you select the **Enforce Referential Integrity** checkbox, Access will automatically make sure that there are no orphan records in the "many table." Access will not let you do the following:

✳ Add a record to the related table (Billing) unless there is a record with that number in the main table (contractors).

✳ Change a value in the primary key field of the main table if there are records in the related table that use that value as their foreign key.

✳ Delete a record from the main table if there is a record in the related table that refers to it.

Unless you have some special reason not to, you should select the **Enforce Referential Integrity** checkbox to make sure you do not enter invalid foreign keys by mistake.

Notice that this feature can work only if you use the table on the "one side" of the relationship as the main table and the table on the "many side" of the relationship as the related table. That is why, when you create a relationship, you should click the primary key in the "one table" and drag it to the foreign key in the "many table." You must make the "one table" the main table to use this checkbox.

Notice that this checkbox only protects the integrity of the foreign key in the related table and does not protect the integrity of the primary key in the main table. For example, it would not prevent you from entering the same value as the employee number in two records of the Contractor table. To prevent this error you should use an AutoNumber counter field (or some other field with a unique index) as the primary key.

Cascade Update and Delete

If you select the **Cascade Update** or **Cascade Delete** checkboxes, Access will override the usual protections for relational integrity in the following ways:

✳ If you select **Cascade Update Related Fields**, you will be able to edit the primary key field in the "one" table, and Access will automatically make the same change to the foreign key in the "many" table, so the records will still be related.

✳ If you select **Cascade Deleted Related Records**, you will be able to delete records in the "one" table even if there are related records in the "many" table. Access will automatically delete the related records in the "many" table, so it will not have orphan records.

After a cascading update or delete, the database will still have relational integrity, but there may have been changes to many records in the many table without the user knowing it.

Though this feature can sometimes be useful in applications, it should be used with great care, since you may delete or modify records in the "many" table automatically without knowing it. Non-programmers should avoid Cascade Updates and Deletes, since they override many of the protections built into Access.

You can accomplish the same thing more safely by using an action query. Include the key fields from both of the related tables in the query form, and use the action query to change them both. Using this method to change the data forces you to change the values in the key field of the many table or to delete records from the many table explicitly, rather than doing it automatically. Action queries are covered in Chapter 10.

Join Type

If you click the **Join Type** button in the Relationships dialog box, Access displays the Join Properties dialog box, which lets you specify which records are included in the joined database.

As you can see in Figure 6.11, the radio buttons in this dialog box give you three options.

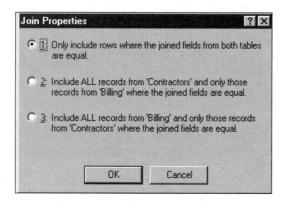

FIGURE 6.11   THE JOIN PROPERTIES DIALOG BOX.

It is obvious how to use these buttons if you are working with a one-to-one relationship. You can include only records that are in both tables or all the records that are in one or the other table.

Join Properties for One-to-Many Relationships

When you are working with a one-to-many relationship, the descriptions in the dialog box are a bit confusing, particularly because they refer to the main and related tables in the relationship that you created with Access, rather than to the "one table" and the "many table" in the logical relationship between the tables.

Assuming that you make the "one table" the main table as you must to enforce referential integrity, you have the following options:

1. Include only records that are in both tables. There will be a record in the joined database only if there is a record with that key in both tables. In the example, there must be a record with the same Employee Number in both the Contractor table and the Billing table for it to be included. If there is a contractor who has not billed or if there is a bill without a contractor to send it to, it is not included. Note that if there were no errors in data entry, there would not be any record in the Billing table without a record in the Contractors table that represents the person who sent you the bill.

2. Include all records from the "one table" and only the records from the "many table" that are related to it. In the example, you would include all records from the Contractor table and only the records from the Billing table that have a related record in the Contractor table. Note that if there were no errors in data entry, this would be all of the records in the Billing table, since each record in this table must have a related record in the Contractors table. Thus, this option would include all the contractors, whether they sent bills or not.

3. Include all records from the "many table" and only the records from the "one table" that are related to it. In the example, this would include all records from the Billing tables and only those records in the Contractor table that are related to it. Thus, this option would include records on the contractors who have sent bills but would leave out the contractors who did not send bills.

When you are working with an ordinary one-to-many relationship, with the "one table" as the main table, options 1 and 3 in the Join Properties dialog box should be equivalent. In the sample application, both would display only the contractors who sent bills, and not the other contractors. The difference between the two is that option 1 would hide records where there is a bill without a contractor and option 3 would not.

NOTE
Since there should never be a bill without a contractor, the two options should give you the same result. If there were an error, though, and there were a bill without a contractor, option 3 would include this bill and option 1 would hide it. In an ordinary one-to-many relationship, the only difference between the two options is that option 1 hides your errors and option 3 reveals them. It is always better to use option 3, so your errors do not go undetected.

Access enforces referential integrity well enough so that errors should not appear, but in the rare cases where errors do slip in, it is best to know that they are there.

When to Use Different Join Properties

The important choice you must make in the Join Properties dialog box is between option 2 and option 3.

If you are using a typical one-to-many relationship with referential integrity enforced, option 2 will include all records in both tables, and option 3 will leave out the records in the "one table" with no equivalent in the "many table." Which of these you should use depends on your reason for joining the tables.

If for example, you want to pay your bills, you should select option 3, and display only the records of contractors who have sent bills.

On the other hand, if you want to produce a report that lets you look generally at how much work your contractors have done, you would probably want to select option 2, so you could also see which contractors have not worked.

You can choose whichever of these is most convenient as the default. You may have to change this property in some forms, queries, or reports.

THE DATA TYPE OF THE FOREIGN KEY

Access gives you a great deal of flexibility in designing key fields. When you create the most common type of relationship, however, a many-to-one relationship with referential integrity enforced, your options become more limited.

As you know, it is usually best to use a counter, like AutoNumber, as the data type of a primary key. If you want to relate a foreign key to a primary key in another table that is a counter and enforce referential integrity, you should make it the Number Data type with the Long Integer length.

WARNING

If you use any other data type, Access displays a rather confusing error message saying that key fields must be the same data type to enforce referential integrity. You will create endless problems for yourself if you try to do as the message says and make the foreign key AutoNumber. Access considers the Long Integer to be the same data type as the AutoNumber because they are both integers of the same size.

Creating a Sample Database

Now that you have enough of a grounding in database theory and in the methods that Access uses to create relationships, it should be easy for you to create a sample relational database.

In this section you create a second table, define its default relationship to the Contractors table, and enter sample data. Then, in later parts of this chapter, you use this sample database in exercises to create queries, reports, and forms for relational databases.

CREATING THE BILLING TABLE

First, you must define the Billing table you will relate to the Contractors table. Since this table was used as an example in the general discussion of database design in the section "One-To-Many Relationships" earlier in this chapter, you have already done most of the analysis needed to design this table. However, the examples did not require you to think about precisely what fields should be in the sample table.

The table needs an Employee Number field as its foreign key and fields for Billing Date and Hours Worked, as shown in the examples. Though it was left out of the example for the sake of simplicity, the table should also have a Billing Number field as its primary key, since Access generally works most efficiently if each table has its own primary key.

Finally, though you might not realize it at first, this table should also have an Hourly Pay field (like the Contractors table), so you can multiply the Hours Worked field by the Hourly Pay field to find the total pay for the period.

At first, you might think you could multiply the Hours Worked field by the Hourly Pay field in that person's record in the Contractors table. This would only be possible if you are sure that the hourly pay will never change. If a contractor ever changed pay rates and you changed the value in the Hourly Pay field in the Contractors table, you would no longer be able to calculate the total pay earned during past periods.

The Hourly Pay field in the Contractors table is the pay rate at the current time, and it can be kept in this table because each contractor has only one current pay rate. However, you also have to record the contractor's pay rates over time, and this is in a many-to-one relationship with the contractor table, because each contractor can have many different pay rates over the years.

You do not need a separate field for total pay earned, because this can be calculated from the values in the Hours Worked and Hourly Pay fields. In

Chapter 8, when you learn about expressions, you will to see how to add this sort of calculated field to a form or report.

To create the Billing table, do the following:

1. If necessary, open the Teach Yourself database, and display its Tables tab. Click the **New** button of the Database Window, select **Design View** in the New Table dialog box and click **OK**.

2. In the Table window, enter the following field definitions. Notice that you use Currency as the data type for hours worked, even though it is not an amount of money. Its values can be entered with one or two decimal places, and calculations using it need to be accurate to less than four decimal places. Thus, these calculations can be done more quickly using the Currency type.

Field Name	Data Type	Properties
Billing Number	AutoNumber	(enter nothing)
Employee Number	Number	Field Size: Long Integer
Date Billed	Date/Time	(enter nothing)
Hours Worked	Currency	Format: General Number, Decimal Places: 2
Hourly Pay	Currency	(enter nothing)

3. Select the Billing Number row and click the **Primary Key** tool (or choose **Primary Key** from the Edit menu).

4. Choose **Save** from the File menu. Access displays the Save As dialog box. Enter **Billing** as the table name and click **OK**. The table is now fully defined, as shown in Figure 6.12. Click the Table window's **Close** box to close the window.

RELATING THE TABLES

Now you must define the relationship between these two tables. This involves creating the most common type of relationship, a one-to-many relationship with enforced referential integrity.

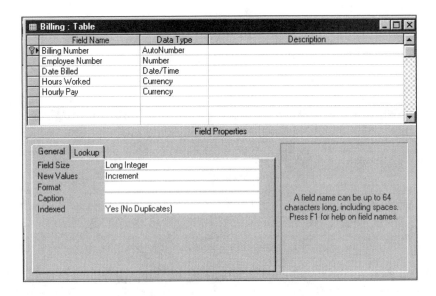

FIGURE 6.12 DEFINING THE BILLING TABLE.

Let's assume that you have a long list of contractors and you do not want to display the ones who are not currently working, because you do not want these records to get in the way during data entry. Thus, you will create a default relationship that displays a record in the Contractor table only if there is a record in the Billing table related to it.

1. Choose **Relationships** from the Tools menu. In the Show Table dialog box, first double-click the **Contractors** table and then double-click the **Billing** table to add both to the Relationships window. Then click **Close**.

2. In the Relationships window, click the Employee Number field in the Contractors field list and drag to the Employee Number of the Billing field list. Access displays the Relationships dialog box. Click the **Enforce Referential Integrity** checkbox, as shown in Figure 6.13.

3. Click the **Join Type** button. In the Join Properties dialog box, select radio button 3, to include all records from the Billing table and only those records from Contractors table where the joined fields are equal. Click **OK**.

4. In the Relationships dialog box, click the **Create** button. Access displays the relationship, as shown in Figure 6.14.

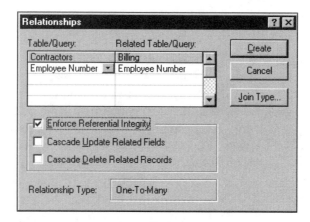

FIGURE 6.13   DEFINING THE RELATIONSHIP.

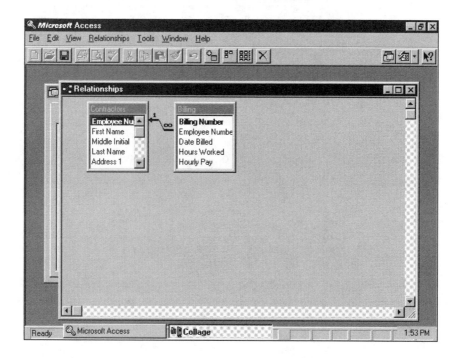

FIGURE 6.14   THE NEWLY-CREATED RELATIONSHIP.

5. Select **Save** from the File menu to save the changes in the Relationships window. Then close the Relationships window.

ADDING SAMPLE DATA

Now you can work with either of the tables individually, just as you always have. Try adding a bit of sample data to the Billing table:

1. In the Database window, double-click the Billing table name to open it in Datasheet View. First, try entering invalid data, to test the way in which Access enforces referential integrity. Press **Tab** to move to the Employee Number field, and type **99**. Of course, no employee has that number in the Contractors table. Press the **Down Arrow** key to try to move to the next record. Access displays the error message shown in Figure 6.15. Click **OK**.

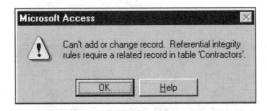

FIGURE 6.15 ACCESS ENFORCES REFERENTIAL INTEGRITY.

2. Edit the Employee Number field so it reads 1, and continue entering the sample data listed below. (Of course, Access enters the billing number for you.)

Billing Number	Employee Number	Date Billed	Hours Worked	Hourly Pay
1	1	1/31/96	95.5	95
2	1	2/28/96	32	95
3	1	3/31/96	150.5	95
4	3	3/31/96	28.5	55
5	4	2/28/96	162.5	9
6	4	3/31/96	22	9

3. The table should look like Figure 6.16. Click the Table window's **Close** box to close it.

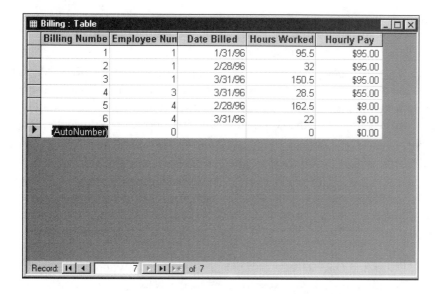

FIGURE 6.16   SAMPLE BILLING DATA.

Queries with Relational Databases

As you entered data in the Billing table, you understood that the Employee Number field linked it to the Contractor table. However, in an actual application, you would not want to look at just the Employee number in the Billing table and try to remember which person it applies to. You would want to see the contractor's name.

It is easy to display fields from both tables by using a query. Queries with relational databases are almost identical to ordinary queries. Once the related tables are included in the Query window, you add fields to the Design grid and use other features of the Query window much as you do when you are creating a query based on a single table. It is so simple that you will be able to learn how to do it simply by looking at an example.

CREATING THE QUERY

First create a query, which you will use to display all the fields of the Billing table along with the contractor's name.

This query is really just an extended version of the record in the Billing table with the Name field as a bit of extra information, so it should use the Join Type in the default relationship. Remember that when you related the tables, you said that records in the Contractor table would be displayed only if there was an equivalent record in the Billing table.

In this case, the query will include a record for each record in the Billing table and will just add the names from the Contractor table where there is a record in the Billing table, which is just what you want. You do not want to clutter it with records for all the contractors who have not worked recently.

To define the query, simply include both tables and drag the fields you want into the Design grid. As always, you can also use the drop-down lists in the Design grid to select the field name. Try displaying one when you do the following exercise, and you will see that each list includes the names from both tables, beginning with the table name, followed by a dot, then followed by the field name.

1. Click the **Queries** tab of the Database window. When the Queries List is displayed, click the **New** button. In the New Query dialog box, make sure **Design View** is selected and then click **OK**.

2. Access displays the Query window and the Show Table dialog box. In the dialog box, double-click on both the Contractors table and the Billing table to add both to the Query window, then select **Close**. Access automatically displays the default relationship between the two, as shown in Figure 6.17.

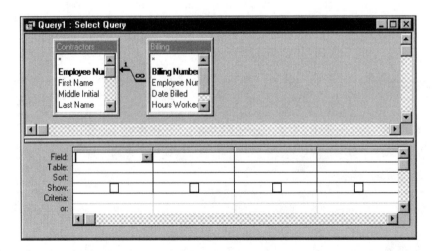

FIGURE 6.17   ACCESS ADDS THE DEFAULT RELATIONSHIP BETWEEN THE TABLES.

3. Double-click the title of the Billing field list to select all fields. Then click and drag them to the first field cell of the Design grid to place all the fields in the grid.

4. Scroll right to display blank cells in the Design grid. Click and drag the Last Name, First Name, Middle Initial, and Hourly Pay fields from the Contractors field list to the Design grid, as shown in Figure 6.18.

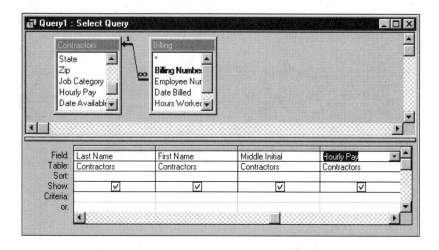

FIGURE 6.18   ADDING FIELDS FROM THE CONTRACTORS TABLE.

5. Choose **Save** from the File menu. Access displays the Save As dialog box. As the Query Name, enter **Bills with Contractor Names**, and click **OK**.

6. Click the **View** tool to toggle to Datasheet view. When Access displays the result of the Query, click and drag the edges of the column headers to resize the columns so you can view them all, as shown in Figure 6.19.

Of course, in addition to specifying which fields to include, you could have used the other features of the Query window to filter records or specify sort order, just as you do with single-table queries.

N O T E

Often, this sort of query looks best if you change the field order, which you can do by clicking and dragging columns, as you do in any query design. In the example, you might want to move the name to the left columns and the billing data to the right. You can do this even though you still use the join property that includes all records from the Billing table and only some from the Contractor table.

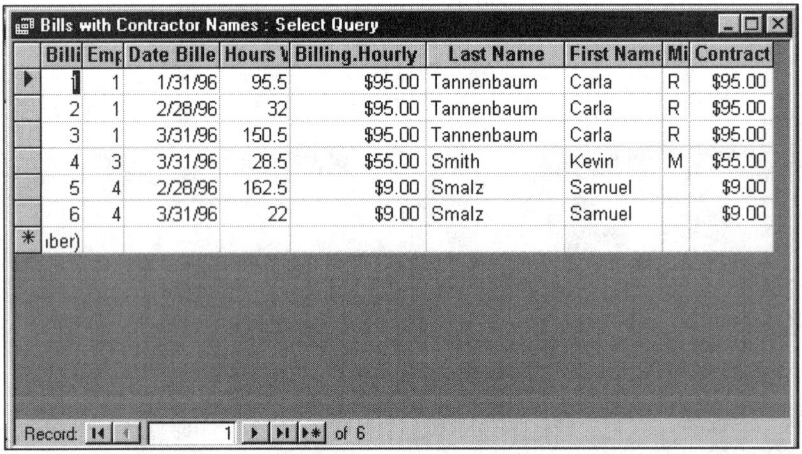

	Billi	Emp	Date Bille	Hours V	Billing.Hourly	Last Name	First Name	Mi	Contract
▶	1	1	1/31/96	95.5	$95.00	Tannenbaum	Carla	R	$95.00
	2	1	2/28/96	32	$95.00	Tannenbaum	Carla	R	$95.00
	3	1	3/31/96	150.5	$95.00	Tannenbaum	Carla	R	$95.00
	4	3	3/31/96	28.5	$55.00	Smith	Kevin	M	$55.00
	5	4	2/28/96	162.5	$9.00	Smalz	Samuel		$9.00
	6	4	3/31/96	22	$9.00	Smalz	Samuel		$9.00
✳	ıber)								

Record: I◀ ◀ | 1 | ▶ ▶I ▶✳ | of 6

FIGURE 6.19   THE QUERY DISPLAYS THE NAME WITH EACH BILL.

WORKING WITH THE QUERY

You can add records, edit records, find values, and work with the result of this query in other ways, just as you work with any table or query in Datasheet View.

There are just a few differences that are results of the one-to-many relationship that the query is based on:

✳   If you change the Employee Number field (taken from the Billing table), the values in the Last Name and First Name fields also change, as they are looked up in the Contractor table on the basis of the Employee Number field.

✳   If you edit one of the fields taken from the Contractors table, the value changes in that table, and therefore changes in all the fields where it appears in the query.

Take a look at these two unusual features in the sample query you just created:

1. Move the cursor to the Employee Number field of the new record. Type **5** and press **Tab** to move to the next field. The first and last name and hourly pay fields from the Contractors table are filled in automatically, as shown in Figure 6.20. As the Date Billed, enter **3/31/96**, and as Hours Worked enter **54**. As Hourly Pay in the Billing table, enter **50** (the same as the value of the field in the Contractors table).

	Billi	Emp	Date Bille	Hours W	Billing.Hourly	Last Name	First Name	Mi	Contract
	1	1	1/31/96	95.5	$95.00	Tannenbaum	Carla	R	$95.00
	2	1	2/28/96	32	$95.00	Tannenbaum	Carla	R	$95.00
	3	1	3/31/96	150.5	$95.00	Tannenbaum	Carla	R	$95.00
	4	3	3/31/96	28.5	$55.00	Smith	Kevin	M	$55.00
	5	4	2/28/96	162.5	$9.00	Smalz	Samuel		$9.00
	6	4	3/31/96	22	$9.00	Smalz	Samuel		$9.00
	7	5		0	$0.00	Smythe	Jessica		$50.00
*	ıber)								

Record: I◀ ◀ [7] ▶ ▶I ▶✳ of 7

FIGURE 6.20 THE FIRST AND LAST NAME FIELDS ARE ENTERED AUTOMATICALLY.

2. Move the cursor to the First Name field of record 1, and edit it so it reads **Carl** instead of **Carla**. Move the cursor to another record. The change is saved and the name is also changed in the next two records, as shown in Figure 6.21. Choose **Undo** from the Edit menu (or click the **Undo** tool) to get rid of the change.

SHORTCUT

This sort of Query gives you a simple way of entering records in fields like the Hourly Pay field of the Billing table, where the value is copied from the other table. Because you included both Hourly Pay fields in this query, the value automatically appears in the Hourly Pay field of the Contractor table, and you can copy it into the Hourly Pay field of the Employee table.

To enter this value automatically, you can use an expression to create a Default Value for the field. Expressions are covered in Chapter 8.

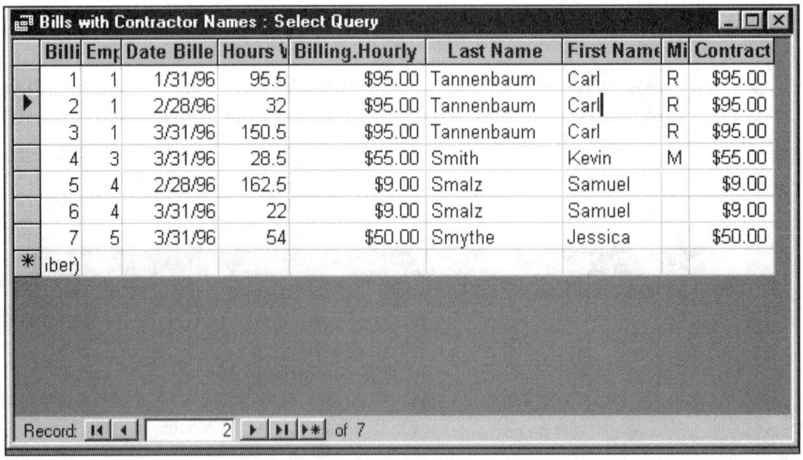

FIGURE **6.21** CHANGING THE FIELD IN ONE RECORD CHANGES THEM ALL.

CHANGING THE RELATIONSHIP IN THE QUERY

As you learned earlier, you define the relationship you need most frequently as the default relationship between tables, but there might be cases where you want to use a different relationship as the basis of the Query.

In Design View you can select **Show Table** from the Query menu, or click the **Add Table** tool to add new tables to the Query window at any time. You can relate these tables to other tables by clicking and dragging a key field from one table to another as you do when you create a default relationship. Likewise, you can select a line representing a join and press **Delete** to delete it.

It is most common to want to change the Join Properties of the relationship. You can double-click the line representing the join or you can select the line and choose the **View** menu, then **Join Properties** to display the Join Properties dialog box, as you did when you created the default query.

In the sample database, you might want some queries that display all the contractor records, even if there are no related billing records. Try changing the join properties in this query:

1. Click the **View** tool to switch the Query window to Design View. Double-click the line that represents the join (or select it and choose **Join Properties** from the View menu) to display the Join Properties dialog box.

2. Select button 2 which includes all records from the Contractors table, and click **OK**.
3. Click the **View** tool to display the data shown in Figure 6.22, including all the names from the Contractor table. Some do not have entries in the fields from the Billing table.

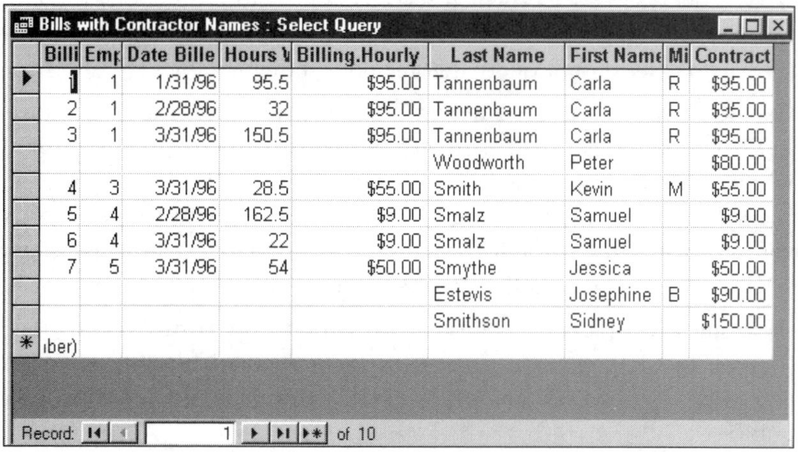
Bills with Contractor Names : Select Query

Billi	Emp	Date Bille	Hours V	Billing.Hourly	Last Name	First Name	Mi	Contract
1	1	1/31/96	95.5	$95.00	Tannenbaum	Carla	R	$95.00
2	1	2/28/96	32	$95.00	Tannenbaum	Carla	R	$95.00
3	1	3/31/96	150.5	$95.00	Tannenbaum	Carla	R	$95.00
					Woodworth	Peter		$80.00
4	3	3/31/96	28.5	$55.00	Smith	Kevin	M	$55.00
5	4	2/28/96	162.5	$9.00	Smalz	Samuel		$9.00
6	4	3/31/96	22	$9.00	Smalz	Samuel		$9.00
7	5	3/31/96	54	$50.00	Smythe	Jessica		$50.00
					Estevis	Josephine	B	$90.00
					Smithson	Sidney		$150.00
ıber)								

Record: 1 of 10

FIGURE 6.22 **THE QUERY WITH ALL THE RECORDS FROM THE CONTRACTORS TABLE.**

4. As you can see, this is not a very useful way to display the data from these tables. Close the Query window and select **No** so you do not save this change in its design.

As you can see, when you are using a query to display fields from two tables, it is generally best to use them in the way that was described in the section “Many-To-One Relationships” earlier in this chapter. You should generally include all the records in the “many table” and look up extra data from each record in the “one table.”

There are exceptions, and there might well be times when you want to use this sort of query and display all the records in the “one table,” as you did in the exercise. This would be useful if you wanted to see which contractors have not worked for you.

As a general rule, when you are keeping all the related fields on a single line, it usually does not look right to have records with some fields blank. To include all the records from the "one table," it is generally better to use a Form/Subform form, as described later in this chapter.

Reports and Forms on Relational Databases

You learned in Chapter 5 that you can create a report or a form based on either a table or a query, to specify which records appear in the Report or Form. Now you can see why it would be useful to create a report or form for a relational database that is based on a query that includes multiple tables.

In general, you can use the Report Wizard and Form Wizard with this sort of query as you do with any query. However, you should bear in mind that, as you saw when you edited the query itself, changes you make in the "one table" in one record can also cause changes in the same field in other records, and changes you make in the foreign key of the "many table" can cause changes in the fields of the same record that are taken from the "one table."

There are a couple of features of the Report and Form Wizards that were not covered in Chapter 5 because they are particularly useful when you are working with relational databases, summary and grouped reports, and forms with subforms.

GROUPED REPORTS

Because they have repetitive data, it is often useful to create grouped reports on queries based on a one-to-many relationship. Chapter 5 discussed how to use the Report Wizard to create this type of report.

In the sample database, you could use this type of report to summarize all the hours worked by each contractor. In the exercise that follows, you create a grouped report with total hours for each contractor. You will also use this grouped report in exercises in Chapter 9, where you learn to design custom reports.

As you will see in this exercise, when you work with a query of this sort, the Wizard displays a step that lets you group by either of the two tables; in addition, it displays its ordinary grouping step to let you add subgroups.

1. If you have not already done so, close the Query you just created, saving changes.

2. Click the **Reports** tab of the Database window, and then click the **New** button. When Access displays the New Report dialog box, use the drop-

down list to select **Bills with Contractor Names**, the query on the relational database that you just created. Then select **Report Wizard** and click **OK**.

3. In the first step of the Report Wizard, as the fields to include, select **Last Name**, **First Name**, **Date Billed**, and **Hours Worked**. Add them all to the Selected fields list, and click **Next>**.

4. In the next step, be sure that **Contractors** is selected as the basis of the grouping, as shown in Figure 6.23. Then click **Next>**. In the next step, simply select **Next>**, since you do not want to add subgroups.

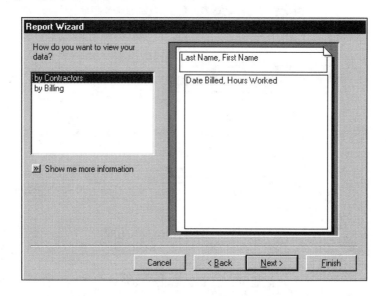

FIGURE 6.23 GROUPING THE RECORDS IN THE REPORT.

5. In the next step, use the top drop-down to select **Date Billed** as the basis of the sort order of detail records. Click the button to its right to sort in descending order, so the most recent billings for each contractor are displayed first. Then click **Next>**.

6. In the next step, select the **Outline 1** radio button, and click **Next>**. In the next step, keep the default style, and simply select **Next>**.

7. In the final step, enter the title, **Hours Worked by Contractors**. Click the **Finish** button.

6. When Access displays the new report, scroll through it, maximizing the window so you can see more of the report, as shown in Figure 6.24. When you are done, click the **Close** button to display the Report Window, and click its close box to return to the Database window. Click the **Restore** button of the Database window to return it to its default size.

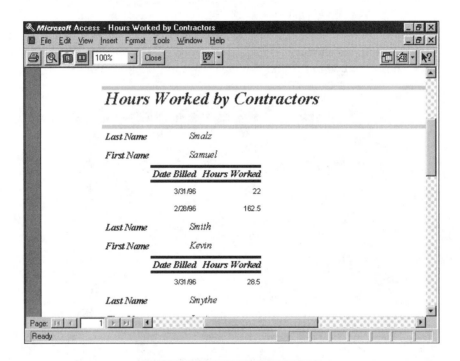

FIGURE 6.24   THE GROUPED REPORT.

You can see that it would improve this report if the contractors' names were placed on a single line in the group header, rather than two lines. You cannot do this using the wizard, but in Chapter 9 you will learn to design custom reports, and to make this change.

MAIN/SUBFORM FORMS

As you saw earlier, if you use two joined tables as the basis of a query, it is usually best to take the many-to-one approach—to include all records from the "many table" and only the related records from the "one table."

You saw that it looks a bit awkward to create a query with all the records from the "one table," some with fields missing because there are no equivalent records in the "many table." The Bills with Contractors Names query did not look as good when it had all records from the Contractors table, some with blank fields for Date Worked, Hours Worked, and Hourly Pay.

The same is true of forms and reports based on this query. As a general rule, it is best to include all records from the "many table" and only related records from the "one table." There are exceptions, and you know how to change the Join properties of queries to include all records from the "one table" to accommodate them, but it is usually best to follow this rule.

If you want to use a one-to-many approach with all the fields from the "one table" and related fields from the "many table," it is generally best to use a main form and subform. The main form holds a record from the "one table," and the subform holds any related records from the many table. Because the emphasis is on the record from the "one table," it does not seem awkward when there is not a matching record from the many table.

The Form Wizard makes it easy to create this sort of form. In the first step, include fields from both tables in the form. Then the second step has an option that lets you choose the grouping of the form: if you group by the "one" table, you can create a form with a subform or linked forms.

As you can see in Figure 6.25, if you select **Form with subforms**, the wizard will create a single form with fields from the one table in its upper half and corresponding fields from the many table listed under it. For example, you could create a form with the name of the contractor in the upper half and all the records from the Billing table for that contractor in a panel in the bottom half. If there are there are too many Billing records for that contractor to display at once, a scroll bar will be added to the panel to let you view them all.

As you can see in Figure 6.26, if you select **Linked forms,** the wizard will create a form with fields from the one table that has a button you can click to display a second form with the corresponding fields from the many table. This is useful if you want to display so many fields that not all of them can fit in a single form.

In both cases, the wizard will let you enter two titles in its final step, one for the main Form and one for the subform or linked form.

NOTE

In both cases, also, the wizard relates the tables using the default relationship you established earlier, so you should not use this wizard unless you have created a default relationship.

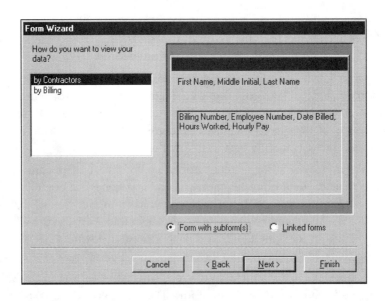

FIGURE 6.25   USING THE WIZARD TO CREATE A FORM WITH A SUBFORM.

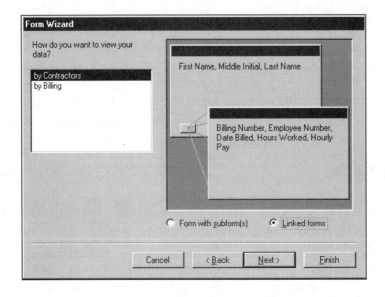

FIGURE 6.26   USING THE WIZARD TO CREATE LINKED FORMS.

In the exercise, you will create a form with a subform for the sample database. Since the two types of multi-table forms use the same principles, it will be easy for you to create Linked forms on your own:

1. Click the **Forms** tab of the Database window, and then click the **New** button. When Access displays the New Form dialog box, select **Form Wizard** and click **OK**.

2. The first step of the Wizard lets you select fields. Choose the **Contractors table** from the Tables/Queries dropdown, and add the First Name, Middle Initial, Last Name, Address 1, Address 2, City, State, and Zip fields to the Selected fields list. Then select the **Billing table** from the Tables/Queries dropdown and add the Date Billed, Hours Worked, and Hourly Pay fields to the Selected fields list, as shown in Figure 6.27. Then click **Next>**.

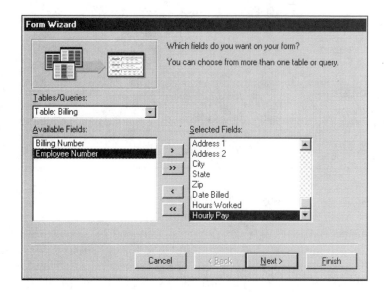

FIGURE 6.27   ADDING FIELDS TO THE FORM

3. In the next step, to create a form with a subform, simply click **Next>**. In the next dialog box, to keep the default Datasheet layout for the subform, select **Next>**. Likewise, in the next step, keep the default Standard style and click **Next>**.

4. In the final dialog box, enter the title, **Contractors with Hours Worked by Each** for the Form, and enter the title **Billing Data** for the Subform. Click the **Finish** button.

5. After a moment, Access displays the new form, as shown in Figure 6.28. Try using this form, and close it when you are done.

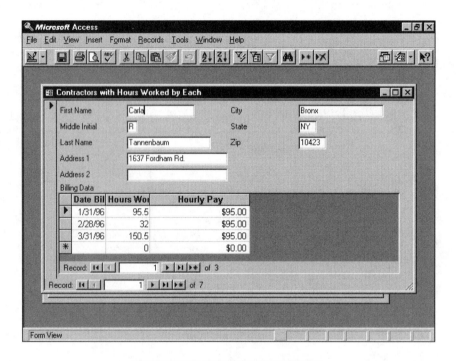

FIGURE 6.28 **THE FORM AND SUBFORM.**

Notice that this form has two sets of arrow tools and two record numbers displayed at once: one for the main form and one for the subform. Try using the arrow tools to scroll through the records of the Contractors table, and notice that the related records from the Billing table (or a blank record, if there are no records entered yet in the billing table) are displayed in the subform.

It is very easy to work with this new form. Use the main form to work with the data in the Contractor table, just as you would with its quick form or most other forms you create for it. The subform is tabular, and you can use it to work with the data for a given contractor in the Billing table just if you were working with any datasheet.

Using Lookup Fields for Data Entry

If you read the section on Lookup fields in Chapter 1, you should realize how convenient it is to use a lookup field as the foreign key field of the "Many" table of a relational database and enter data in it by using a drop-down that displays the values of the primary key field of the One table. If you did not read that section, you might want to go back to the end of Chapter 1 and read it, and then do the following optional exercise, which will make it clear how to use this wizard:

1. Select the **Billing table** in the Tables panel of the Database window and then click the **Design** button to display it in Design view.

2. From the Data Type drop-down of the Employee Number field, select **Lookup Wizard**.

3. In the first step of the Wizard, be sure that you have selected the radio button that says: *I want the lookup column to look up the values in a table or query.* Then click **Next>**.

4. In the second step, leave Contractors selected as the table that is used as the source of the values. Click **Next>**.

5. In the third step, choose the **Employee Number**, **Last Name**, **First Name**, and **Middle Initial** as the fields to be included in the lookup column, and click **Next>**.

6. In the fourth step, narrow the columns, as shown in Figure 6.29, and keep the key column hidden, as recommended. Click **Next>**.

7. In the final step, keep Employee Number as the title of the lookup column and click **Finish**. When the Wizard displays a dialog box that prompts you to save changes in the table, click **Yes**.

8. Click the **View** tool to display the table in Datasheet view. Click the **Employee Number** field of the new record to see that it lets you add the Employee Number to the Billing Table by selecting from a drop-down with a list of all contractors' names, as shown in Figure 6.30. When you are done experimenting with it, close the table.

You can see that the lookup field makes it easy and foolproof to add an Employee Number. The user simply selects the employee's name and does not even have to know that the Employee Number exists.

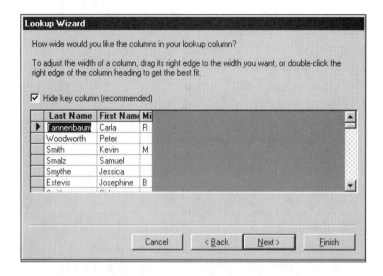

FIGURE 6.29   PLEASE SUPPLY A CAPTION.

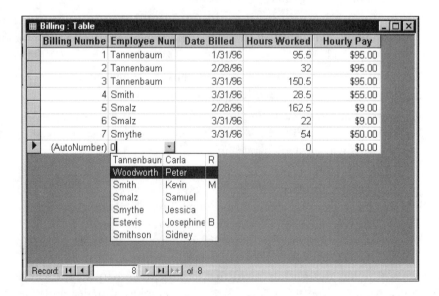

FIGURE 6.30   ADDING AN EMPLOYEE NUMBER USING A LOOKUP FIELD

To Sum Up

In this chapter, you learned simple methods of normalizing data, breaking up complex data into multiple tables. You learned to look for many-to-one, one-to-many, and many-to-many relationships, to use a primary key and a foreign key to relate two tables that are in a many-to-one relationship, and to break down a many-to-many relationship into two many-to-one relationships.

After looking at how to analyze data, you learned to work with multi-table databases in Access. You saw that it is best to begin by creating a default relationship that enforces referential integrity. You also learned to create queries based on multi-table databases, to use the Report Wizards to create reports on multi-table databases, and to use the Form Wizard to create a form for a multi-table database.

Now you have learned all the basic features of Access that you need to manage your own data in most business applications. Part II of this book covers power features of Access. You can go on and read it now, or you can begin doing practical work with Access and come back to this book and work with Power Features whenever you find it useful.

PART II

Adding Power

CHAPTER 7

Designing Custom Forms

This chapter covers form design in general, but it focuses on the basic techniques that you will find most helpful in your own work, and it concludes with an exercise that uses these basic techniques to modify the design of a form. You may also want to try out some of the more advanced techniques of form design on your own. In this chapter, you learn to:

* Select, resize, add and delete bands (sections) of the form
* Select, resize, and move individual or multiple controls of the form
* Use layout tools such as the Ruler, the Grid, Automatic Alignment, and Automatic Sizing to help place controls properly
* Edit and change the typeface and style of text in the form
* Change the colors and special effects used in the form
* Add fields to the form
* Use the toolbox to add objects such as labels, text boxes, lines, and rectangles

✳ Use the toolbox to add objects such as checkboxes, radio buttons, and combo boxes, which can replace fields to ease data entry

✳ Specify default properties of the objects you add

✳ Display and make some changes in the Property sheets of objects

The Basics

In Chapters 5 and 6, you created forms using Form Wizards. Though these are adequate for many purposes, it is often useful to customize the forms that the Wizards create. For example, you will find that if a table has many fields, the forms you create for the table using the Wizards do not fit all the table's fields on a single screen. The table would be easier to work with if you rearranged the fields so you could see them all at once.

In this chapter, as you learn to design custom forms, you will see that Access' Form window in Design View gives you tremendous power. For example, you can rearrange the fields in the forms created by Wizards simply by clicking and dragging them to the location where you want them.

Displaying Forms

As with other objects, you select the **Forms** tab of the Database window to display the forms list and then select its **New**, **Open**, and **Design** buttons to create new forms and work with existing ones. You can also create a new form by selecting a table or query in the Database window and then clicking the **AutoForm** or the **New Form** tool on the toolbar.

Once you have created a form, you can use the toolbar to display it in Design View, Form View, or Datasheet View using the tool drop-down shown in Figure 7.1. Chapter 5 discussed how to use Form View and Datasheet View; in this chapter, you learn how to work with forms in Design View.

In general, it is best to begin by using a Form Wizard or creating an AutoForm, even when you are creating a custom form. When you create a new form, the New Form dialog box gives you the option of using the Form Wizards or creating a new form. If you select **Design View**, Access displays a blank form. You can add fields of the table or query that it is based on to the form design, using the methods you will learn below.

FIGURE 7.1   DESIGN VIEW, FORM VIEW, AND DATASHEET VIEW TOOLS.

However, it is easier to use a Wizard to select fields, so you have all the fields that you need placed in the Form window when you begin. The last dialog box of every Form Wizard has a button that lets you display the form you defined in Design View, so you can customize it. To create a form with all the fields, it is often easiest to start with an AutoForm.

You should begin by displaying the AutoForm you created in Chapter 5 in Design View and saving it under a different name, so you can try the techniques of form design on it as you read about them in this chapter:

1. If necessary, open the Teach Yourself database. Click the **Forms** tab of the Database window to display the list of forms. Select **Contractors** and click the **Design** button to display it in Design View.

2. Click the **Maximize** button of the Form window so you have more room to work in.

3. Choose **Save As/Export** from the File menu. When Access displays the Save As dialog box, leave the **Within the current database** radio button selected, and edit the New Name so it reads **Contractors: Custom Form**. Then select **OK**.

Your screen should display the form in Design View, as shown in Figure 7.2.

Getting Oriented

All the items included in a form, such as fields, labels (text objects), and check-boxes, are called *controls*. In Access, there are three fundamentally different types of control:

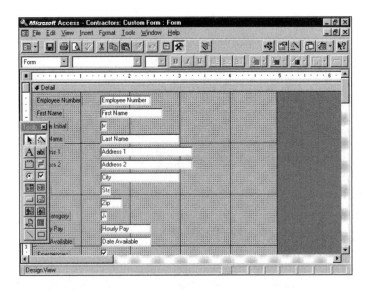

FIGURE 7.2   THE FORM WINDOW IN DESIGN VIEW.

✳ **Bound controls** are associated with data in the table. All the fields displayed in the AutoForm are bound controls. This name is used because the information displayed in them depends on the data in the table. They are connected (or bound) to the table.

✳ **Unbound controls** are independent of the data in the table. If you add the word *Contractors* in the header of the AutoForm, it would be an unbound control. It always remains the same, regardless of the data in the table.

✳ **Calculated controls** are created using expressions. For example, you can create a calculated control that displays the sum of the values in several numeric fields. Because calculated controls require expressions, they are described in Chapter 8, "Working with Expressions."

THE VIEW MENU

There are a number of features of the Form window in Design View that you can display or hide by using the View menu, shown in Figure 7.3. The Toolbox, Grid, and Ruler are displayed by default. Beginners should not select Code from the View menu, but should use the other features, such as Properties, Field List, and Tab Order, which are all covered in this chapter.

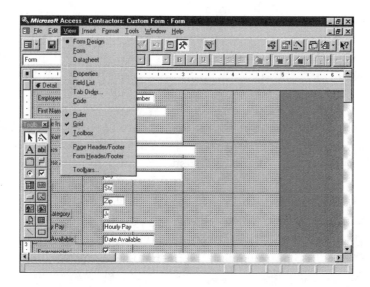

FIGURE 7.3 **THE VIEW MENU.**

After a feature is displayed, you can choose the menu option or click the tool again to close it.

Take a quick look at the features controlled by the View menu to get an overview of how you design forms:

✳ The first three menu options, **Form Design**, **Form**, and **Datasheet** (like the first three drop-down tools on the first tool of the toolbar) let you toggle among views of the form. As you learned in Chapter 5, you can display forms in Design View, in Form View as a form with data, or in Datasheet View as a table with data.

✳ Choose **Properties** from the View menu or click the **Properties** tool to display a property sheet with properties for selected object. You can display properties for the entire form, for bands, or for controls.

✳ Choose **Field List** from the View menu or click the **Field List** tool to display or hide a field list similar to the one you used in the Query window, which you use to add fields to the form.

✳ Choose **Tab Order** from the View menu to control in what order the cursor will move from field to field when you press the **Tab** key. This feature is covered later in this chapter.

✳ Choose **Code** from the View menu or click the **View Code** tool to display programming code associated with the form. Programming is not covered in this book, and beginners should not use this option. If you do select this option by mistake, Access displays code in a window that covers the Form window. Close this window in one of the usual ways (for example, by choosing **Close** from the File menu) to return to the Form window.

✳ Choose **Ruler** from the View menu to display or hide the rulers above and the left of the Design window, which make it easier for you to lay out controls. By default, this option is checked and the rulers are displayed.

✳ Choose **Grid** from the View menu to display or hide a grid of dots in the Design window. Controls are automatically aligned to this grid when you move them, so they will be lined up with each other.

✳ Choose **Toolbox** from the View menu or click the **Toolbox** tool to display or hide the toolbox that you use to add new controls. By default, this option is checked and the toolbox is displayed.

✳ Choose **Page Header/Footer** and **Form Header/Footer** to control what bands the form has. Bands will be discussed later in this chapter.

Open these using the View menu or the tools shown in Figure 7.4. The menu option is checked and the tool button is depressed to show they are in use. Access remembers which are open and closed when you stop designing the form. It displays the same ones the next time you open the Form window in Design View.

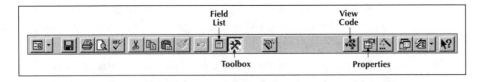

FIGURE 7.4 **TOOLS THAT LET YOU USE FORM DESIGN FEATURES.**

Although the toolbox is displayed by default, other important features of the Form window, such as the Field List, are not automatically displayed the first time you begin to design a form. Always keep the View menu and these tools in mind when designing a form, so you can use all the features needed for designing forms.

THE FORMATTING TOOLBAR

When you are working with a Form, Access also displays a second toolbar, called the Formatting toolbar, which you can use to select objects or to specify their colors and other special effects. This toolbar is shown in Figure 7.5, with labels that explain how its tools are used. The tools that are used to format text are accessible only when a text object is selected.

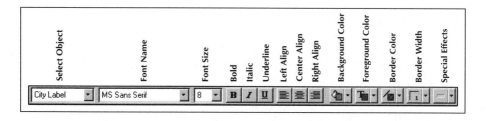

FIGURE 7.5   THE FORMATTING TOOLBAR.

You learn more about all these features of form design in the course of this chapter.

Working with the Form

In the next few sections, you'll see how to select and work with the form as a whole, with bands (or sections) of the form and with individual controls on the form.

You can tell which object is selected because its name is displayed in the Select Object drop-down of the Formatting toolbar. You can also select objects by choosing them in this toolbar.

Selecting the Form

To select the form, choose **Select Form** from the Edit menu or choose **Form** in the Select Object drop-down. As you will see near the end of this chapter, you can display a property sheet for the whole form—as you can for other objects that you select—but this is useful primarily for programmers. After selecting the form, you cannot manipulate it in many of the simple ways that you can bands and controls.

Resizing the Form

Most users work with the entire form only by resizing it. To resize the form, simply place the pointer on its right edge, where it is displayed as a vertical line with arrows pointing in both left and right directions. Then drag left or right to make the form narrower or wider. (If you have maximized the form, you can use the horizontal scrollbar to display the form's right edge.)

To change the height of the form, you must resize its individual bands, as described below.

Working with Bands

The Form design window is divided into *bands* or *sections*, as shown in Figure 7.6, where the Form Header band and Detail Band are both displayed. Which band you place a control in determines how that control is used when you print the form or report or display it on the screen.

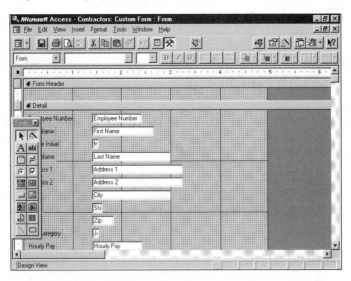

FIGURE 7.6   TWO SECTIONS (BANDS) OF THE FORM ARE VISIBLE.

Many forms have three sections:

> ✳ **Form Header** is displayed at the top of the screen when you view the form on the screen and remains in that location when you scroll

through a record. When you print the form, it is printed once at the beginning of the printout.

✳ **Detail** scrolls when you scroll through the forms on the screen and is repeated for each record when you print the form. In an AutoForm, the Detail band includes all the fields of the table.

✳ **Form Footer** is displayed at the bottom of the screen, if space permits. When you print the form, it is printed once at the end of the printout.

In most forms generated by Access, the Form Header and Form Footer band have nothing in them and have a size of zero, but you will see how to resize them in a moment. After expanding them, you can add text or other controls to them using the methods described later in this chapter.

Selecting a Band

You can select a band simply by clicking it or by choosing it in the Select Object drop-down of the Formatting toolbar. You can also press **Tab** or **Shift-Tab** to select the bands in turn.

The bar with the band's name on it is shaded when it is selected. After you have selected it, you can change the color or other properties of the band using methods described later in this chapter.

Resizing Bands

You will often have occasion to change the size of bands when you are designing custom forms—for example, to make the Header band larger so it can hold a company logo and form title.

You resize a band by clicking and dragging its lower border. When the mouse pointer is in the location where it can be used to resize the band, it is displayed as a horizontal line, with arrowheads pointing up and down. Then you can click and drag downward to make the band larger or upward to make it smaller. While you resize the band, the rulers are highlighted, to show the size of the band.

Adding and Deleting Bands

A form must have a Detail band, but you can remove the Form Header and Form Footer bands. In addition, you can add Page Header and Page Footer bands to a form. These bands are not displayed on the screen, but they are printed at the top and bottom of every page if you print the form.

Use the Format menu to add or remove bands. The two final options on this menu are Page Header/Footer and Form Header/Footer.

When you first create the AutoForm, the Form Header/Footer option from the View menu is checked to show that the form includes a form header and footer. Choose **Page Header/Footer** from the View menu to add a page header and footer. This option will also be checked after they are added.

These options are toggles. If they are checked, you can choose either of them to remove the form or page header and footer. Choose them again to add the form or page header and footer.

WARNING

If you remove form or page header and footers, Access also removes all the controls in them, so that you lose any previous work you did designing them. Access displays a warning telling you this before removing headers and footers. Because Access cannot undo this change, it is best to save your work before removing a header and footer. Then you can undo the change after seeing its effect by closing the Form window without saving changes.

Working with Controls

As you know, all the individual items included in a form, such as fields, text boxes, and checkboxes, are called *controls*. This chapter covers Bound controls (such as the fields in the AutoForm), which are associated with data in the table, and Unbound controls (such as text you add to the header of the AutoForm), which are independent of the data in the table. (Calculated controls, which are created using expressions, are covered in Chapter 8.)

Later in this chapter, you learn to use the toolbox to add many other types of controls, such as list boxes, option buttons, and OLE objects.

Selecting and Manipulating Controls

To select a control, simply click it, or choose it from the Select Object drop-down of the Formatting toolbar. To deselect a control, click anywhere in the Form window outside of that control.

Once a control is selected, you can press **Tab** or **Shift-Tab** to deselect it and select the next or previous control in turn.

When a control is selected, it has two types of handles, the *Resize handle* and the *Move handle*, as shown in Figure 7.7. In this section, you learn to resize and move selected controls. Later in this chapter, you learn to change many properties of controls after selecting them.

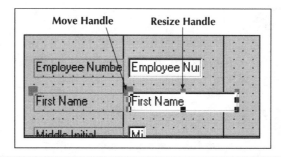

FIGURE 7.7   THE SELECTED CONTROL HAS TWO TYPES OF HANDLES.

Notice that in the illustration, the **First Name** field is selected and has both the Resize and Move handles. The box that holds the fields name has only the Move handle. Whenever you select a control or its label, the other one has the Move handle added in this way. As you will see in a moment, this lets you move the two controls either independently or together. Remember, though, that a control must have Resize handles to be selected. The control with just a Move handle is not selected.

The easiest way to tell if you're ready to move a control is that the mouse cursor changes to a little hand.

TIP

DELETING A CONTROL

Press **Delete** to delete the selected control. Access does not display a warning before deleting it. In case of an error, you can select **Undo Delete** from the Edit menu or click the **Undo** tool to return the control to the form.

If you delete a control, its label is automatically deleted, but you can delete a label without deleting the control.

RESIZING A CONTROL

Click and drag the Resize handles to change the size of the control. When you put the pointer on one of these handles, it is displayed as a two-headed arrow, indicating the directions you can drag that handle.

✳ Click and drag the top or bottom handle up or down to change the height of the control.

✳ Click and drag the side handles left or right to make the control wider or narrower.

✳ Click and drag the corner handles diagonally to change both the height and width of the control.

After resizing, you can choose **Undo Sizing** from the Edit menu or click the **Undo** tool to get rid of the change.

MOVING A CONTROL

To move a control, you can simply click and drag its Move handle in any direction. When the pointer is on the Move handle, it is displayed as a hand with its index finger extended.

Use this method to move a field's name or text box. Only the control whose Move box you drag will be moved, and the other will remain in place.

You can also move a control by placing the pointer anywhere on its edges except the handles. The pointer is displayed as a hand with all its fingers extended when you can click and drag to move the control.

Use this method to move a field name and text box together. You must move the one that is selected—the one that has both Move and Resize handles—but the other one, which has just a Move handle, will move along with it so they always remain the same distance apart.

After moving a control, you can choose **Undo Move** from the Edit menu or click the **Undo** tool to get rid of the change.

SPECIAL TECHNIQUES FOR WORKING WITH CONTROLS

In addition to these basic methods of selecting, moving, and resizing controls, there are a few special techniques that make your work easier.

Selecting Multiple Controls

In general, a control is deselected when you select another control (or click anywhere in the Form window). There are times, however, when you want to select multiple controls—for example, to change the color of a group of controls.

You can also move or resize a group of controls simultaneously by selecting them all, and it is necessary to do this when you move or resize controls that consist of two controls to create a special effect, such as a shadowed look.

There are several ways to select multiple controls:

✳ To select adjacent controls, click and drag to form a square around the entire group of the controls you want selected. Click somewhere outside of any control (beyond one corner of the group), hold down the mouse button, and drag to the opposite corner of the group. Access displays a line, as shown in Figure 7.8, to indicate the area you are dragging around. When you release the mouse button, all the controls within the line are selected.

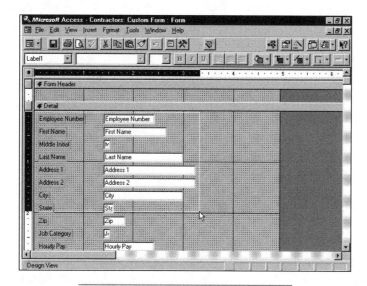

FIGURE 7.8 **SELECTING ADJACENT CONTROLS.**

✳ To select controls that are *not* adjacent, hold down the **Shift** key as you click them. When you shift-click a control, other controls are not deselected, so you can select an indefinite number of controls in this way.

✳ To select all the controls in all the bands of the form, choose **Select All** from the Edit menu.

You can press **Delete** to delete all the selected controls, and you can also resize or move them in tandem.

Resizing Multiple Controls

With multiple controls selected, resizing one of them resizes all the others, as if you had clicked and dragged the same Resize handle for each of them.

Moving Multiple Controls

If you place the pointer on any one of the selected controls, it will be displayed as a hand, and you can click and drag the control to move it and all the other selected controls the same distance in the same direction. You can move just one of the selected controls and leave the others in place by using its Move handle.

Layout Tools

There are a few special layout tools that may make it easier for you to work with controls.

THE RULER

The ruler above or to the left of the grid is highlighted when you move an object to help you align it.

Choose **Ruler** from the View menu to display or hide these rulers. By default, this option is checked and the rulers are displayed.

THE GRID

As you learned earlier, a grid of dots is displayed in the Design window by default and controls are automatically aligned with this grid to make it easier to align them with each other.

Choose **Grid** from the View menu to display or hide this grid. If you hide it, controls are still aligned to it; hiding simply makes it easier to see some effects in the Form design. By default, this option is checked and the grid is displayed.

Choose **Snap to Grid** from the Format menu to turn this automatic alignment on and off. By default, this option is checked and controls are aligned to the grid. You might want to turn off this feature when you move one or two controls to make them stand out by **not** being aligned with the others.

You can change the granularity of the grid by using its property sheet, covered later in this chapter.

AUTOMATIC ALIGNMENT

You can select a number of controls and align them with each other automatically. When you choose **Align** from the Format menu, Access displays the submenu shown in Figure 7.9.

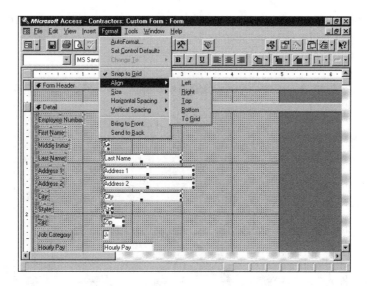

FIGURE 7.9   USING AUTOMATIC ALIGNMENT.

Choose **Left** to align the left edge of all the selected controls with the left edge of the leftmost one. Likewise, select **Right**, **Top**, or **Bottom** to align all the controls with the rightmost, highest, or lowest edge of any selected control.

Choose **To Grid** to align upper-left corners of the selected controls to the nearest grid points. This is useful if you had turned off Snap to Grid when you placed them.

AUTOMATIC SIZING

You can select controls and have Access automatically size them by choosing **Size** from the Format menu and one of the following options from its submenu, shown in Figure 7.10:

✳ Select one or more controls and choose **to Fit** to adjust the size of the control to fit the text it contains.

✳ Select one or more controls and choose **to Grid** to adjust the size of the control so all of its edges fit the grid. This is useful if you have changed the granularity of the grid, so that controls that you placed earlier do not fit exactly into the new grid.

✳ You can also use this command to make a number of controls the same width or height. Select several controls and choose **to Tallest**, **to**

Shortest, **to Widest**, or **to Narrowest**, in order to make them all as high as the tallest or shortest or to make them all as wide as the widest or narrowest.

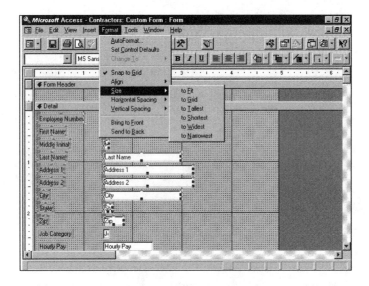

FIGURE 7.10   USING AUTOMATIC SIZING.

SPACING

You can adjust the spacing of controls by choosing **Horizontal Spacing** or **Vertical Spacing** from the Format menu. Both of these have a submenu with the options **Make Equal**, **Increase**, and **Decrease**, which you can use to space all the controls evenly or to increase or decrease the spacing between them uniformly.

Changing Stacking Order

When you place objects in the form, the ones that you place later appear to be above ones that you placed earlier. If two objects overlap, the one that was placed later will hide the one that was placed earlier. The order in which objects cover one another is sometimes called their *stacking order*.

To change this order, select an object and then:

✳ Choose **Bring to Front** from the Format menu to make that object appear to be in front of all other objects.

✴ Choose **Send to Back** from the Format menu to make that object appear to be behind all other objects.

These options are only needed if objects overlap.

Changing Tab Order

You can also specify the tab order of controls in the form—that is, the order in which the user can access them by pressing **Tab** and **Shift-Tab** (rather than clicking them with the mouse). This is useful if you have moved controls or added new controls, so that the order in which the user accesses them by pressing **Tab** is not the same as the order in which they are displayed on the screen.

To do this, choose **Tab Order** from the View menu to display the Tab Order dialog box, shown in Figure 7.11. Use the Section radio buttons to specify which band's controls are displayed in the Custom Order list.

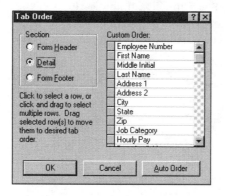

FIGURE 7.11   THE TAB ORDER DIALOG BOX.

In general, it is easiest to click the **Auto Order** button. Access automatically sets the tab order based on the location of the controls in the form, so the user tabs through from top to bottom and from left to right. The order of controls in the Custom Order list is changed to reflect this order when you select this button.

To set tab order by hand, move the rows in this list as you move the rows in a table. Use the selection boxes on their left to select one or more rows, and then click and drag the selection box to move the rows to specify tab order.

Working with Text

You can edit the text in a label or change the typeface and style of any text in the form in much the same way that you do with most Windows word processors.

Editing Text

You can edit the text in a label directly in the Form Design window. The text in some controls, such as fields, depends on what you enter in the table. You can edit the text on some other controls, such as push buttons that you add to the form. You can also edit the label that is attached to any type of control.

To edit text, first click the label (or other control) to select it. You must select only the control that you want to edit, and not select multiple controls.

Once the Label (or other control) is selected, the mouse pointer is displayed as an insertion bar when you move it over the label, as in any Windows word processor or editor. You can click in any location in the label to place an insertion point there, or click and drag to select text. Edit using the usual Windows editor techniques, described in Chapter 3.

Changing Typeface, Style, and Alignment

Though you can only edit the text in a label, you can specify the typeface (font), style, and alignment of most controls that contains text. For example, you can change the typeface, style, and alignment of the data displayed in fields. You can also change the typeface of text on push buttons that you add to the form—but not its alignment, as it is always centered.

When you select one or more controls that contain text, the tools on the Formatting toolbar used for working with text are enabled, as shown in Figure 7.12. You can work with them as you do with similar controls in Windows word processors.

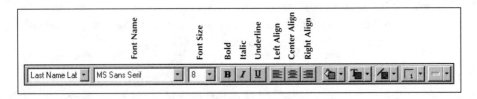

FIGURE 7.12   TOOLS USED FOR WORKING WITH TEXT.

✳ Use the **Font Name** drop-down list to select a typeface, such as Arial, Courier, or Times Roman. The fonts available in this list depend on the fonts you have installed under Windows.

✳ Use the **Font Size** drop-down list to specify the size of the type, in points. You may have to resize a control to hold a larger font size.

✳ Use the **Font Bold** and **Font Italic** buttons to display the text in bold-face and/or italic type. The button appears to be pressed when it is selected, and you can click it again to deselect it, so the text is no longer bold or italic.

✳ Use the **Left Alignment**, **Center Alignment**, or **Right Alignment** buttons to determine how the text is aligned within its control. For example, data is ordinarily aligned to the left of the field it is displayed in, but you can use these buttons to center or right-justify it within the field.

All these features must be applied to an entire control. They are not enabled when you are editing text in a control, and so you cannot (for example) use a different typeface for some of the letters in a label. They can be applied to many controls at once simply by selecting all of the controls before applying them.

Working with Colors and Effects

You also use the Formatting toolbar to specify the colors of objects, to specify the type of border they have, and to create special effects, such as raised or lowered look.

First, you must select a band of the form or one or more controls, using the methods described earlier in this chapter. (Not all options on the palette are available if you select a band.)

Most controls have three elements whose color you can specify:

✳ The **foreground**, for example, the text displayed in a label

✳ The **background**, for example, the area within the label around the text

✳ The **border**, for example, the box displayed around the label

You can specify colors for all of these and you can also specify the type of line used and special effects used in the border.

Use the three color tools to select the foreground, background, or border color. Simply click the tool's drop-down arrow to display a color palette, as shown in Figure 7.13, and select a color to apply it to the selected objects.

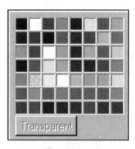

FIGURE 7.13   APPLYING A COLOR.

Notice that the Back Color and Border color tools both have a **Transparent** button. If you select this, the background or border will be transparent. That is, you will be able to see other objects through the background of the control or the control will appear not to have any border.

The Border Width tool, shown in Figure 7.14, lets you specify the thickness of the border. You can select a hairline or a border from 1 to 6 points thick.

FIGURE 7.14   SPECIFYING THE WIDTH OF THE BORDER.

The Special Effect tool, shown in Figure 7.15, lets you shade the border to create a lowered or raised effect, or leave it unshaded to create a boxed effect.

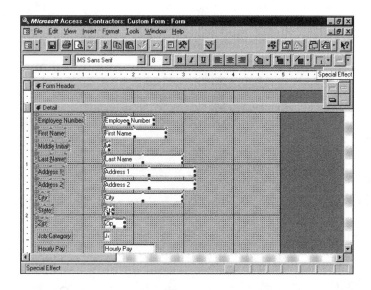

FIGURE 7.15 **SPECIFYING A SPECIAL EFFECT.**

Adding Controls

Even if you begin by creating a form with a Wizard—which places all the fields you want on it—you may well want to add extra controls to it. Most obviously, you might add rectangles, lines, or OLE objects as graphic enhancements; you might add new labels with help text or other descriptive text; or you might replace fields with controls such as list boxes to make data entry easier.

Adding a Field

You may need to add fields to a form design if you are starting with a blank form, if you forgot to include a field when you first defined the form, or if you deleted a field by mistake.

To add a field, first display the field list, if necessary, by choosing **Field List** from the View menu or selecting the **Field List** tool. This field list, shown in Figure 7.16, is used like field lists in queries, though it does not have an asterisk representing all fields.

To add a single field to the form, simply click and drag it from the field list to the form.

FIGURE 7.16 **THE FIELD LIST.**

After you have selected multiple fields in the field list, you can click and drag any of them to the form, and all of the others will be dragged along with it. To select multiple fields:

✳ Click a field to select it. Then hold down the **Shift** key and click another field to select all the fields between it and the first field.

✳ Hold down the **Ctrl** key as you click fields, to select additional fields without deselecting ones that are already selected.

✳ Double-click the title bar of the Field List to select all fields.

Fields that you add in this way are made up of a label and a text box for data entry, like the fields that Access places in the form initially. When you select the label or text box, a Move handle is automatically added to the other, and you can move them in tandem or separately, as described earlier in this chapter.

Using the Toolbox

You can add many other types of control using the toolbox. The tools available in the toolbox are shown in Figure 7.17.

In general, you add a new control to the form by clicking a tool in the toolbox and then clicking and dragging on the form to define the size and location of the control.

After you click one of these tools, the pointer changes its form to indicate that it is being used to add a control. In general, the pointer changes to crosshairs and an icon that indicates the type of control that you are adding. For example, when you are adding a rectangle button the pointer consists of crosshairs and a rectangle icon.

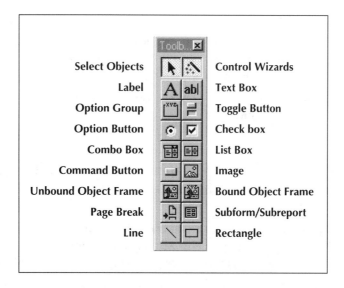

FIGURE 7.17   TOOLS IN THE TOOLBOX.

Place the crosshairs on the location where you want one corner of the new control to be. Then click and drag to the opposite corner to specify the location and the size of the control.

When you release the mouse button after clicking and dragging to place a new control, Access may display a Wizard to let you define the control. No Wizard is displayed when you add a rectangle, for example, because no information beyond its size and location is needed to define it. However, if you are adding an Option Group, Access displays a Wizard to let you specify options.

All the tools in the toolbox are described below, along with details on placing each type of control. Remember that after they are placed, you can use the methods described earlier to move, resize, delete, and, when applicable, to specify the colors and fonts of these new controls.

SELECT OBJECTS

The Select Objects tool returns the pointer to its usual form, an arrow.

It can be used to cancel the operation of adding a new control. After you click a tool, the pointer changes to the form that lets you add that control. Click the **Select Objects** tool to return the pointer to its usual form, so you are no longer adding that new control.

CONTROL WIZARDS

The Control Wizards tool enables or disables the wizards used to define new controls that you add to the form. Only programmers should work with this feature disabled. Most users should work with the wizards.

All of the instructions in this section assume that the Wizards are available when you create new controls.

LABEL

To add new text to the form, click the **Label** tool and click and drag to create a label box. After you release the mouse button, simply type text and it will be displayed in the box.

If the box is large enough for several lines of text, the text automatically wraps to the next line when necessary. It also automatically wraps to fit if you resize the text box later. To start a new paragraph, press **Ctrl-Enter** rather than **Enter**.

If you type too much text to fit, the box automatically expands to accommodate your entry. If your entry is on one line, the box gets wider. If your entry is already on multiple lines, the box expands vertically. Remember that you can always resize the box after you have finished typing and the text is automatically rejustified to fit in it.

When you are done entering text, press **Enter** or click anywhere outside the label box to continue designing the form. You can still edit the text at a later time, as you do any text, by selecting it and then clicking it to put an insertion bar in it.

You can also specify the font and style of the text by selecting the label box, as you do any label, and then using the methods described in the section "Working with Text." You cannot specify font or style when you begin entering the text.

Automatically Sizing the Label

Rather than clicking and dragging to define the label box, you can automatically size it to fit the text you type.

Simply click the **Label** tool, click anywhere on the form, and begin typing. The box gets wider as you type to accommodate the text.

If you press **Ctrl-Enter** to add a new line, the box keeps that width and adds new lines to accommodate the text you type.

Attaching a Label to a Control

If a Bound control does not already have a label attached to it—for example, if you deleted the label for a field—you can use the **Text** tool to create a label and attach it to the control using the **Cut** and **Paste** options.

Create the label as usual. When you are done, select it and choose **Cut** from the Edit menu. Then select the control you want to attach it to and choose **Paste** from the Edit menu. Finally, use its Move handle to adjust its location.

The label is attached to the control in the same way that fields' labels are attached to them. When you select the label or control, a Move handle is automatically added to the other, and you can move them together or separately, as you learned to do earlier in this chapter.

TEXT BOX

To add a text box to the form, click the **Text Box** tool and then click and drag to place the text box. When you release the mouse button, Access displays a text box like the one you use to enter data in a field. The word *Unbound* is in the text box to indicate that it is not attached to a field. Its label has an arbitrary name made up of the word *Text* followed by a number, as shown in Figure 7.18.

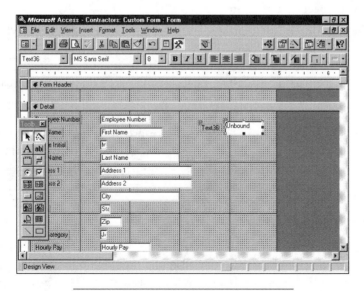

FIGURE 7.18 ADDING A TEXT BOX TO A FORM.

You can use a text box to display a calculated value. For example, you could display a value that is the sum or product of numbers in other fields.

After placing the text box, click inside it to remove the word *Unbound* and place an insertion point in it. You can also select it and then click in it at any time to place an insertion point in it, as you do with labels. Type an Access expression; and the result of that expression will be displayed in the form. (See Chapter 8 for more information about expressions.) Click anywhere outside of the text box to finish typing in it.

The value it displays in Form view is read-only. The user cannot edit it.

OPTION GROUP

The Option Group tool is used to create a group of controls that work together to let the user enter data in a field that has only a few possible entries.

Types of Option Group

The most common type of Option Group is made up of radio (option) buttons, but this tool also lets you create a group of checkboxes or a group of toggle buttons (which can appear to be raised or pushed down). In any case, if the user selects one of the options, the others are automatically deselected. The Wizard lets you assign values to each option, which you can store in the field of a table or use later in a program.

If the Option Group replaces one of the fields on the form, you should delete that field from the design, if it was initially included in it.

N O T E

The main limitation of the Option Group is that the values assigned to the options must be numbers. If you are working with a numeric field with several possible values, you can use this type of control to enter these values in it. Developers can use these numbers to control other actions of an application. Beginners who want to use a control to enter data in a field should use a combo box rather than an Option Group, as combo boxes make it is easier to enter values of various data types.

Adding an Option Group

To add an Option Group, click the **Option Group** tool, and click and drag to place the box that will be the border around all the option buttons in the group. When you release the mouse button, Access displays the Option Group Wizard, which lets you do the following:

✳ Enter names of all the options in the first dialog box. You can add and edit these in the same way that you add and edit records in a table. Each name you add will be displayed next to one of the buttons, so enter names that help the user decide which button to choose.

✳ Use the radio buttons in the second dialog box to specify whether or not there will be a default value. If you do create a default value, you must use the drop-down list to select the name you gave to one of the buttons. This button will be selected by default when the form is displayed.

✳ The third dialog box lists all the names you entered and has a text box next to each where you can enter the value associated with it. This is the value that will actually be entered in the field if the user selects that button.

✳ Use the radio buttons in the fourth dialog box to decide whether or not to bind the option group to a field. Only developers should select **Save the value for later use**. Nonprogrammers should select the radio button called **Store the value in this field** and use the drop-down list to its right to select one of the fields in the table or query that the form is based on. The value of the option the user selects will automatically be entered in this field.

✳ The fifth dialog box lets you choose whether the buttons will be option buttons, checkboxes, or toggle buttons, and what style the group will have. It displays the final appearance of the option group.

✳ The final dialog box lets you enter a label for the entire option group.

Which Control to Use

In general, it is best to use radio buttons in option groups, because users are accustomed to selecting options in this way.

Groups of toggle buttons can be used to create special effects, though you should be careful to use them in ways that do not confuse users who expect push buttons to initiate actions.

WARNING

Option groups made of checkboxes can confuse users and should be avoided unless there is a special reason for using them. A checkbox is conventionally used to enter data in a field that can have only two values, most often a Yes/No field. They are not conventionally associated with groups, where one is deselected when others are selected.

Because they use only integers as their values, Option Groups are useful primarily for developers, who control later actions of an application on the basis of the selection in the option group.

TOGGLE BUTTONS, OPTION BUTTONS, AND CHECKBOXES

In addition to associating them in groups to let the user choose among several values, you can place a single toggle button, option button, or checkbox to let the user enter a value into a Yes/No field.

If the control is selected, **Yes** is entered in the field, and if it is not, **No** is entered in the field.

Adding these Controls

To create one of these controls, first display the Field List. Then click the **Toggle Button**, **Radio Button**, or **Checkbox** tool in the Toolbox. As always, the pointer will be displayed as a crosshair with an icon next to it representing the type of control you are adding. Use this pointer to click and drag a Yes/No field from the Field List to the form. Access creates a toggle button, radio button, or checkbox bound to that field.

You can also click the appropriate tool and click and drag on the form to create an unbound toggle button, radio button, or checkbox. This is useful for developers who want to control some later action of an application on the basis of the option selected in one of these controls, but is not advisable for nonprogrammers.

Which Control to Use

For nonprogrammers, it is best to use these controls to enter values in a Yes/No field.

A checkbox is best for this use, since this is the conventional method of selecting Yes or No in Windows applications, and users are accustomed to it. Use a toggle button for special effects.

WARNING

You can confuse users by using a radio button for this purpose, because radio buttons are conventionally used in groups to let users select one of several options. Be particularly careful not to use several radio buttons near each other to enter values in several Yes/No fields. Users expect to be able to select only one of them at a time.

COMBO BOXES AND LIST BOXES

In Access and other Windows applications, you often choose items from lists. Access lets you add two of these types of lists to forms, combo boxes and list boxes.

The Difference between Combo Boxes and List Boxes

A *combo box* is a combination of a drop-down list and a text box. The user can enter a value in the text box, or select a value from the drop-down to display it in the text box. This is the same way that drop-down lists generally work in Windows applications, but Access calls this control a combo box to emphasize the fact that, by default, users can enter a value in the text box that is not on the list. (You can change this default by using the property sheet of the combo box and selecting **Yes** as the Limit to List property, but this property is No by default.)

A *list box* displays choices and lets the user select one, but unlike a drop-down list, the options in the list box are always displayed. If there are more choices in the list than can be displayed in the area you define for the box, Access adds a scrollbar to its right edge to let the user display all the options. Unlike a combo box, a list box does not let the user type in a value. Only the values in the list may be chosen.

Combo boxes and list boxes are very similar, then. Combo boxes are useful when you do not have much room on a form because the options are not always displayed; they can also let users type in values that are not available on the list. However, the mechanics of defining a list of items to be displayed in a combo box or list box are the same, and the Wizards that you use to create them are identical.

Multiple-Column Combo and List Boxes

Access lets you create combo boxes or list boxes with multiple columns. In a combo box, the value in the first column is displayed in the text box when the drop-down list is closed. In either case, you can select the column whose value will be entered in the table.

For example, you can create a combo box with the full names of all the states in its first column and the two-letter abbreviation for each state in a second column next to the name. The full name of the state will be displayed in the text box. When the drop-down list is displayed, it will have a two-column list of state names and their abbreviations. You can define the combo box so the abbreviation is entered in the table.

Two Ways of Adding these Controls

To add one of these controls, click the **Combo Box** tool or **List Box** tool, and click and drag to define its size and location the form.

When you release the mouse button, Access displays the Combo Box Wizard or List Box Wizard, which are used in the same way. The first dialog box of both lets you choose among two fundamentally different ways of defining the values in the list. You can type values in the Wizard when you define the control or you can have the control display the values in a table or query.

In general, you type in the values if there are a small number of them that will not change. You could do this to let the user enter a title such as Mr., Ms., Mrs., Dr., and so on. There are a limited number of these titles, and it is not difficult to type them in the Wizard when you are defining the control.

Use the values in a table or query when there are a larger number of values to choose among and when the available values may change. This is particularly useful in a relational database.

For example, in the relational database that you worked with in Chapter 6, you could create a data-entry form for the Billing table that includes a list box with three columns. It would display the last name, first name, and employee number from all the records of the Contractor table. The user could select the contractor by name, and the form could enter the employee number in the Billing table.

NOTE You could also create special tables to be used as the basis of combo or list boxes. For example, you could create a table with the names and abbreviations of all the states, which you use as the basis of a two-column combo box. It would display the state name in its text box, include both state name and abbreviation in its drop-down list, and enter the abbreviation in the table. If you create this special table once, you can import it into any database you are working on, and then you can add this extra touch with very little effort. Chapter 12 discusses importing tables.

Entering Values in the Wizard

If you indicate in the first dialog box of the Combo Box Wizard or List Box Wizard that you are typing in the values to be displayed, then you use the remaining dialog boxes as follows:

✳ Enter the values to be displayed in the same way that you enter data in a table, as shown in Figure 7.19. The figure uses just one column. You can also enter any number up to 40 in the # of columns box and define values for all the columns. After entering a number, press **Tab** or click to move the cursor to the table; the number of columns you indicated is displayed. Remember that the values you enter in the first column will be displayed in the text box, but you can enter values from any of the columns in the table.

✳ Use the same dialog box to specify the width of the columns displayed in the combo box or list box by clicking and dragging the right edge of the column headings, as you do when you are resizing the columns of a table.

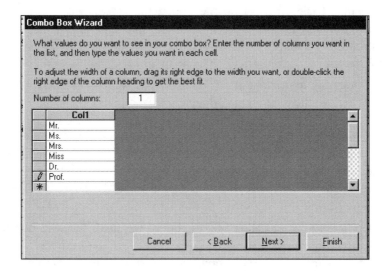

FIGURE 7.19   ENTERING VALUES TO BE DISPLAYED.

✳ If you are working with multiple columns, select which column of the combo box has the value you want to store in the table. (If you are working with one column, the Wizard skips this dialog box.)

✳ Enter a label for the combo box and select the **Finish** button to place it in the form.

Creating a list box or combo box in this way is very straightforward.

However, to use the list box or combo box, you must display its Property Sheet and use its Control Source property to bind it to a field, as described in the section "Useful Properties for Beginners" later in this chapter.

Using Values from a Table or Query

It is a bit more complicated to create a list box or combo box based on a table or query.

To make it clearer, examples are included in the steps that follow which you could use to create a three-column list box in the data-entry form for the Billing table. This list box displays the last name, first name, and employee number from all the records of the Contractor table, and enters the appropriate selected employee number in the Billing table.

Rather than basing this list on the Contractors table itself, you could begin by creating a query that sorts the records in alphabetical order by name and includes the Last Name, First Name, and Employee Number fields, so it will be easier for the user to look up the names in an alphabetical list.

After indicating in the first dialog box that you want to use values looked up in a table, you use the remaining dialog boxes as follows:

✳ Select a table or query in the database which the values will be taken from. For example, if you were creating a form for the Billing table, the query with an alphabetical listing of contractors table would be displayed in this list, because it is in the same database, and you would select it.

✳ Use a field picker dialog box to choose the fields that will be displayed in the columns of the combo box or list box. The number of fields you select is the same as the number of columns. For example, select the **Last Name**, **First Name**, and **Employee Number** fields.

✳ Specify the width of the columns displayed in the combo box or list box by clicking and dragging the right edge of the column headings, as you do when you are resizing the columns of a table.

✳ If you are working with multiple columns, select which column of the combo box or list box has the value you want to store in the table. (If you are working with one column, the Wizard skips this dialog box.) For example, select the **Employee Number** field.

✳ Select a field of the table that the combo box or list box is bound to. In the example, the Wizard would display a list of all the fields in the

Billing table, and select the **Employee Number** field. (Nonprogrammers should always select the **Bound** radio button and select a field in this dialog box. Only programmers should create an unbound control.)

✳ Enter a label for the combo box or list box and select the **Finish** button to place it in the form.

COMMAND BUTTON

A *command button* (also called a *push button*) executes some action.

The Command Button Wizard makes it easy to create buttons that perform many standard actions. For example, you can easily add buttons to the form that let you move to the first, previous, next, and last records, like the controls at the bottom of the Form window. You can also add buttons that let you search for a record, like the Search tool on the toolbar. Many of these are useful primarily for developers, who are creating applications that do not have the usual toolbar or other features of the Access interface.

You can also use command buttons to perform custom actions that you cannot perform in one step using the Access interface. The easiest way to do this is to use a button to run a macro. Macros are covered in Chapter 11.

To add a command button to a form, click the **Command Button** tool and click and drag to define the location and size of the command button. When you release the mouse button, Access displays the Command Button Wizard, shown in Figure 7.20.

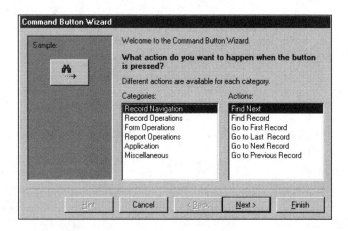

FIGURE 7.20 THE COMMAND BUTTON WIZARD.

The first dialog box of this Wizard lets you select categories (types of action) the button can perform. For each category, it displays a different list of actions. As you can see in Figure 7.21, the actions it allows for record navigation are all similar to things you can do from the Access Interface and they are easy to understand. The same is true of actions in most other categories. Only custom actions are difficult to create and require you to write an Access macro or a program.

The first dialog box displays a picture of the push button with the standard icon (binoculars) representing that action.

The second dialog box lets you replace this picture in several ways:

✳ **Standard Pictures** lets you choose from the standard icons that come with the Command Button Wizard. The **Show All Pictures** checkbox lets you display all available standard pictures or display only the pictures that are suggested for that control.

✳ You can choose the **Browse** push button to display a dialog box that lets you select any bitmap (BMP) file to use as the picture on the button.

✳ The **Picture** radio button is selected by default. You can use text rather than a picture on the push button by selecting the **Text** radio button and entering the text in the box to its right.

The final dialog box lets you name and create the command button.

IMAGE FRAME

The Image tool lets you insert a picture into the form. After you click and drag to define the frame for this picture, Access displays the Insert Picture dialog box, which you use just like the Open dialog box to select the file that contains this picture. You can add graphics files, Windows metafiles, bitmap files, or icon files to the form.

UNBOUND OBJECT AND BOUND OBJECT FRAMES

You can add OLE objects to the form by selecting the **Unbound Object Frame** or **Bound Object Frame** tool and clicking and dragging to define the size and location of the frame that will hold the OLE object.

A bound OLE Object frame displays the contents of an OLE object field of your database and changes as you move through records. An unbound OLE Object frame displays an OLE object that remains the same as you move through the records. It is most commonly used to add a business' logo to its data entry forms. Both of these tools are discussed in Chapter 12, which covers OLE objects.

PAGE BREAK

Use the **Page Break** tool to add a page break to the form. The page break is significant only when you print the form.

For example, if you want to print the form with each record on a separate page, add a page break in the Detail band, below the form's last field. When Access prints the form or displays it in Print Preview, it begins a new page whenever it reaches the page break.

The page break is displayed as a short, dark dotted line, at the left margin of the form design. You can select it and move it as you do other controls. To remove the page break, select and delete it.

SUBFORM/SUBREPORT

You learned about subforms in Chapter 6, when you created a form with a subform using the Form Wizard. As you know, if a form is used to display records from a table on the one side of a one-to-many relationship, it can include a subform with all the related fields from the table on the many side of the relationship—for example, all the bills from each contractor.

 In general, if you want to include a subform in a graph, it is best to use this Wizard to create it. You then can move and resize the subform as you do any other object in Design View.

NOTE

To add a subform in Design View, you must use the property sheets of objects in fairly advanced ways.

If you are working with a relational database, you can use the **Subform** tool to add a frame or a subform to a form, simply by clicking and dragging. Attaching to the subform to the frame requires more advanced techniques. You must use the property sheet for the subform/subreport and select an existing form as its source object. That previously defined form will be displayed in the frame. You must also use the Link Child Fields and Link Master Fields properties to link the forms, so the right records of the subform are displayed when you change the record displayed in the main form.

You can also add a subform to a form by dragging a form's name from the Database window to the Form Design window. Again, you must set the Link Child Fields and Link Master Fields properties to link the forms.

Though these properties will be filled in automatically if you set up the database properly, it is generally easier for beginners to begin by using the Main/Subform Wizard and then to customize the form, if necessary.

For more information on more advanced methods of creating a subform, search for the topic *Creating Subforms* in Access Help.

LINE

To add a line to the form, simply click the **Line** tool and click and drag on the form. Access adds a straight line connecting the places where you begin and end dragging. It may be horizontal, vertical, or diagonal.

Lines are useful to underline or emphasize parts of the form or to divide the form visually into several parts.

You can use the **Border Color** tool and the **Border Width** tool, as described earlier in this chapter, to define the colors and thickness of the line.

RECTANGLE

To add a rectangle to the form, simply click the **Rectangle** tool and click and drag on the form. Access adds a rectangle with opposite corners in the locations where you begin and end dragging. The edges of the rectangle are always horizontal and vertical.

Rectangles are useful to emphasize parts of the form or for visually grouping several controls by adding a box around them.

You can use the **Back Color** tool, the **Border Color** tool, the **Border Width** tool, and the **Special Effect** tool, as described earlier in this chapter, to define the colors, thickness, type (solid, dotted, or dashed line) of the rectangle.

N O T E   The most common use of a rectangle is to place a box around an area of the form. To do this, use the palette to give it a clear back color, a boxed rather than a sunken look, and a thicker line as its border. You can also use **Send to Back** from the Format menu, rather than giving it a clear back color.

CHANGING CONTROL TYPE

You can change the type of an existing control by selecting it and then choosing **Change To** from the Format menu to display the submenu shown in Figure 7.21. Only the types that the currently selected tool can be converted to are accessible on the submenu.

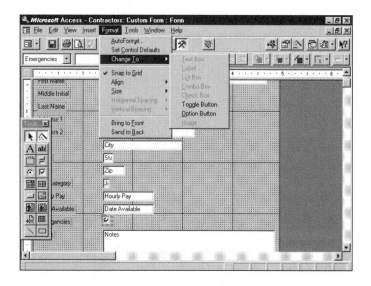

FIGURE 7.21   **CHANGING CONTROL TYPE.**

Saving Time in Formatting

As you can see, you can define many properties of a control. For a label, you can define foreground color, background color, border color, border width, font name, font size, and so on.

Rather than defining all of these for each new control you add, it is often easiest to create default properties for the new control, to paste properties from one control to others, or to use AutoFormats.

Defining a Default Format

To define the default properties for controls, simply select any control that already has those properties, and choose **Set Control Defaults** from the Format menu. Any new control you add automatically has these default properties.

The Format Painter Tool

You can apply the properties of one existing control to other controls by using the **Format Painter** tool. Select the control whose properties you want to use, and click the **Format Painter** tool. The pointer is displayed with a paint brush next to it. Then click any other control to apply these properties to it.

Using AutoFormats

You can apply any of a selection of predefined formats to objects by choosing AutoFormat from the Format menu or clicking the AutoFormat tool to display the AutoFormat dialog box, shown in Figure 7.22. Simply select a format from the Form Styles list; this is illustrated in the Sample area.

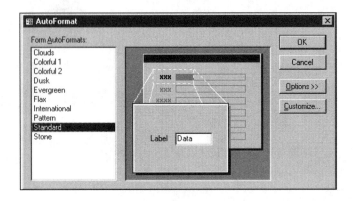

FIGURE 7.22   THE AUTOFORMAT DIALOG BOX.

A Look at Property Sheets

You can display a property sheet for an object, such as the entire form, a band of the form, or a control, by selecting it and choosing **Properties** from the View menu. It can also be displayed by clicking the **Properties** tool of the toolbar, or by right-clicking it and selecting **Properties** from its shortcut menu.

Once you display a property sheet, Access keeps it open and displays the properties of any object you select. To hide the property sheet, choose **Properties** from the View menu or click the **Properties** tool again, or click the property sheet's close box.

Typical Property Sheets

Some property sheets are useful primarily for programmers; others will be covered in later chapters of this book. For now, you should just glance at a few to get an idea of what sorts of properties objects have.

Figure 7.23 shows the property sheet for a label which has relatively simple properties. Notice that it lists features such as the label's name, its caption, whether it is visible, its location and size, and its colors (stated as code numbers). You can change these features on the property sheet, but you can change most of them more easily using the methods described earlier in this chapter. This property sheet lets you create an invisible control, which you cannot do using the interface, but there is usually no reason for a nonprogrammer to want to do that.

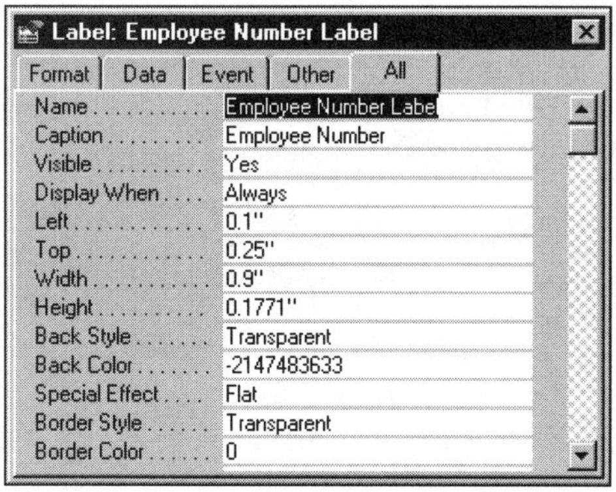

FIGURE 7.23 **THE PROPERTY SHEET FOR A LABEL.**

Though labels do not have event properties, many objects do. Event properties for a text box are shown in Figure 7.24. You can use a macro or program as one of these properties to have it executed before or after the control is updated, when it is clicked or double-clicked, and so on. In general, only developers use these event properties.

Since objects often have many properties, you can use the tabs at the top of the property sheet to limit the type of properties displayed. You can select **Format**, **Data**, **Event**, **Other Properties**, or select **All** to display all the Properties in a single list.

FIGURE 7.24   EVENT PROPERTIES FOR A TEXT BOX.

Useful Properties for Beginners

As you can see, property sheets are meant to be used by developers, but there are also features of property sheets that the typical user may find useful. Some are covered here, and others in later chapters.

CHANGING THE FINENESS OF THE GRID

The property sheet for the form as a whole has Grid X and Grid Y as two of its format properties, as shown in Figure 7.25. You can edit the values in them to change the granularity of the grid that Access automatically aligns controls to.

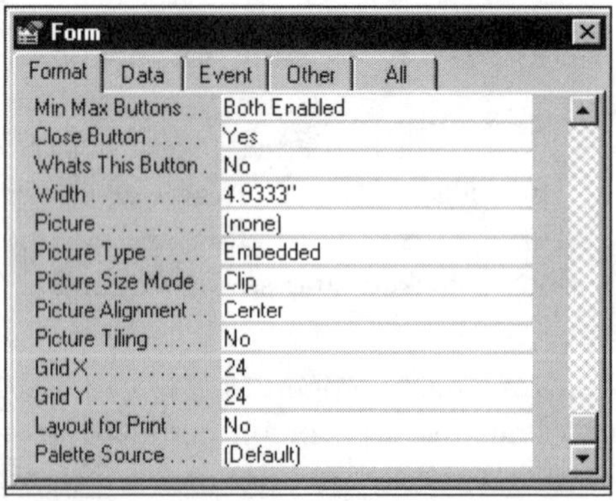

FIGURE 7.25   FORMAT PROPERTIES OF A FORM.

To use this property sheet, choose **Select Form** from the Edit menu and display the property sheet (if it is not already displayed), click the **Format** tab, and scroll down to find the Grid X and Grid Y properties. Then simply edit the number. These numbers represent the number of gridlines per inch. You can enter **4**, for example, to place gridlines 1/4 inch apart.

LIMITING CHOICES IN A COMBO BOX

You learned earlier that the property sheet of the combo box has a Limit to List property. You can select **Yes** as this property instead of the default **No** to prevent users from typing a value that is not on the list into the combo box. This is one of its Data properties.

BINDING A CONTROL TO A FIELD

One useful Data property of many controls is the Control Source property, which lets you bind the control to a field. As you can see in Figure 7.26, you can display a drop-down list for this property and select any of the fields in the table or query that the form is based on to bind the control to that field. You can delete the value in the field and leave it blank to create an unbound field. This can be useful if you forget to bind a control to a field when you first place it in the form.

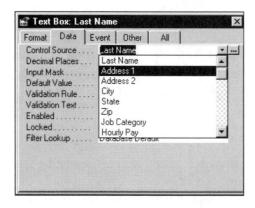

FIGURE 7.26   SETTING THE CONTROL SOURCE PROPERTY.

GETTING HELP ON PROPERTIES

Property sheets have many features like this one, which may be useful on occasion, but are not generally needed by most people. You might want to look through the property sheets to get a general idea of what they contain. You can display help for any individual property by moving the cursor to it and pressing **F1**.

Designing a Sample Form

In this exercise, you display the AutoForm that you created in Chapter 5, save it under a different name, and modify it using the techniques you have learned in this chapter. The exercise includes a relatively small number of changes in the design of the form, which you will find useful in practice: rearranging the fields to make the form more readable, adding a header, and adding a combo box. You might want to try other changes yourself.

1. If you have not already done so, open the Teach Yourself database. Click the **Forms** tab of the Database window to display the list of forms. Be sure the AutoForm named **Contractors** is selected, and select the **Design** button to display it in Design View. Choose **Save As/Export** from the File menu. When Access displays the Save As dialog box, edit the form name so it reads **Contractors: Custom Form** and select **OK**. Then click the **Maximize** button of the Form window so you have more room to work in.

2. Now, make the layout a bit more compact. Move the text boxes for all the fields left, so their left edge is just right of the one inch mark. After you have moved them all, choose **Align** from the Format menu and **Left** from the submenu to be sure they are properly aligned. Next, select the text boxes of the Address 1 and Address 2 fields and drag click and drag the right edge of one to narrow them, so they are no wider than the Last Name field.

3. Now, click and drag the Notes field upward, so its top edge is to the right of the City field. Resize it so its right edge is left of the 5-inch line. Click the **Move** box of its label, and drag the label so it is just above the Notes field and aligned with its left edge. In addition, click and drag the Emergencies field and the Date Available field and their labels so they are just above the Notes field; you are just moving these here temporarily, to make them easier to work with later, and so you can put them on top of each other. The new location and sizing of the fields is shown in Figure 7.27.

4. Click and drag the right edge of the form so it is 5 inches wide.

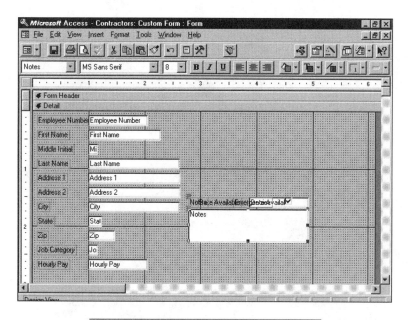

FIGURE 7.27   MOVING AND RESIZING THE FIELDS.

5. Click the **First Name** label to select it and click it again to place an insertion point in it. Edit it to read **Name**. Then click outside of it to stop editing, click it to select it, and choose **Size** from the Format menu and **To Fit** from the submenu, so the box is just large enough to fit the word Name.

6. Select the label **Middle Initial** and press **Delete**. Then select the label **Last Name** and press **Delete**. Then resize the text box for the Last Name to make it a bit larger. Now, click and drag both of these fields on the same line as the First Name field.

7. Click and drag around the **Address 1**, **Address 2**, and **City** fields to select them all. Then drag them up so they are just under the Name field. Do not use the Move handle to drag just one; be sure to drag them all together. There should be just two lines of the grid between the Name and Address 1 fields, as there are between fields in the initial AutoForm.

8. Click outside the selected fields to deselect them. Then click the label of the **State** field and press **Delete**. Likewise, select and delete the label of the Zip field. Then click and drag these fields so they are to the right of the City field. Finally, edit the label of the City field so it reads **City/State/Zip**, as shown in Figure 7.28.

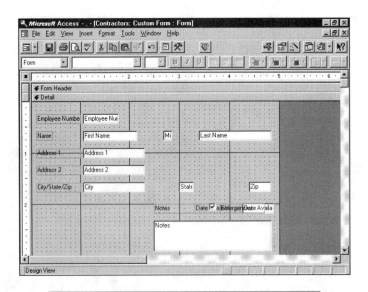

FIGURE 7.28   PLACING CITY, STATE, AND ZIP ON ONE LINE.

9. Now, if necessary, display the toolbox and move it to the right, so it is out of the way. Then click the **Line** tool, and click and drag to place a line two gridlines below this basic data. The line is selected after you place it. Use the **Border Width** tool of the Formatting toolbar to select **2 points** as the thickness of this line.

10. Next, rearrange the Job Category, Hourly Pay, Date Available, and Emergencies fields so they are lined up to the left of the Notes field, under the line, with one gridline spacing between them, as shown in Figure 7.29.

11. Now, you can add a drop-down list to make it easier to select Job Category. First, select the **Job Category** field and press **Delete** to delete it and its label. Click the **Combo Box** tool in the toolbox, and click and drag to locate the list where the field label and field were (near the left edge of the form under the line you added). In the first dialog box of the Combo Box Wizard, select the radio button that lets you type in values; then click **Next>**.

12. In the next dialog box, enter **2** as the number of columns. On the first line, enter **Programmer** in Column 1 and **P** in Column 2. Likewise, on the next two lines, enter **Writer** and **W** and **Clerical** and **C**. Then narrow Column 1 a bit, and narrow Column 2 until it is the right width to hold a single letter, as shown in Figure 7.30. Then click **Next>**.

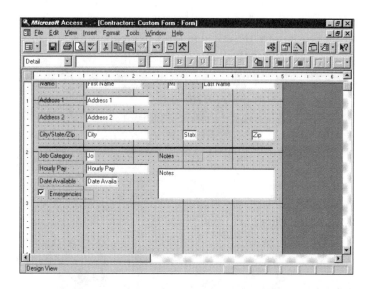

FIGURE 7.29 REARRANGING THE FIELDS UNDER THE LINE.

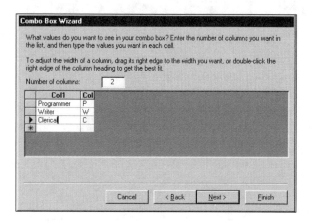

FIGURE 7.30 DEFINING THE COMBO BOX.

13. In the next dialog box, as the value you want to store in your database, select **Column 2** then click **Next>**. In the next dialog box, select **Job Category** from the drop-down menu to store the value in that field and then click **Next>**. In the following dialog box, as the label, type **Job Category** and click the **Finish** button to place the control.

14. Resize and move the control and its label as necessary to display their data and align them with the other controls (see Figure 7.31).

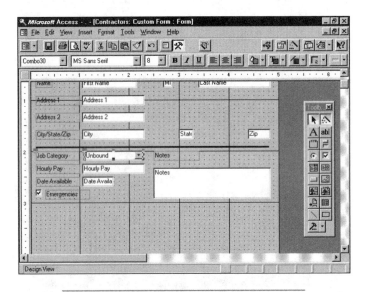

FIGURE 7.31 **PLACING THE LABEL AND COMBO BOX.**

15. Scroll down as necessary, and click and drag the bottom edge of the detail band upward so it is just below these fields, as shown in Figure 7.32. You can see that using a drop-down list for the Job Category field (rather than a list box or radio buttons) makes it easier to fit all the fields in the window.

16. Because you have laid out the fields in this way, you have room to add a title to the form. Scroll upward to see the header band. Then, click and drag the bar with the name of the Detail band on it downward until the Form Header band is about one-half inch wide.

17. Click the **Label** tool. Then click at the left edge of the Form Header band to place an insertion bar there, and type **Contractors: Data Entry Form**. Press **Enter** to stop editing and select this label. Use the **Font Size** tool of the Formatting tool bar to select **24**. Click the **Bold** tool. Select **Size** from the Format menu and **To Fit** from the submenu. Click and drag the label to place it in the Form Header band properly, and, if necessary, resize the band so it just fits the title, as shown in Figure 7.33.

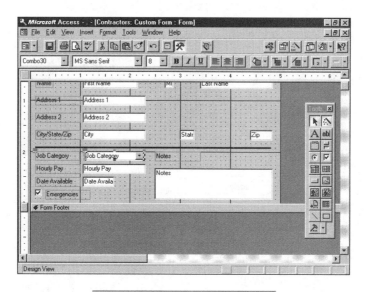

FIGURE 7.32   RESIZING THE WINDOW.

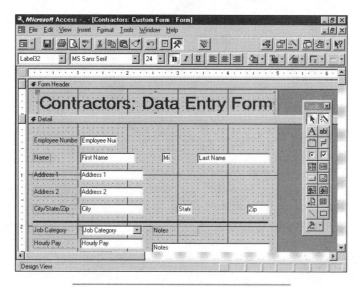

FIGURE 7.33   THE FINAL DESIGN OF THE FORM.

18. Click the **Form View** tool and, after a moment, Access displays the newly designed form. Click the **Restore** button of the Form window and resize the Form window to fit the new form, as shown in Figure 7.34. Select **Save** from the File menu to save the changes.

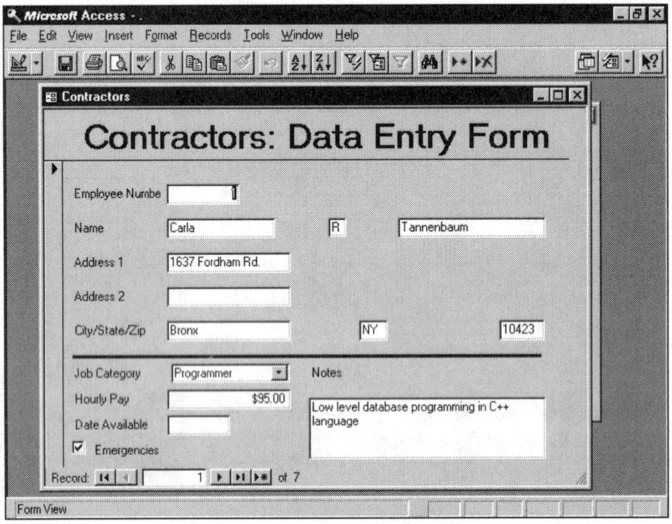

FIGURE 7.34   USING THE FORM.

You can see how clear and easy this custom form is to work with.

In an actual application, you might want to make the heading a bit more elaborate. For example, you might want to include a company logo in it and in any other forms used in this database.

To Sum Up

In this chapter, you learned to create custom forms. You learned to add, select, resize, move, and delete controls, to use layout tools such as the ruler and the grid to line up controls more precisely, and to use the palette to specify colors and effects for controls. You also learned special techniques for working with text controls. Finally, you learned to use the toolbox to add new controls, including simple controls such as text boxes, lines, and rectangles, and advanced controls such as option groups, combo boxes, and command buttons. You also looked briefly at the properties of controls, bands, and the form as a whole.

Report design is similar to Form design, and you will look at how to use these features in more powerful ways in Chapter 9, "Designing Custom Reports." First, though, you will learn about Access expressions, which you must use to add advanced features, such as calculated fields, to forms and reports.

CHAPTER 8

Working with Expressions

xpressions are a feature of virtually every programming language and of every database management system used by developers. They let you create many different types of results based on your data—calculations based on numeric data, transformations of text data, sums or averages of all the values in a field, and much more.

Expressions are one of the more complex features of Access that the ordinary user must work with. Programmers use them regularly. Users can gain extra power by using expressions to validate data, enter default values in fields, and create calculated fields in forms and reports. Access includes an Expression Builder that you can use in these situations to make it easier to create expressions.

This chapter provides a basic overview of the elements that make up an expression. It also provides simple examples of the way that you use expressions as a non programmer. Chapter 9, which covers report design, includes more complex examples of expressions used in calculated fields of reports. In this chapter, you'll learn the following:

✳ What elements are used in expressions

✳ How to use the Expression Builder to create expressions

✳ How expressions use identifiers to refer to objects or their properties

✳ How expressions use literals and constants

✳ How expressions use the arithmetic, comparison, logical, and assignment operators

✳ How expressions use functions

✳ What basic types of built-in functions are available in Access

✳ What the common Access expressions are, such as those used to add page numbers to reports

✳ How to use expressions to validate data as it is being entered

✳ How to use expressions to enter default values in fields

✳ How to use expressions in calculated fields in forms and reports

Understanding Expressions

An Access expression is something like a calculation. Just as you perform a calculation in arithmetic and come up with a result, Access evaluates an expression and comes up with a result.

When you use expressions, Access displays the result rather than the expression. For example, later in this chapter you use an expression to create a calculated field that displays the total pay in a contractor's monthly bills. As the field's value, you use the following expression:

```
= [Hours Worked] * [Hourly Pay]
```

This expression calculates the total that is billed by multiplying the amount in the Hours Worked field by the amount in the Hourly Pay field. The calculated field based on this expression displays the result of this calculation, rather than displaying the expression itself.

Unlike calculations in arithmetic, Access expressions can evaluate to true or false, to dates, or to text, as well as to numbers. Expressions can also use many more elements than ordinary calculations, including the following:

✳ **Identifiers** let you refer to objects from the Access database, such as tables, forms, reports, controls, and their properties. You use identifiers primarily to refer to fields in the table you are working with. An ! is used between the identifier and field name: for example, the First Name field of the Contractors table can be referred to as `[Contractors]![First Name]`, using Contractors as the identifier.

✳ **Literals** are values that are used as they appear in the expression. For example, if you multiply the value in some field by the number 5, the field name is used to refer to the value in the field, but the number 5 is used literally.

✳ **Constants** are values that have constant, predefined values, such as Null.

✳ **Operators** are symbols that tell the expression what operations to perform on other values in it. For example, the + operator means that the other values are added.

✳ **Functions** are special calculations you can use to give expressions more power. For example, there are functions that perform financial calculations such as Present Value and Future Value, and functions that return the current date and time. Access has a large number of built-in functions, and programmers can also create their own user-defined functions.

In the rest of this section, you'll look at all of these elements of expressions in more detail before you practice using expressions.

The Expression Builder

Access generally lets you type in expressions or create them using the Expression Builder window, shown in Figure 8.1.

Many cells that can have expressions in them have a button (called the Build tool) to their right with three dots on it, which you can click to display the Expression Builder. The expression you create here is entered in the cell when you select **OK**.

N O T E

The Expression Builder gives you hints about elements that are still needed as you are creating the expression. It does not display elements that are not appropriate in the current location, and it even takes care of some details of syntax. It is best to use the Expression Builder to create expressions until you become familiar enough with them to be able to create them correctly yourself.

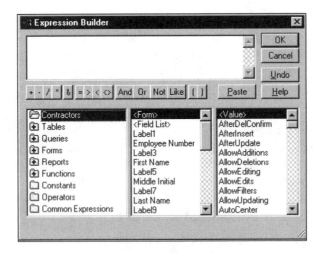

FIGURE 8.1   THE EXPRESSION BUILDER.

HOW TO USE THE EXPRESSION BUILDER

You may type elements of the expression in the Expression Builder's text box at the top of the dialog, or you may enter them there by clicking the operator buttons (which represent the most commonly used operators). You can also add elements by selecting them from the lists of Access objects, functions, constants, operators, and common expressions. Notice that there is no list of literals, since it is impossible to provide a list of all the words and numbers you might want to use literally. You must type literals in the text box.

To copy elements of the expression from these lists, first click one of the folders on the left to display the type of element you want, such as operators or constants. Exactly which folders are included depends on what you were doing when you displayed the Expression Builder, and what types of elements are appropriate in expressions used there.

Some of these folders have a + sign on them to indicate that they have child folders, which you can display by double-clicking them. For example, the Functions folder has a child folder listing the built-in functions of Access, and may have other child folders. Double-click a folder with a + on it to display its child folders; when you do so, the + becomes a –, and you can double-click the folder to close its children.

Folders with + or – on them are used only to display child folders. When you click any other folder, a list of elements you may use in the expression is displayed to its far right.

In some cases, the center panel also includes elements you can add to the expression. In general, however, it is used to limit the list displayed at the far right. For example, if you select the **Operators** folder, all operators are displayed by default. You can use the center panel, as shown in Figure 8.2, to display all the operators or only certain types of operators (such as the arithmetic operators displayed in the illustration).

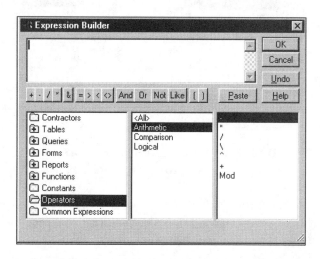

FIGURE 8.2   **DISPLAYING ONLY ARITHMETIC OPERATORS.**

To add an element from a list to the expression text box, simply double-click it, or select it and click the **Paste** button.

To add commonly used operators, simply click one of the operator buttons above this list.

If there is an obvious gap in the expression you create, Access includes a word enclosed in angle brackets in the expression to tell you what type of element is missing. For example, if you add two fields to the expression text box one after another, Access adds `<<Expr>>` between them, as shown in Figure 8.3, to show you where an expression is needed.

You can edit the expression in the text box using the usual Windows editing techniques. Click to place the insertion bar in the expression and then edit it.

In general, double-clicking selects an entire element of the expression rather than just a single word as it usually does with Windows editors. For example, if a field name is made up of two words, double-clicking it will select the entire field name.

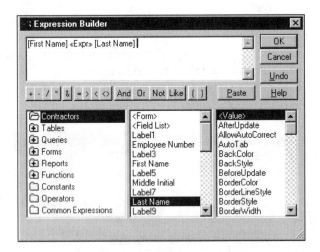

FIGURE 8.3   THE EXPRESSION BUILDER GIVES YOU

HINTS ABOUT MISSING ELEMENTS OF THE EXPRESSION.

In addition, to make it easier for you to replace words such as <<Expr>> added by Access, you can select them simply by clicking them. You cannot place an insertion bar in them and edit them, as you usually can in this text box.

After you select text in this text box, it can be replaced by adding a new element, as well as by typing text. For example, if Access adds <<Expr>> between two fields, you can click that word to select it, and then click an operator button to replace it.

DISPLAYING THE EXPRESSION BUILDER

You should display the Expression Builder now so you can practice as you read the sections about the different elements of expressions.

The Expression Builder does not include elements inappropriate to the place where you invoked it. It is displayed in a complete version when you use it to enter the Control Source property of a field in a form. Remember that you learned in Chapter 7 that you can use the Control Source property of a control to bind it to a field. You can type it in or simply select the field from this property's drop-down list. You can also use an expression rather than just a field as the source of the data displayed in a control of a form: type it in or generate it using the Expression Builder.

Later in this chapter, you'll base a field on an expression in this way. For now, simply display the Expression Builder, as follows:

1. In the Database window, click the **Forms** tab, select **Contractors** and click the **Design** button.

2. Access displays the Auto-Form in Design View. Click the **Properties** tool to display a Property List. Select the **Data** tab in this dialog.

3. Click the text box in the form where the Zip field is entered. Click the **Control Source** property, which should be the first property listed in the property sheet. Click the **...** button on the right of the property to display the Expression Builder. Use the Expression Builder to display the different types of elements as they are discussed.

Identifiers

Identifiers are the names of Access objects. They can be any of the following:

* The name of any field in the current object
* The name of any control in the current object
* The name of any control in any object in the database
* The name of a table or query
* The name of the property of an object

As a nonprogrammer, you use identifiers almost exclusively to refer to fields in the current object—that is, fields in the current table, query, form, or report.

HOW TO READ AN IDENTIFIER

To refer to fields or other controls in the current object, you can simply use their names. To use any other identifiers, you must write out their names in full. As a nonprogrammer, you do not generally need to do this, except occasionally when working with multi-table databases. Even then, you can generate the identifiers easily with the expression builder.

This section describes how identifiers are named so you can read full names when you come across them.

When you write an identifier out in full length, it may consist of an object type (such as forms or reports), the name of an object of that type, the name of a control in the object, the name of a property, and the symbols summarized in Table 8.1.

TABLE 8.1   SYMBOLS USED IN IDENTIFIERS.

Symbol	Use	Example
[ ]	Encloses an object name longer than one word	`[First Name]`
!	Separates object names	`[Contractors: Auto-Form]` `![First Name]`
.	Separates object names from a property	`[Contractors: Auto-Form]!` `[First Name].OnClick`

For example, to refer to the OnClick property of the First Name field of the Contractors Auto-Form, you would use the identifier:

```
Forms![Contractors: Auto-Form]![First Name].OnClick
```

The example shows the two identifier operators. The ! (exclamation point) operator is generally used before the name of an object such as a table, form, or control. The . (dot) operator is generally used before the name of a property.

The example also shows how identifiers use square brackets to enclose object names longer than one word. These brackets may be omitted for objects with single-word names. However, it is generally best, as a matter of style, to include them so the object name is obvious when you look at the expression that this identifier is used in.

SHORTCUT

The square brackets are the only symbols that non programmers need to use in most identifiers. If you leave out the rest of the identifier, Access assumes that the object is a control in the current object; for a form or report, a control in the table or query on which it is based.

When you use the Expression Builder to create identifiers, it uses the shortest form possible. Most of the identifiers that you generate in the Expression Builder will simply be field names enclosed in square brackets.

PAGE NUMBERS

The only properties you use frequently in expressions are the ones that refer to page numbers. The Expression Builder makes it easy to use these by listing them under the Common Expressions folder.

Access forms and reports have the following two page number properties:

✳ **Page** refers to the current page number, as the form or report is being printed.

✳ **Pages** refers to the total number of pages in the form or report.

These are useful for numbering pages when you print a report, and are discussed in more detail, in the section "Common Expressions" later in this chapter.

USING THE EXPRESSION BUILDER TO CREATE IDENTIFIERS

The first five folders in the Expression Builder are all used to select identifiers.

The first folder represents the current object (in this case, the Auto-Form for the Contractors table). The folders that follow represent all the other tables, queries, forms and reports in the database. Their children are the names of individual tables, queries, forms, and reports.

Select any object to display its fields and other controls in the center panel. Select one of these controls to display its properties in the right panel.

If the current object is a form or report, it also has a Record Source option in the center panel. You can select the option to display the names of controls in the table or query that the form or report is based on in the right panel.

For example, Figure 8.4 shows an identifier for the BorderColor property of the First Name field of the form you created using the Wizard in Chapter 5. To generate this, double-click the Forms folder to display its children, double-click **All Forms** to display its children, and click **Contractors Data Entry** to display the objects of this form in the center panel. Then click **First Name** in the center panel to display its properties in the third panel, and double-click the **BorderColor** property (or highlight it and select **Paste**) to place the identifier in the expression text box.

NOTE

This example is meant to let you look at a complex identifier, but in reality, beginners generally use fields from the current object or the table or query it is based on. In general, you either select a field from the center panel or select **Record Source** from the center panel, so you can use the right panel to select a field from the table or query it is based on.

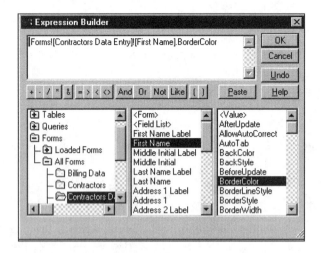

FIGURE 8.4   A COMPLEX IDENTIFIER.

Literals and Constants

You simply type literals into the Expression Builder text box. As you learned in Chapter 4, you must use delimiters around a literal that depends on its data type:

✳   Text literals must be surrounded by the " delimiter.

✳   Date literals must be surrounded by the # delimiter.

✳   Number literals do not need delimiters and must not include the thousands separator or number sign.

In queries, you used literals such as "NY" and #1/31/94#.

Access expressions also let you use constants. These are like literals because they do not change depending on the content of the table. As you can see in Figure 8.5, the Expression Builder includes the following constants:

✳   " " (Empty String) matches a text expression with nothing in it.

✳   **Null** matches any expression with nothing in it.

✳   **False** matches a logical expression that evaluates to false.

✳   **True** matches a logical expression that evaluates to true.

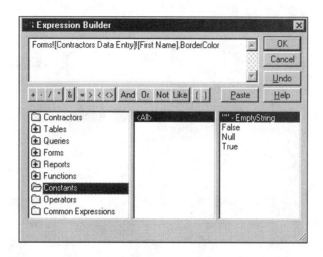

FIGURE 8.5   **DISPLAYING CONSTANTS IN THE EXPRESSION BUILDER.**

You also used constants in queries, but notice that here they match any expression, not just the content of a field. For example, you could have a function that returns Null as well as a field with no value entered in it.

Operators

You also used operators in queries, but you may be confused by the way that operators are used in expressions unless you remember that queries use abbreviated expressions. Queries let you leave out the identifier and enter the rest of the expression in a column under a field name. The field name is assumed as the identifier before the rest of the expression.

For example, if you enter **>=#1/1/96#** under the Date Available field in the QBE grid, that is equivalent to using the expression `[Date Available]` `>=#1/1/96#`.

Many of the operators were covered in Chapter 4, but they are summarized here for reference; details are included that were left out of the earlier chapter. Of course, the examples given are full expressions, rather than the abbreviated expressions used in queries.

If you select the **Operators** folder in the Expression Builder, all the expressions are displayed in the right panel, as shown in Figure 8.6. However, you can use one of the options in the center panel to display only one of the operator types described next.

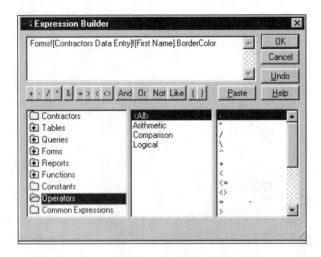

FIGURE 8.6   DISPLAYING OPERATORS IN THE EXPRESSION BUILDER.

ARITHMETIC OPERATORS

The Arithmetic Operators, shown in Table 8.2, are used for ordinary mathematical calculations.

TABLE 8.2   THE ARITHMETIC OPERATORS.

Operator	Meaning
–	subtraction (or negation of a single number)
*	multiplication
/	division
\	division with an integer result (decimal places are truncated)
^	exponentiation (raising a number to a power)
+	addition
Mod	modulo division (returns only the remainder)
( )	used for grouping

When used with numeric data, the data type of the result is generally the same as that of the most precise operand. For example, if you multiply an integer by a double, the result will be a double.

All of these operators require two operands except for the – (minus) operator. This operator can be used with two operands to indicate subtraction—for example, `[Date Available]` - `30`. It can also be used with a single operand to negate its value—for example, – `[Hours Worked]`, which returns the value in the Hours Worked field as a negative number.

ORDER OF PRECEDENCE

In arithmetic calculations, by default exponentiation comes first, then multiplication and division, then addition and subtraction. However, you can change this default order of precedence by using parentheses, just as you do in ordinary mathematics.

For example, let's say that you give a contractor a $100 bonus for a month. You could use the expression `[Hours Worked] * [Hourly Pay] + 100` to calculate the total earned for a month. Because there are no parentheses, this expression uses the default order of precedence. First it multiplies hours worked by hourly pay to get the total earned for that month. Then it adds the $100 bonus to the total.

You could include parentheses and write the expression as (`[Hours Worked] * [Hourly Pay]`) + `100`, but it would not make any difference in the result.

On the other hand, let's say that you give an employee a $1 per hour bonus for a month. You would use the expression `[Hours Worked]` * (`[Hourly Pay] + 1`) to calculate the total earned. Here, you must use the parentheses to make Access add 1 to the hourly pay before multiplying it by hours worked. This is not the same as the default order of precedence; the result would be different if you left out the parentheses.

For example, if someone worked 10 hours and earned $50 per hour, then `[Hours Worked] * ( [Hourly Pay] + 1 )` would have the result 510—first add 50 + 1, and then multiply the result by 10. On the other hand, `[Hours Worked] * [Hourly Pay] + 1` would have the result 501—first multiply 50 times 10, and then add 1 to the result.

DATE ARITHMETIC

The addition and subtraction operators can also be used to perform calculations on dates, to add or subtract a number of days to a date.

STRING CONCATENATION

The arithmetic operator + can also be used to combine, or concatenate, two text strings.

Access also provides a special operator **&**, which can be used only for string concatenation. It is generally considered the best style to use & for concatenation for the sake of clarity.

COMPARISON

The comparison operators are shown in Table 8.3. Expressions based on these operators return a value of true or false

TABLE 8.3   THE COMPARISON OPERATORS.

Operator	Meaning
=	is equal to
>	is greater than
>=	is greater than or equal to
<	is less than
<=	is less than or equal to
<>	is not equal to
Between...And	is within the range indicated

These operators can be used with numbers, text, and dates, but both operands must be the same data type. For example, it makes sense to use the expression `[Date Available] >=#1/1/96#` or the expression `[Last Name] < "M"`, but it obviously does not make sense to use the expression `[Last Name] < #12/1/96#`.

The Between...And operator lets you find a range of values. For example, the expression `[Date Available] Between #1/1/96# And #12/31/96#` evaluates to true for all records with the Date Available field that has a value in 1996. Notice that the range includes the two values you enter. In the example, it would include the dates 1/1/96 and 12/31/96.

The comparison operators listed in the table are all included in the Expression Builder. There are also a few special comparison operators, which are described below.

THE LIKE OPERATOR

The Like operator lets you create expressions with literals that use the wildcard characters:

✳ * represents any group characters

✳ ? represents any single character

For example, if the expression `[Last Name] Like "A*"` is evaluated as true for any record with a value in the Last Name field that begins with A.

In Operator

You can use the operator In to find values in a list that you specify. The list must be in parentheses following the word In, with its items separated by commas. For example, `[State]` In ("NY", "NJ", "CT") would be evaluated as true if the value in the State field is included in this list of three states.

The Is and Is Not Operators

The Is and Is Not Operators are used only in comparisons that use the constant Null. For example, `[First Name] Is Null` would evaluate as true for records that have no entry in the First Name field.

The Logical Operators

Use the logical operators, listed in Table 8.4, to combine two expressions that evaluate to true or false into a single expression.

TABLE 8.4   THE LOGICAL OPERATORS.

Operator	Meaning
And	Both expressions must be true for the combined expression to be true.
Or	Either expression may be true for the combined expression to be true.
Xor	One of the expressions, but not both, must be true for the combined expression to be true.
Not	The following expression must be false to evaluate as true or true to evaluate to false.
Eqv	Equivalence is a bitwise operation used in programming.

continued

Operator	Meaning
Imp	Implication is a bitwise operation used in programming.
( )	Parenthesis are used for grouping.

All of these logical operators require two operands, except for Not, which has a single operand that follows it.

You can create more complex logical expressions by using these operators with operands that are already complex logical statements.

For example, the expression `[Job Category] = "P"` Or `[Job Category] = "W"` would evaluate as true for anyone who is a programmer or writer. Notice that it is made up of two expressions that can evaluate to true or false—the expression `[Job Category] = "P"` and the expression `[Job Category] = "W"`. Because they are connected using Or, the entire expression evaluates as true if either of these evaluates as true.

Now, suppose that you want this expression to find only programmers and writers who earn $80 or more per hour. You would use this expression:

```
( [Job Category] = "P" Or [Job Category] = "W" ) And
Hourly Pay >= 80
```

Notice how important the order of precedence is with logical expressions. The expression above would give you a different result from this expression:

```
[Job Category] = "P" Or ( [Job Category] = "W" And
Hourly Pay >= 80 )
```

If a programmer earned less than $80 per hour, the first expression would evaluate as false, but the second would be true.

N O T E

In general, when you create logical expressions of this sort, it is best to use parentheses to indicate precedence, rather than trying to rely on default precedence. Create one expression at a time, and enclose it in parentheses before you relate it to other expressions in order to see the more complex expression as a combination of two expressions.

THE ASSIGNMENT OPERATOR

The = operator assigns a value to a control.

If you want a text box to display the first and last name, you can use the expression = [First Name] & [Last Name]. The & operator concatenates the values in the First Name and Last Name fields, and the = operator assigns that value to the control.

Access supplies the assignment operator for you when you are using the Expression Builder. For example, if you use the Expression Builder to select a field name as the control source of a control, Access will supply the = before it when you place the expression.

Do not confuse this assignment operator with the = comparison operator. The comparison operator compares two existing values, and the assignment operator gives an object a new value. The assignment operator = is always unary—used with only one operand, which follows it. The comparison operator = is used with two operands, one before and one after it. However, in the QBE grid, it may be used with only the second of these operands because the first one is understood to be the field name at the top of the column.

Functions

In Chapter 5, you learned the function Date( ), which returns the current date. All functions must include the open and close parentheses after them, like Date( ). In most functions, these parentheses contain arguments that the function acts on. For example, if you use a function to capitalize text, you would include the text that is to be capitalized in the parentheses as the argument of the function. If a function has multiple arguments, they are all included in the parentheses, separated by commas. Even if a function does not take an argument, however, you must include the parentheses after it, so Access knows that it is a function.

Two other functions are used almost as commonly as Date( ):

* ✳ **Now( )** returns the current date and time.
* ✳ **CurrentUser( )** returns the name of the person who is currently using Access.

It is obvious how you might use these three functions on forms; by adding text boxes to the form that display the date and/or time, and (if you are working on a network) the name of the person using the form.

Now( ) is invaluable when you are designing printed reports. You usually must print them out several times to get them exactly the way you want them, and you can avoid confusion by being able to see at a glance which report was printed most recently. In the final report, where you want to include only the date, you can either replace Now( ) with Date( ) or format Now( ) so it displays only the date. In Chapter 9, you will learn to use its property sheet to format it in the same way that you do a Date/Time field.

Access includes two types of functions. In addition to its built-in functions, it allows developers to create user-defined functions. This advanced feature of Access is not covered in this book. When beginners are working with the Expression Builder, they should always use the Built-In Functions child folder of the Functions folder.

Access has over 100 built-in functions, many of which are useful primarily for programmers. Here, we summarize the different types of functions included in Access to give you a general idea of the program's capabilities. We also describe some of the important functions.

You can learn about functions by looking through the Expression Builder to see which are available and by using the help system to search for function by name or type.

To display functions in the Expression Builder, first double-click the **Functions** folder and then click the **Built-In Functions** folder. As you can see in Figure 8.7, the Expression Builder begins by displaying all the functions in the right panel, but you can use options in the center panel to display only one type of function.

Notice also that when you highlight a function in the right panel, the function and the types of argument it takes are displayed in the lower left of the Expression Builder. In the illustration, the Abs( ) function, which returns the absolute value of a number, is selected, and Abs(number) is displayed below to show that it requires a number as an argument. When you add functions to the expression text box, they include words indicating the arguments they need, which you must replace with the actual arguments.

MATH FUNCTIONS

In addition to the arithmetic operators which perform the basic mathematical operations, Access has a complete set of math functions that perform more advanced mathematical operations:

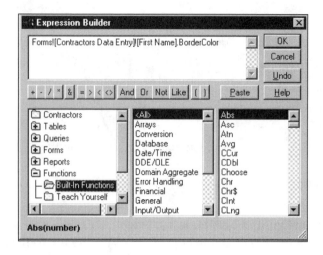

FIGURE 8.7 **DISPLAYING FUNCTIONS IN THE EXPRESSION BUILDER.**

✳ **Sqr( )** returns the square root of the argument.

✳ **Abs( )** returns the absolute value of the argument.

✳ **Log( )** returns the natural logarithm of the argument.

✳ **Cos( )**, **Sin( )** and **Tan( )** are trigonometric functions that return the cosine, sine, and tangent of the argument.

For complete information, search in the help system for the topic "Math Functions."

FINANCIAL FUNCTIONS

Access includes a complete set of functions used in financial analysis:

✳ **PV( )** returns the present value of a series of payments.

✳ **FV( )** returns the future value of a series of payments.

✳ **IRR( )** and **MIRR( )** return the internal rate of return and the modified internal rate of return.

✳ **SLN( )** returns straight-line depreciation **DDB( )** uses the double-declining balance method, and **SYD( )** uses the sum of years' digits method to calculate depreciation.

For complete information, search in the help system for the topic "Financial Functions."

TEXT FUNCTIONS

Access has a complete set of string handling text functions similar to those used in most programming languages:

✳ **LCase( )** converts all the alphabetic characters in the argument to lower case.

✳ **UCase( )** converts all the alphabetic characters in the argument to upper case.

✳ **Left( )**, **Right( )**, and **Mid( )** isolate a number of characters from the beginning, ending, and middle of the text string use as their argument.

✳ **LTrim( )**, **RTrim( )**, and **Trim( )** remove unnecessary blank leading spaces, trailing spaces, and both leading and trailing spaces from the string used as their argument.

NOTE

When you concatenate strings in Access, it generally removes unnecessary trailing blanks automatically, so you do not need to use the functions that do this as you do in other database management programs. For example, if you use the expression [First Name] & " "& [Last Name], Access prints the names with only one blank space between them. It automatically trims any trailing blank spaces that follow the first name in the first name field.

For more information on string functions, search in the help system for the topic "String Handling."

DATE/TIME FUNCTIONS

Apart from Date( ) and Now( ), Access' most useful date and time function is DateDiff( ), which returns the time interval between two dates. For more information on this complex function, search in the help system for the topic "DateDiff."

AGGREGATE FUNCTIONS

The aggregate functions are listed as *SQL Aggregate* functions, as they are based on Structured Query Language (SQL). SQL is a query language used by many database management systems. These functions are very useful for creating controls to display summary calculations in reports, and include the following:

✳ **Avg( )** returns the average (arithmetic mean) value in the specified field.

✳ **Count( )** returns the total number of records.

✳ **Max( )** and **Min( )** return the highest and lowest value in the specified field.

✳ **Sum( )** returns the total of all values in the specified fields.

There are also functions for standard deviation and variance.

Access also includes a set of domain aggregate functions that can be used in some situations where the aggregate functions cannot. These are similar to the aggregate functions but begin with a **D**—for example, DAvg( ), DCount( ), and so on.

The SQL aggregate functions are adequate for most users, and can be used in calculated controls on forms or reports (except in controls added to the page header or footer band). For complete information, search in the help system for the topic "Aggregate Functions."

OTHER FUNCTIONS

Access also includes equivalents for virtually all other functions you might be familiar with from using other database or spreadsheet programs. For example:

✳ **Asc( )** returns the ASCII value of the first character of a string argument.

✳ **CCur( )** converts the argument to the Currency type; **CInt( )** converts the argument to the Int type; and **CStr( )** converts the argument to the text (string) type. These are not needed as often as they are in other database programs, however, because Access generally lets you concatenate values of different data types without conversion.

✳ **IIF( )** is the Immediate If (or Inline If), which takes three arguments, and returns the second argument if the first evaluates to true, or returns the third argument if the first evaluates to false.

✳ **Format ( )** lets you control the format of the data that is returned. For example, `Format ( [Date], "mmmm" )` returns the month of the data field as a word. See the Help system for the codes for all the available formats.

This section has given you a brief description of the functions available in Access. You will use some functions in the exercises later in this chapter and in Chapter 9. If you want to become a more advanced user, you should browse through the Expression Builder and the help system to learn more functions. Start by searching for the topic "Functions Reference" in the Help system.

Common Expressions

If you open the Common Expressions folder, the Expression Builder displays the meaning of commonly-used expressions in the center panel, as shown in Figure 8.8. If you select one of these, the expression itself is displayed in the right panel, and you may add it to the expression in the usual ways.

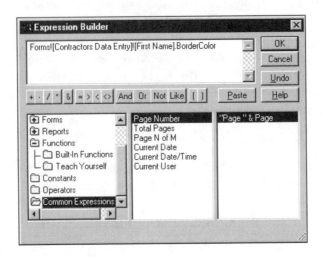

FIGURE 8.8   DISPLAYING COMMON EXPRESSIONS.

The list includes the following common expressions:

* **Page Number** uses the expression `"Page " & Page`, which is made up of the text literal for the word page, followed by the concatenation operator, followed by the identifier Page, which specifies the current page in a form or report as it is being printed.

* **Total Pages** uses the expression `Pages`, an identifier that specifies the total number of pages in a form or report.

✳ **Page N of M** uses the expression `Page & Page & of & Pages`. The text literals Page and of are concatenated with the identifiers that represent the current page of a form or report being printed and the total number of pages in the report.

✳ **Current Date** uses the Date( ) function.

✳ **Current Date/Time** uses the Now( ) function.

✳ **Current User** uses the CurrentUser( ) function.

All of these common expressions are particularly useful in printed reports. You will look at them again in Chapter 9.

Using Expressions

Now that you have a general overview of expressions, you can look at some practical uses of expressions. The following sections look at the some common uses of expressions among users: validating data, creating a default value, and creating a calculated field.

All of these features of Access were mentioned in earlier chapters of this book. Now you have the background to work with them. The first few examples use simple expressions that are the easiest for you to type. Then you will use slightly more complex expressions, easiest to enter by using the Expression Builder.

Other uses of expressions are covered later in this book. Chapter 9 discusses their use in reports, and Chapter 10 discusses their use in queries. The exercises in Chapter 9 give you the opportunity of working with more complex expressions than this chapter.

Validating Data

One common use of expressions is validation of data. In Chapter 2, you learned that fields have validation rules and validation text properties, which let you test the data that is entered. The validation rule is an expression that is evaluated whenever data is entered or edited in the field. You must use an expression that evaluates to true or false. The validation text is displayed if the entry does not conform to the validation rule.

N O T E

When you enter a validation rule, however, you do not use the entire expression. The name of the field that you are validating is assumed as the identifier, as it is when you enter criteria in the Design grid of the Query window.

One field in your sample application that should be validated is the Job Category field. Currently, a user can enter any letter in this field (except in the custom form, where the entry is made using a drop-down list), though it should allow only a P, W, or C to be entered. The easiest way to do this is by entering the validation rule `In("P", "W", "C")`. This is such a simple expression that it is easier to type this criterion into the Validation Rule cell than to use the Expression Builder:

1. In the Database window, click the **Tables** tab to display the Tables list, select **Contractors**, and click the **Design** button, to display this table in Design View.

2. Scroll down through the field list, and click the **Job Category** field to display its properties. Click the **Validation Rule** cell. Type **In("P","W","C")**.

3. Click the **Validation Text** cell and type **You must enter a P, W, or C in this field**, as shown in Figure 8.9

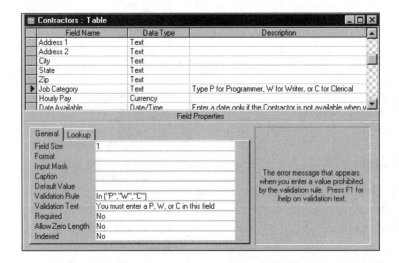

FIGURE 8.9   THE NEW PROPERTIES OF THE JOB CATEGORY FIELD.

4. Now, make an entry to test these new properties. Click the **View** tool. When Access prompts you to save changes in the table, click **Yes.** When Access displays the next dialog box, click **No** to skip checking existing data.

5. Scroll right and click the **Job Category** field of the new record (marked by an asterisk). Type **X**, and press **Tab** to move the cursor to the next field. Access displays the message box shown in Figure 8.10.

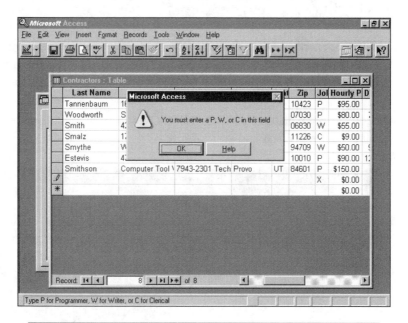

FIGURE 8.10 ACCESS WILL NOT LET YOU ENTER INVALID DATA IN THE FIELD.

6. Select **OK** to return to the table. Delete the **X** from the Job Category field, and type **P** instead. Press **Tab** and Access lets you move the cursor to the next field. Now that you are done testing, press **Esc** to eliminate the new record.

Default Values

You will also find expressions useful as a way of entering a default value in a field. To do this, use the Default Value property of the field, and enter an expression in it that begins with the = (assignment) operator. If you use the Expression Builder to create this expression, Access supplies the = operator.

In some cases, the = can be omitted when you assign a default value, but it is best to use it to make it clear that you are assigning a value.

Try a simple example of a default value. Let's say that you realize that most of your contractors are from New York and want to enter this by default in the State field. You can edit this value if a contractor is from another state, and you can save time by using it for contractors from New York. Since this value is a literal, you can simply type it in as the property, rather than using the Expression Builder.

1. If necessary, click the **Tables** tab of the Database window to display the Tables list; then select the **Contractors** table and click the **Design** button. If you are already using the Contractors table, simply click the **View** tool.

2. Click the **State** field. Click the **Default Value** property. As the default value, type **="NY"**, as shown in Figure 8.11.

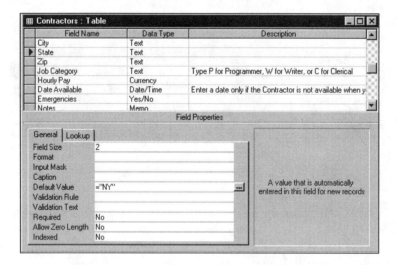

FIGURE 8.11   ASSIGNING A DEFAULT VALUE.

3. Click the **View** tool. Click **Yes** to save the change in the table design. Notice that NY is displayed as the default value in the State field of the new record, as shown in Figure 8.12.

Em	First Name	Mi	Last Name	Address 1	Address 2	City	Stat	Zij
▶ 1	Carla	R	Tannenbaum	1637 Fordham F		Bronx	NY	1042
2	Peter		Woodworth	Star Consultant	4152 Front St.,	Hoboken	NJ	070:
3	Kevin	M	Smith	42 Elm Circle		Greenwich	CT	068:
4	Samuel		Smalz	1701 Albemarle		Brooklyn	NY	1122
5	Jessica		Smythe	WordSmiths	910 University A	Berkeley	CA	9470
6	Josephine	B	Estevis	47 Bleeker St.		New York	NY	1001
7	Sidney		Smithson	Computer Tool \	7943-2301 Tech	Provo	UT	8460
✱	ɔer)						NY	

Record: ◄◄ ◄ 1 ► ►◄ ►✱ of 7

FIGURE 8.12   THE DEFAULT VALUE IS DISPLAYED IN THE NEW RECORD.

N O T E

When you create a default value in a table in this way, it is also used in all the objects based on this table. For example, all the forms that include this field will also use NY as its default value when you add a new record. On the other hand, if you create a default value for a field in another object, such as a form, it only applies to the field when you are using that object to add new records.

Calculated Fields

One of the most important use of expressions is to create calculated fields in forms and reports. You learned in Chapter 7 that the three basic types of fields in forms are bound, unbound, and calculated. You created the first two types of field in that chapter, and now you will create a calculated field.

To create a calculated field, simply add a text box to the form and use the appropriate expression as its Control Source property. You learned in Chapter 7 that you can use the Control Source property to select the field that a control is bound to. You can also use this property to base the control on an expression.

A SAMPLE CALCULATED FIELD

Here, you can create a field that uses a simple numeric calculation. Your Billing table includes fields for Hourly Pay and Hours Worked for each bill. You can multiply the values in these fields to display the total billed.

If you use the Expression Builder to generate this expression, Access automatically adds the = (assignment) operator, because you are assigning this value to the text box:

1. Close any open windows except for the Database window. In the Database window, select the **Tables** tab, and select the **Billing** table. Then click the **Auto-Form** tool.

2. After Access displays the Auto-Form, click the **Design View** tool so you can customize this form. Resize the window if necessary. Click and drag the lower border of the form window and the form to add room for a new field below the ones already included.

3. If necessary, display the toolbox. Click the **Text Box** tool in the toolbox. Then click and drag to add a text box below the Hourly Pay field. It should be the same size and use the same spacing as the Hourly Pay and Hours Worked field, as shown in Figure 8.13.

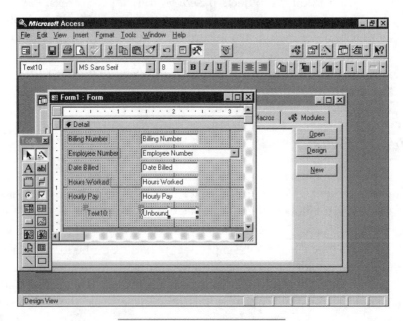

FIGURE 8.13   ADDING A TEXT BOX.

4. Be sure the new text box is still selected. If necessary, display the property sheet by selecting **View Properties** and display its **Data** tab. Click the **Build** tool (the tool with three dots on it) to the right of its Control Source property to display the Expression Builder.

5. In the center panel, double-click the **Hours Worked** field to add it to the expression. Then click the button with the * operator on it. Finally, scroll down the center panel and double-click the **Hourly Pay** field to finish generating the expression, as shown in Figure 8.14. Click **OK**. Access places the expression in the property sheet, with the assignment operator added before it.

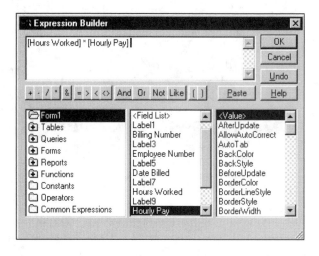

FIGURE 8.14 **CREATING THE EXPRESSION USED IN THE CALCULATED FIELD.**

6. This value is a dollar amount and you want it displayed accordingly, so display the **Format** tab of the property sheet, and use the Format drop-down list to select **Currency**.

7. Close the property sheet. Click the label of this calculated field to select it, and click it again to place an insertion bar in it. Edit it so it reads **Total Pay**. Move the label as necessary to line it up with the other labels above it. The final design is shown in Figure 8.15.

8. Click the **Form View** tool to display data in this form, and resize the Form window as necessary, as shown in Figure 8.16. (This figure assumes you did the optional exercise in Chapter 6 to substitute a drop-down for the Employee Number.) Click the value in the **Total Pay** text

box, and try to edit it. Access displays a message in the status bar saying that it cannot be edited.

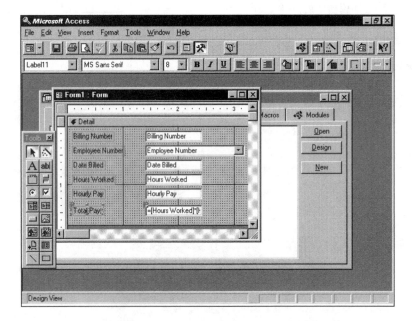

FIGURE 8.15 **THE FINAL DESIGN OF THE FORM.**

9. Close the Form window. Select **Yes** to save the form and give it the name **Billing**. You can see that calculated fields in forms cannot be edited because they are based on the value of the expression. This sort of arithmetic calculation is even more useful in reports than in forms, and you will look at it again in Chapter 9.

OTHER TYPES OF CALCULATED FIELDS

Remember that calculated fields can contain any expression, not just an arithmetic calculation. In Chapter 9, when you design reports, you will work with calculated fields that:

✳ Display the date and time, using the Now( ) function

✳ Display the page number, using the Page property

✳ Display text concatenated with field contents in a text box

✳ Display summary calculations using the Sum( ) function

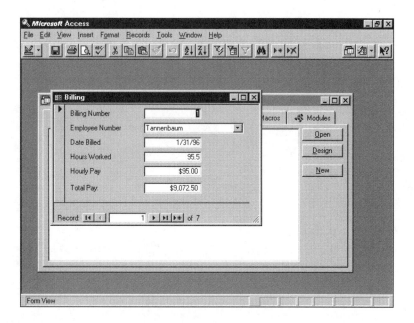

FIGURE 8.16   USING THE FORM.

All of these are calculated field, created by entering expressions in text boxes.

To Sum Up

Expressions can consist of identifiers, literals and constants, operators—including arithmetic, comparison, logical, and assignment operators—and a wide variety of functions. The Expression Builder makes it easier to create expressions by letting you select their elements using push buttons and lists.

After learning how to create expressions, you learned to use them as the default value and validation rule properties of a field when you are designing a table, in order to make data entry faster and more accurate. You also looked at how to use expressions to create calculated fields. You will look at some other uses of expressions in Chapter 9, where you will learn to design custom reports with calculated fields, and in Chapter 10, where you will use them in queries.

CHAPTER 9

Designing Custom Reports

As you read this chapter, you will see that report design is similar in many ways to form design (covered in Chapter 7). However, reports are different from forms in a few important ways, because they are meant to be printed rather than viewed on the screen.

This chapter includes a brief summary of the features that report design has in common with form design, but it concentrates on special features of reports. Because you have now learned about expressions, this chapter also looks at how they are used in report design. What you learn about expressions in reports also applies to forms. In this chapter, you learn the following basics of report design, quickly reviewing the points that are similar to form design and emphasizing the points that are different. You also learn to:

* Create sorted and grouped reports
* Create reports that are grouped on a range of values
* Create subgroups within grouped reports
* Control how groups are printed

309

✳ Set up the printer to print a report or form

✳ Set margins for the printed report or form

✳ Print only the data of a report or form, without graphic elements

✳ Create reports that use a repeated item

✳ Create form letters

The Basics of Report Design

Figures 9.1 and 9.2 show a simple report in Design View and in the Print Preview window. You should be able to see, simply by looking at them and comparing them with what you learned about forms in Chapter 7, how similar report design is to form design.

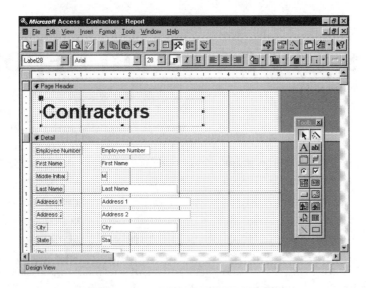

FIGURE 9.1   A REPORT IN DESIGN VIEW.

However, there are also differences between the two, the most important of which are:

✳ **Grouping**: Because they are used to view a large number of printed records rather than a single record displayed on the screen, reports let you group records and add headers and footers with summary data on the groups. For example, you can design a report that groups contractors by job category and includes a group footer with the average wage for contractors in each category.

✳ **Page Setup**: Because reports are meant to be printed, you must also know how to set margins and set up the page in other ways to take full advantage of them. Though you can print forms, this feature is most important for reports.

You should review the features of the report design window, and particularly its differences from the form design window, before creating a sample report.

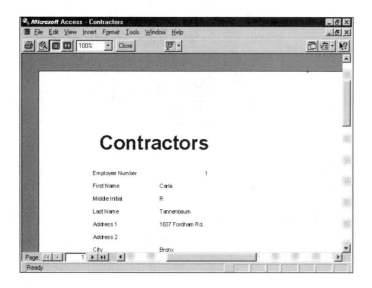

FIGURE 9.2   PREVIEWING THE REPORT.

Changing Views

As you learned in Chapter 1 and Chapter 5, reports are displayed in Print Preview rather than in Datasheet View, because they are meant to be printed rather than edited. When you display the Reports list in the Database window, it has the following buttons instead of the New, Open, and Design buttons that other objects have:

✳ The **New** button creates a new report. When you create a new report in this way, you must select the table or query it is based on in the New Report dialog box.

✳ The **Preview** button displays an existing report in the Print Preview window.

✳ The **Design** button displays an existing report in Design View.

You can also create a report by selecting a table or query in the Database window and selecting the **New Report** or **Auto-Report** tool.

In addition, when you display a report in Design View, the View tool dropdown, shown in Figure 9.3, includes the following options:

FIGURE 9.3   THE VIEW TOOL FOR REPORT DESIGN.

✳ **Design View** lets you change the design of the report

✳ **Print Preview** displays the report in the Print Preview window

✳ **Layout Preview** displays the report in the Print Preview window, with only a small amount of sample data available

These options are also available on the View menu, though the menu option **Layout Preview** is equivalent to the **Sample Preview** tool.

SHORTCUT

If your report is based on a table or query that has a large amount of data in it, Access can be slow at displaying the Print Preview, and you can save time by using Layout Preview instead.

Working with Objects

When you are designing reports, you select objects as you do when you are designing forms:

✳ To select the report, choose **Select Report** from the Edit menu or select **Report** from the Object drop-down.

✳ To select a band, simply click it, select it from the object dropdown, or press **Tab** or **Shift-Tab** to select the bands in turn. The bar with the band's name on it is shaded when it is selected.

✳ To select a control, simply click it or select it from the object dropdown. To deselect a control, click any place in the Form window outside of that control. You can also select multiple controls, using the methods described in "Special Techniques for Working with Controls" in Chapter 7.

WORKING WITH BANDS

You add and remove Page and Report Header/Footer bands for reports as you do for forms. Choose **Page Header/Footer** and **Report Header/Footer** from the View menu. Both these options are toggles. They are checked if the header and footer are displayed, and you can choose them again to remove the header and footer.

Report headers and footers appear once at the beginning and end of the report, and Page headers and footers appear at the top and bottom of each page. You can add page numbers to the page header or footer by using the Page property, which is in the Common Expressions folder of the Expression Builder. Refer to Chapter 8 for more information on the Page property.

Reports also have group headers and footers, which are not available in forms. They are controlled using the Sorting and Grouping dialog box, described later in this chapter.

RESIZING BANDS

To resize a band, simply click and drag its lower border up or down.

DISPLAYING JUST A HEADER OR FOOTER

Both Page and Report headers and footers must be added to the report design in pairs. You can display just a header or just a footer by using the Format menu to add both and then resizing the one you do not want so its size is zero.

Group headers and footers can be added individually.

WORKING WITH CONTROLS

When a control is selected, it has two types of handles; the Resize handles and the Move handle, as shown in Figure 9.4.

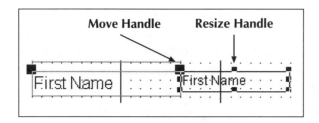

FIGURE 9.4   SELECTING A CONTROL.

You work with controls in reports as you do in forms:

✳ To resize a control, click and drag one of the Resize handles.

✳ To move a control, click and drag on the Move handle or anywhere on the control where the pointer is displayed as a hand.

✳ To delete a control, select it and press **Delete**.

To edit text, first select the control and then click to place an insertion point in it.

Notice that it is less common to have labels attached to fields in reports than in forms. This is because in a columnar report the label with the field's name is in the Page Header band, and the field itself is in the Detail band.

OTHER FEATURES OF REPORT DESIGN

The Report Design window has the same features controlled by the View menu as the Form Design window, and the equivalent tools.

These are the options you can choose from the View menu:

✳ Choose **Field List** or click the **Field List** tool to display or hide a field list, which you can use to add fields to the report.

✳ Choose **Properties** or click the **Properties** tool to display a property sheet with properties for selected objects, for the entire form, bands, or controls.

✳ Choose **Ruler** to display or hide the rulers above and to the left of the window.

✳ Choose **Grid** to display or hide a grid in the design window. Controls are automatically aligned to this grid when you move them, so they will be lined up with each other. Choose **Snap to Grid** from the Format menu to turn this automatic alignment on and off. Use the property sheet of the entire report to change the granularity of the grid. In reports, horizontal and vertical lines one inch apart are displayed in addition to the grid of dots.

✳ Choose **Toolbox** or click the **Toolbox** tool to display or hide the toolbox that you use to add new controls.

All of these features work in the same way in report design as in form design. See Chapter 7 for more information on these features.

The toolbox is the same in reports as it is in forms, though you will never need to use some of its tools in reports. There is no reason to use the Combo Box tool to create a drop-down control in a report for quicker data entry, as you did in the sample form you created in Chapter 7. Access keeps these features consistent in form and report design in order to make it easier for you to learn to use these two windows.

The Formatting toolbar is also the same in Reports as in forms, and can be used in the same ways to specify the colors, fonts, and other properties that affect the appearance of report controls.

A Sample Report

Though many of the techniques used are the same, you create reports differently than forms, simply because they are meant to be printed rather than viewed on screen. Before going on to more advanced features of report design, such as grouped reports, you should try creating a sample report. The sample report will help you solidify your understanding of the basics and get some sense of the design elements involved in laying out reports. In addition, it gives you an opportunity to use expressions, which you had not yet learned when you laid out forms.

Let's suppose that you want to produce a simple report listing the names and addresses of contractors in columns. To improve the report's appearance, you want the name to be listed in a single column, rather than having separate columns for first, middle, and last names.

You can place the First Name and Last Name fields in a single column by using a text box with the expression:

```
[First Name] & " " & [Last Name]
```

As you learned in Chapter 8, **&** is the concatenation operator used to combine text strings. This expression is made up of the value of the First Name and Last Name fields with a blank space added as a text literal (enclosed in quotation marks) between them. If you did not add this literal, the two names would run into each other. Adding the middle initial requires a more complex expression, which is described later in this chapter.

GENERATING THE INITIAL REPORT

As always, it is easiest to begin by using a Wizard to place fields on the report, and then to use Design View to customize it.

If you only used the Wizard to add the address, city, state, and zip fields, you would have to move them all to the right to make room for the name. Instead, you begin by using the Wizard to add the First Name and Last Name fields, which will hold a place for the new expression you are creating.

1. Open the Database window and click the **Tables** tab to display the Tables list. Select the **Contractors** table, then click the **New Report** tool of the New Object tool drop-down.

2. Access displays the New Report dialog box, with **Contractors** already selected in the drop-down list as the name of the table. Select **Report Wizard** and click **OK**.

3. The first step of the Wizard lets you select the fields to include. Double-click **First Name**, **Last Name**, **Address 1**, **Address 2**, **City**, **State**, and **Zip** to move them into the Selected Fields list, as shown in Figure 9.5. Then click **Next>**.

4. Click **Next>** in the next step to skip groupings. Grouped reports will be covered later in this chapter. In the following step, click **Next>** to skip sort order.

5. In the next step, keep **Tabular** as the layout, but select **Landscape** as the Page orientation, so all the fields will fit in the width of the page. Click **Next**. In the following step, click **Next** to keep the default style.

6. In the final step box, enter **Contractors' Names and Addresses** as the report title. Select the **Modify the report's design** radio button. Then select **Finish** to generate the report.

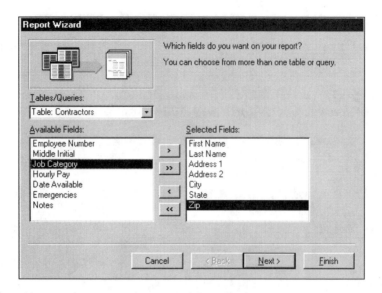

FIGURE 9.5   **INCLUDING FIELDS IN THE REPORT.**

7.   Access takes a moment to generate the report and then displays it in Design View. Click the **Maximize** button to maximize the window. If necessary, make the text box that holds the title wider, so the entire title is displayed. The report design is shown in Figure 9.6. Click the **Print Preview** tool to display the report in the Print Preview window, and zoom the window, as shown in Figure 9.7. After you have looked at the initial report in Print Preview, click the **Close** tool to return to Design View.

Notice that, in Design View, the field names are in the Page Header band, so they are displayed at the top of each page, while the fields themselves are in the Detail band, so they will be displayed for each record in the table. This combination gives you the tabular layout, with the data in columns and the field name at the top of each.

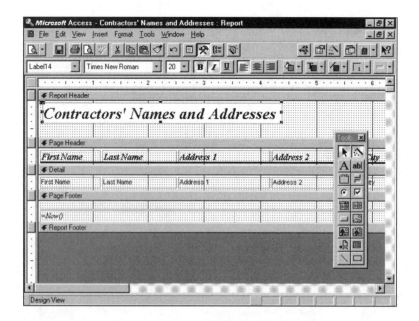

FIGURE 9.6   THE INITIAL DESIGN OF THE REPORT.

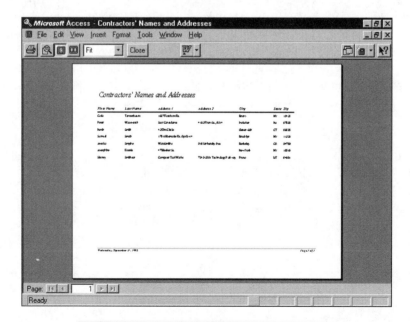

FIGURE 9.7   A PRINT PREVIEW OF THE INITIAL DESIGN.

WORKING WITH EXPRESSIONS

Now you can modify the initial report to get some practice working with expressions.

Notice that the Print Preview has the date in the report title band, but that the initial design has the expression =Now( ) in the page footer band (the assignment operator followed by the Now( ) function). Though this function returns both the date and time, it is formatted to display only the date. Let's assume that you want both the date and the time on the sample copies that you print as you design this report, since you will print out many sample copies during one day as you work on the design. You can change its format temporarily, assuming that you will change it back when you have the finished report.

You must also add a text box that includes the First and Last Name field to replace the actual fields. As you know, you do this by adding a text box to hold the expression and then entering the expression as its Control Source property. The easiest way to do this is to move the First Name and Last Name fields out of the way, then add the text box, and finally delete the First Name and Last Name fields. As long as the fields are still in the report, you can select them in the Expression Builder. You will see later how to type in field names even if they are not in the expression builder, but for a beginner it is easier to select them.

1. Select the text box that contains the expression =Now( ). Click the **Property Sheet** tool to display its property sheet, and select the **Format** tab. The first property is Format, and it is currently Long Date. Display this cell's drop-down list. Scroll upward in the drop-down list, and select the first format in the list, **General Date**, as shown in Figure 9.8.

Text Box: Text15	
Format	Data	Event	Other	All
Format	General Date
Visible	Yes
Hide Duplicates . . .	No
Can Grow	No
Can Shrink	No
Left	0.1"
Top	0.3333"
Width	1.5521"
Height	0.1979"
Back Style	Transparent
Back Color	16777215
Special Effect	Flat
Border Style	Transparent

FIGURE 9.8   CHANGING THE FORMAT OF A DATE/TIME EXPRESSION.

2. Now that you have the property sheet displayed, you can also use it to add a text box with an expression that displays the name. Click and drag the **First Name** and **Last Name** text boxes in the Detail section right to get them out of the way. Click the **Text box** tool and click and drag to place a new text box where these fields used to be. Click the **Data** tab of the Property Sheet. Click the **Control Source** property, the first property in the list, and then click the **...** button to its right to display the Expression Builder.

3. Scroll down and double-click **First Name** in the center panel, which contains the objects in the report, to add [First Name] (in square brackets) to the expression. Then click the **&** button. Then you must enter the Literal " " by hand. Then click the **&** button again. Finally, double-click **Last Name** in the center panel to add it to the expression, as shown in Figure 9.9. Click **OK**. Click anywhere in the design window to place the expression in the text box, and then close the property sheet.

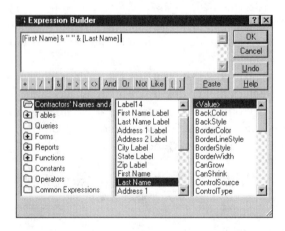

FIGURE 9.9 AN EXPRESSION TO DISPLAY THE ENTIRE NAME.

4. Now, delete the First and Last Name fields, which you dragged right to get out of the way. In addition, delete the default name Access gives to the new text box. If necessary, resize the new text box, so it can hold the entire name and align it with the other fields.

5. Delete the Last Name label from the page header.

6. Finally, select the **First Name** label, then click it again to place an insertion point in it. Edit it so it just reads **Name**, as shown in Figure 9.10.

Click the **Print Preview** button to view the report as it is currently designed.

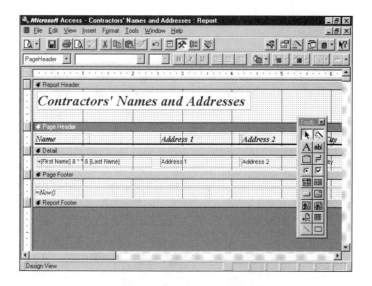

FIGURE 9.10 **THE DESIGN OF THE REPORT.**

The report includes both the date and the time in the footer and has the first and last names concatenated as a single name.

ADDING GRAPHIC ENHANCEMENTS

Looking at the report in Print Preview, you might want to add a few more graphic enhancements. Try adding lines under the heading under the data, in order to make the detail lines of the report stand out.

1. Select the **Close** tool to return to design mode. If necessary, close the Property sheet and display the Toolbox. Click the **Line** tool, and click and drag to draw a line in the Report Header band, below the title. Continue dragging right beyond the right edge of the screen. The report scrolls automatically to let you continue the line. Keep dragging right until the line goes almost to the right edge of the report. After placing the line, select **3** from the Border Width tool of the Formatting toolbar to create a heavy line.

2. Now you must add a similar line near the top of the Page Footer band to be displayed under the data. Click the **Line** tool in the toolbox. Click

and drag near the top of the Page Footer band, beginning near the right margin to the left margin. After you have placed the line, select **3** from the Border Width tool to create a second heavy line.

3. The final design is shown in Figure 9.11. Click the **Print Preview** button to display the report shown in Figure 9.12.

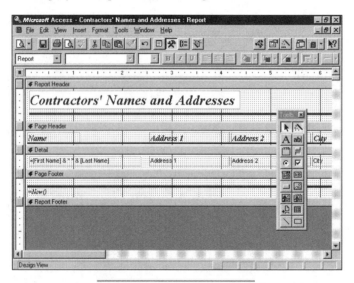

FIGURE 9.11   THE FINAL DESIGN.

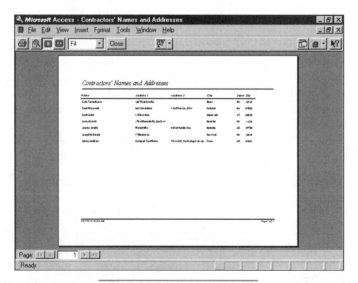

FIGURE 9.12   THE FINAL REPORT.

In an actual quality report, you would also want to adjust the spacing of the columns. Because the First and Last Name expression took the place of two fields, it has too much white space to its right, and some of the other fields are too narrow to hold the names. You should click and drag the other fields and labels left in order to even out the spacing, and resize the other fields where necessary. This is so easy to do that there is no need to include it in an exercise, but you can do it on your own if you want.

USING A COMPLEX EXPRESSION

The next exercise adds the Middle Initial field to the expression that displays the name in this report—a much more difficult problem.

Your first impulse might be simply to use the concatenation operator to add the Middle Initial field, expanding the expression from the current

```
[First Name] & " " & [Last Name]
```

to

```
[First Name] & " " & [Middle Initial] & "." & [Last Name]
```

Here, you use both a period and a space as the text literal after the middle initial, rather than just a space, to display names in the form *Carla R. Tannenbaum.*

The problem is that some people do not have a middle initial entered in the table, and this expression would also include the extra period and space after the first name for them. What you need is an expression that displays nothing if there is no entry in the Middle Initial field, and displays the middle initial followed by a period and a space if there is an entry in the Middle Initial field.

To create this expression, you use the IIF( ) function, covered in Chapter 8. This function takes the form:

```
IIF( expr, truepart, falsepart )
```

The initial expression must evaluate as true or false. If it evaluates as true, the function returns the **"truepart"** expression that follows. If it evaluates as false, the function returns the final **"falsepart"** expression.

To display the middle initial in the way you want, you can use the following expressions within the IIF( ) function:

✳ The initial expression: `[Middle Initial] Is Null`. This evaluates to true if there is no entry in the Middle Initial field. You can follow it with the two expressions that you want if there is no entry and if there is an entry.

✳ The "truepart" expression: `""`. Two quotation marks with nothing between them represent an empty string—in other words, nothing. If there is no entry in the Middle Initial field, the expression returns the empty string and nothing is displayed.

✳ The "falsepart" expression: `[Middle Initial] & ". "`. If there is an entry in the Middle Initial field, the expression returns that entry followed by a period and a space.

Now that you have looked at each element in the expression used to display the middle initial, you should be able to understand the function used to display the middle initial:

```
IIF( [Middle Initial] Is Null, "" , [Middle Initial] &
". " )
```

This is a bit hard to read because the commas that are used as separators do not stand out as strongly as they should, but it becomes clear if you look individually at each of the three expressions used in the function.

Remember that this function just handles the display of the middle initial, and to display the entire name, you must concatenate it with the First Name and Last Name fields to form the expression:

```
[First Name] & " "& IIF( [Middle Initial] Is Null, "",
[Middle Initial] & ". " ) & [Last Name]
```

Notice that there is always a space following the first name. If the middle initial is not included, the last name comes right after this space. If the middle initial is included, it is followed by a period and another space.

The exercise uses what is probably the easiest method of changing the expression that you now have in this text box. It uses the Expression Builder but types the three expressions within the function by hand, rather than generating them. You can try other methods if you want. Sometimes editing in the Expression Builder is tricky. If you delete something, you should make sure that extra elements of the expression were not deleted along with it.

1. If necessary, display the report in Design view. Select the text box that holds the expression that displays the name. If necessary, select the **Properties** tool to display the property sheet; if necessary, also, remove other features of the design window that are in the way.

2. Click the **Control Source** property and click the **...** button to display the Expression Builder.

3. Place the insertion point just before the initial square bracket of Last Name. Double-click the **Functions** folder, click **Built-In Functions**, then scroll down in the right panel until **IIF** is displayed, and double-click it.

4. The Expression Builder adds the IIF( ) function and indicates that there is an expression missing after it, as shown in Figure 9.13. The missing operator is the concatenation operator. To add it, click **<<Expr>>** to select it, and then click the **&** button.

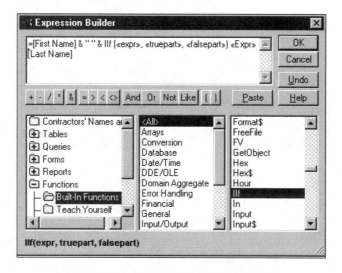

FIGURE 9.13 ADDING THE IIF( ) FUNCTION.

5. Now, type in the initial logical expression of the IIF( ) function. Click **<expr>** to select it, and type **[Middle Initial] Is Null**.

6. Next, click **<truepart>** to select it, and type **""**, the empty string. Finally, click **<falsepart>** to select it, and type **[Middle Initial] & ". "** to create the final expression shown in Figure 9.14. Select **OK**.

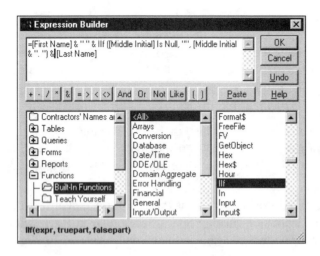

FIGURE 9.14   THE FINAL EXPRESSION.

7. Click anywhere to place the expression in the text box. Then click the **Print Preview** tool to display the report, as shown in Figure 9.15. When you are done, close the Report window and save your changes.

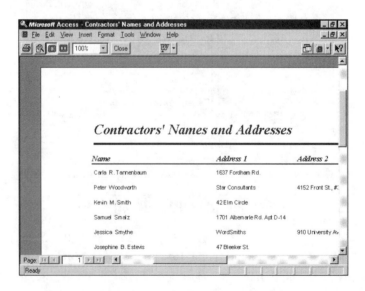

FIGURE 9.15   THE REPORT USING THIS EXPRESSION.

Sorting and Grouping

So far in this chapter you have looked at ways of designing reports that are similar to the ways you design forms. In addition to the basics of report layout, you have used a few different types of calculated fields, which you were not able to use when you designed forms in Chapter 7, because you had not yet learned about expressions. In the future, you can apply what you learned about calculated fields to forms.

Now, you will look at the one major feature of reports that does not apply to forms—sorting and grouping.

When you are designing printed reports, you often want to group records and to include a header and footer for each group. For example, you might want to do a report on your Contractor table that is grouped by job category, so the programmers, writers, and clerical help are listed separately. You could include a header for each group that says something like *Contractors in Job Category "P"*. You might also want a footer for each group that says something like *The average wage for this Category is ... per hour.*

You can include summary data for the group, such as the average wage, by creating a calculated field that uses aggregate functions you learned about in Chapter 8, particularly:

* **Avg( )**, which is the average value in the specified field
* **Count( )**, which is the total number of records
* **Max( )** and **Min( )**, which are the highest and lowest value in the specified field
* **Sum( )**, which is the total of all the values in the specified field

After you look at how to create groups, you will look at how these functions are used.

The Sorting and Grouping Dialog Box

In Chapter 6, you saw how to use the Wizard to create groups for you. You can also create or modify groups from the Report design window by selecting the **Sorting or Grouping** tool or by choosing **Sorting and Grouping** from the View menu to display the Sorting and Grouping dialog box, shown in Figure 9.16.

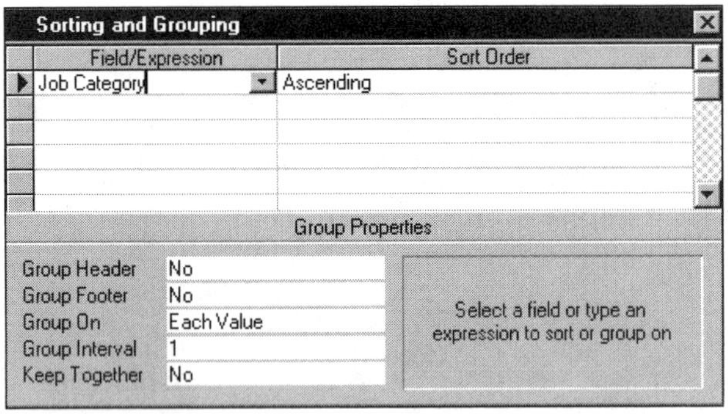

FIGURE 9.16   THE SORTING AND GROUPING DIALOG BOX.

Simply use the drop-down lists in the grid in the upper portion of this dialog box to select the field or fields that the report will be grouped on, and to specify whether they are sorted in ascending or descending order. You may select a field from the drop-down list or type an expression directly in the cell.

You must sort on the fields or expressions specified here in order to group on them. Any fields that you sorted using other methods are automatically included in this list. For example, primary key fields and fields that you sorted on in a query, if the report is based on a query, are listed in this dialog box the first time you open it.

Whether the data also is actually grouped on the fields or expressions that you sort them on depends on the Group Header and Group Footer properties that you specify in the lower half of this dialog box. By default, the Group Header and Group Footer properties are set to No when you add a new field or expression. The report is *sorted* on the field or expression but not *grouped* on it.

To create groups, select **Yes** for one or both of these properties. Access creates a header and/or footer for the group that separates it from the other groups.

For example, if you sorted by job category in ascending order, all the clerical help would be listed first, then the programmers, and then the writers, but the records would just follow one after another without being separated. If you also created a group footer for job category, then the footer after the records in each category would separate it from the records in the other categories. This example shows why you can sort without grouping but cannot group without sorting.

If you have defined a header or footer for the group, Access displays the Grouping symbol to its left, as shown in Figure 9.16.

GROUPING BY RANGE

You learned in Chapter 5 to use the Report Wizard to group on a range of values. If you are working in Design View, you can use the Group On property of the Sorting and Grouping dialog box to group on a range of values. For text or number values, it must be used in combination with the Group Interval property.

Normally the Group On property is set to **Each Value**, so Access creates a new group whenever the value in the field or expression changes—for example, a new group for each job category or a new group for each employee number.

There are also cases where you want similar values to be included in a single group. For example, if you are grouping records by date, you might want all the records in the same month to be grouped together. The month is the range of values that you want to group on.

Grouping Date/Time Data by Range

The drop-down list in the Group On cell, shown in Figure 9.17, lets you select different ranges of values to group on. If the group is based on a Date/Time field, it includes a selection of ranges of dates and times—Year, Qtr, Month, Week, Day, Hour, and Minute.

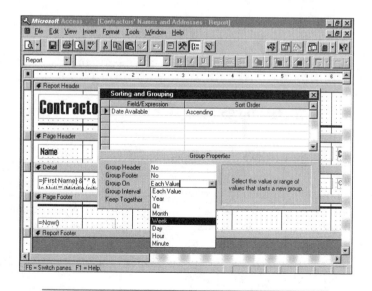

FIGURE 9.17   GROUPING ON A RANGE OF DATE/TIME VALUES.

Grouping Text Data by Range

You can also group text data on a range of values by selecting **Prefix Characters** as the Group On property and using the **Group Interval** property to specify how many characters the group is based on.

For example, if you want to group records by the first letter of the last name, so all names beginning with A, B, and so on are listed together, you would select **Last Name** as the field to group on, **Prefix Character** as the Group On property, and **1** as the Group Interval, indicating that the group is based on one character at the beginning of the last name, as shown in Figure 9.18.

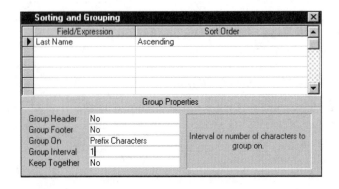

FIGURE 9.18   GROUPING TEXT DATA BY THE FIRST LETTER OF LAST NAME.

To group on the first two characters of the last name, do the same but enter **2** as the interval.

Grouping Numeric Data by Range

To group numeric data (including Number, Currency, or Counter fields) by a range of values, select **Interval** as the Group On property and select the number that represents the range as the Group Interval property.

For example, you could group contractors by their hourly pay, with $10 as the range of values, so contractors who earn less than $10 per hour are included in one group, contractors who earn $10 or more but less than $20 are included in a second group, and so on. To do this, select **Hourly Pay** as the field to group on, select **Interval** as the Group On property, and select **10** as the Group Interval property, as shown in Figure 9.19.

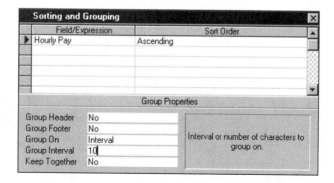

FIGURE 9.19   GROUPING NUMERIC VALUES BY RANGE.

Sorting When You Group by Range

When you group by range, the sort also is based on the range. For example, Access might sort records by year but not by the date within the year, or might sort records by the first letter of the last name but not sort alphabetically by the entire last name.

NOTE

To sort properly, you can use the same field or expression a second time as the basis of a sort grouped on each value. For example, you could select the same Date field in two cells in the grid. In the first, use it just as the basis of a sort, with **Each Value** as the Group On property, so Access sorts all the records by date. In the second, set the Group Header and/or Footer property to **Yes**, and select a range such as **Month** as the Group On property, so Access groups by month.

KEEPING GROUPS TOGETHER

You can specify how groups are organized by page when the report is printed by using the **Keep Together** property, which lets you select among the following options:

✳ **No** prints the report without regard to page breaks. A group may run over onto a second page.

✳ **Whole Group** prints the entire group on a single page if it fits. If a new group will not fit on the remainder of the current page, it is printed beginning at the top of the following page.

✳ **With First Detail** prints at least one detail record on the same page as the group header. If there is no room for a record under it, the group header is printed at the top of the following page.

For presentation-quality reports, it is always better to select **With First Detail** rather than **No**, at least for major groups. The header of a major group should not be printed at the bottom of a page with no records following it.

SHORTCUT

You can also control printing by adding page breaks at the top of a Group Header band or at the bottom of a Group Footer band, so the group always begins on a new page. As you learned in Chapter 7, you can add a page break to a form or report by clicking the **Page Break** tool of the toolbox and then clicking a location on the design. The page break is displayed as a heavy broken line next to the left margin.

CREATING COMPLEX SORTS AND SUBGROUPS

As you know, you cannot always sort on a single field. If you want to sort alphabetically by name, for example, you have to use the first name and middle initial as tie-breakers in cases where the last name is the same.

To create complex sorts like this, simply select all of the fields in the Field/Expression column, from the most important to the least important. For example, to sort alphabetically by name, use the sort order shown in Figure 9.20. The first field is the primary sort order, and the ones below are only used as tie-breakers.

NESTED GROUPS

You create groups with subgroups in the same way. Simply create a complex sort and select **Yes** as the Group Header and/or Group Footer property for all the groups.

For example, you might want to group by state, and have all the records within each state grouped by city, and have all the records within each city grouped by zip code. You can do this by using the sort order shown in Figure 9.21.

You can include Header and Footer bands for all the groups. For example, you might want to include footers for all groups, and use the `Count( )` function in each to display the total number of records from each zip code, from each city, and from each state. After you created this grouping in the Sorting and Grouping dialog box, and specified that a footer should be included in each, Access displays the report as shown in Figure 9.22, and you can add text and expressions to the footer in the usual ways.

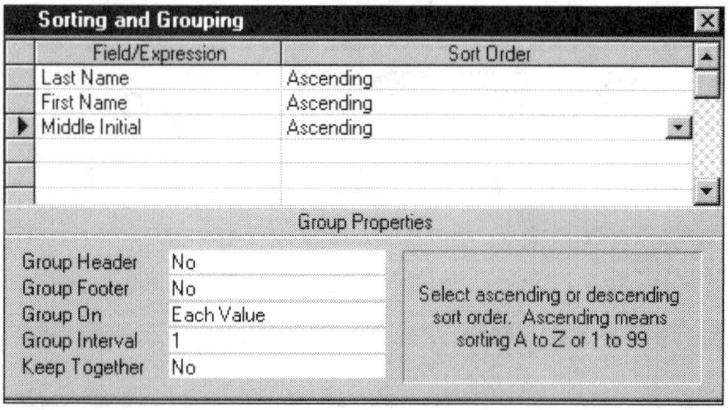

FIGURE 9.20   SORTING ALPHABETICALLY BY NAME.

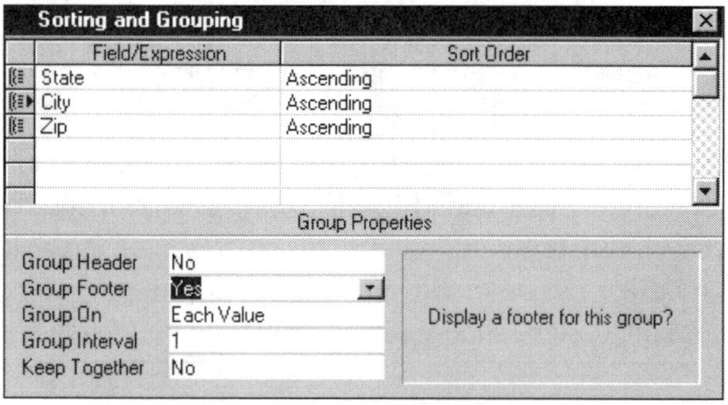

FIGURE 9.21   CREATING GROUPS WITH SUBGROUPS.

CHANGING THE DEFINITION OF A SORT OR GROUP

To change the definition of sorts and groups, you can edit them just as you do when you are changing the design of a table.

Display the Sorting and Grouping dialog box, edit text, and then make selections from drop-down lists in the usual ways.

The select boxes for the rows of the Sorting and Grouping dialog boxes are like the select boxes for the rows of tables, and are used in the same way. Click the select box to select a row. Then, to change sorting and grouping order, click and drag the select box to move the selected row. To remove a group or sort, press **Delete** to delete the selected row.

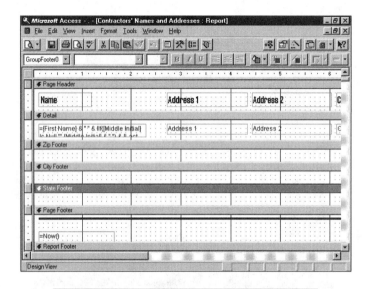

FIGURE 9.22   GROUPS AND SUBGROUPS IN DESIGN VIEW.

WARNING

If you delete a row, you also lose any properties associated with it and any controls you added in that group's header and footer in Design View. You cannot undo this change. As a precaution, it is best to save the design before modifying a complex group or sort. Then you can close the design without saving changes if you made a mistake.

A Sample Grouped Report

To get some experience working with grouped reports, you should try redesigning the report you created earlier in this chapter to turn it into a report on hourly wages by job category. You will add a field for hourly wage, group the report by job category and include a summary band for each group that displays the average hourly wage for that job category.

1. If you have not already done so, save the changes in the report that you created earlier in this chapter, Contractors' Names and Addresses. If you have closed this report, open it in Design View.

2. Choose **Save As/Export** from the File menu. Enter the new name: **Wages by Job Category**, and click **OK**

3. Click the text box that holds the title in the report header, and then click it again to place an insertion bar in it. Edit it so it reads *Contractors' Wages by Job Category.*

4. Now, add the Hourly Wages field to the right of the other fields in the report. Scroll right until you can see the right edge of the report. Display the Field List. Scroll down in the Field list, and click and drag the Hourly Pay field so it is to the right of the Zip field.

5. Now, add the label for this field to the Page Header band. Fists, select this label and press **Del** to delete it. If necessary, display the tool box. Click the **Label** tool and click and drag to add a label box in the Header band above this field. Type **Hourly Pay** in the label box: it should be in the same style as the other labels. Align this field and label with the other fields and labels, resize them as necessary, and resize the report as necessary so it is only 9 inches wide again. In addition, select the line under the field names, and resize it so it is under this new field name, as shown in Figure 9.23.

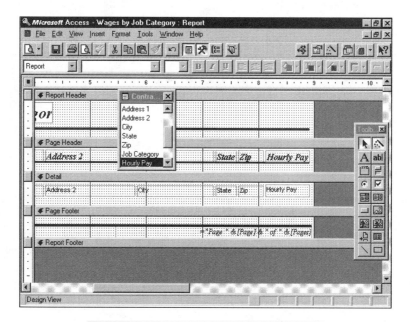

FIGURE 9.23   ADDING THE NEW FIELD AND LABEL.

6. Click the **Sorting And Grouping** tool. In the Sorting and Grouping Dialog box, select **Job Category** as the Field/Expression, leave **Ascending** selected as the sort order, and select **Yes** for both Group Header and Group Footer. Then close this dialog box.

7. Click the **Job Category** field in the Field list, and drag it into the header band. Place it so its label lines up with the left margin. Select both the field and its label. Use the Formatting bar to select **Arial** as the font for both, **10** as the size for both, and to make them both bold. Click the **Italic** button until neither is Italic. Narrow the text box that displays the field's contents, since it only must display one letter, and make sure the field and its label are properly aligned.

8. Now, click the **Label** tool and click and drag to add a label to the Job Category footer band, at its left margin. Type **Average wage for job category**. Click and drag the **Job Category** field from the Field list, so it is to the right of this new label, and then select and delete the label that is automatically placed with the field.

9. Finally, add a calculated field to display the average. Click the **Text** box tool, and click and drag to place an unbound text box in the Job Category footer band, to the right of the fields already there. Select and delete the label that is placed with the field. Select the field. Click the **Property Sheet** tool and display the Data tab of the Property sheet, if necessary. Click the button to the right of its Control Source property to display the expression builder. Open the Built-In Functions folder. Double-click the **Avg** function. Select **<expr>** in the Expression text box. Open the Wages for Job Category folder, and double-click **Hourly Pay** to add it to the expression, as shown in Figure 9.24. Click **OK**. Click the **Format** tab of the Property sheet, and select **Currency** as its format. Close the Property Sheet, Toolbox, and Field list to make the report easier to work with.

10. Select the three objects in the Job Category Footer band. Make them all Arial, 10 point, bold. Resize and align the objects as necessary: remember that the Job Category field holds just one letter. Drag the lower border of the footer down, so there is space after this summary for each job category. The final design is shown in Figure 9.25. Save the changes and click the **Print Preview** tool to display the preview of the report, shown in Figure 9.26.

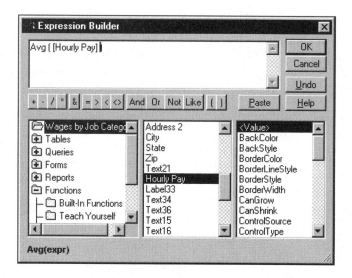

FIGURE 9.24 **CREATING THE EXPRESSION TO DISPLAY AVERAGE HOURLY PAY.**

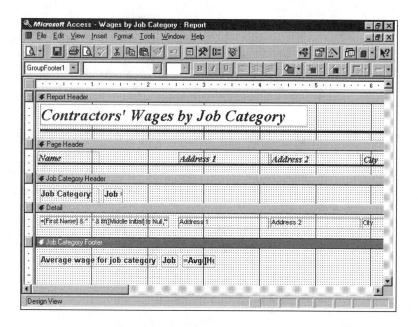

FIGURE 9.25 **THE FINAL DESIGN OF THE REPORT.**

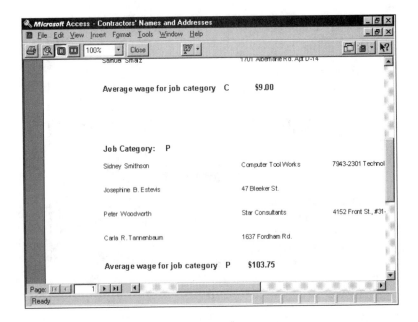

FIGURE 9.26   PREVIEWING THIS DESIGN.

You might want to add some refinements to this report on your own, but the exercise should have made it clear how to create a grouped report with summary data in the group footer.

Page Setup and Reports with Repeated Items

Now that you are designing custom reports, you may need to work with the Page Setup dialog box in either its initial or its expanded form. To display this dialog box, choose **Page Setup** from the File menu.

The Margins and Page tabs let you format the data on the page. The Layout tab is useful when you are creating a report with repeating items, such as mailing labels.

The Margins Tab

Use the four Margin text boxes of the Margins tab, shown in Figure 9.27, to specify the size of the left, right, top, and bottom margins.

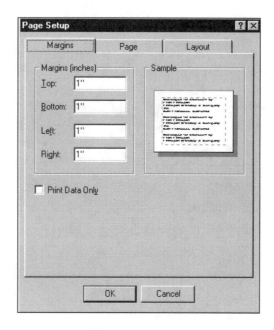

FIGURE 9.27 THE MARGINS TAB.

WARNING

If a Wizard creates unusual settings for the left and right margin, they are probably necessary to fit the data within the width of the page. If you change these margins, make sure the data from each page does not run onto a second page.

Select the **Print Data Only** checkbox of the Margins tab to print only the data in the report, leaving out graphics, borders, and the like. You can use this feature to print a draft report (since graphics take longer to print) or to print the data on a preprinted form.

The Page Tab

Use the **Portrait** or **Landscape** radio button of the Page tab, shown in Figure 9.28, to control the orientation of the items on the paper. You can switch from portrait to landscape to make room for more fields across the width of a page.

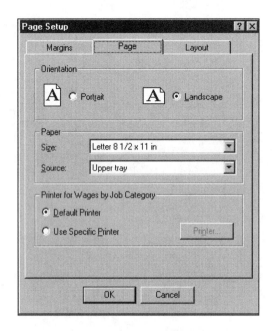

FIGURE 9.28   THE PAGE TAB.

Use the two Paper drop-down lists of the Page tab to specify the Size and Source of the paper you are printing on. The Source drop-down list applies only if your printer has multiple paper sources such as several paper trays, an envelope tray, or the like.

If you select the **Use Specific Printer** radio button, Access displays a dialog box with a drop-down list that lets you choose among all the available printers.

The Layout Tab

The Layout tab is useful if you are creating reports with repeating items, such as mailing labels. As you will see, when you look at mailing labels in Design View, their design only takes up a small portion of the page. The Layout tab indicates how they are repeated on the page.

THE LAYOUT OF ORDINARY REPORTS

Figure 9.29 shows the Layout tab of an ordinary report, which does not contain repeating items.

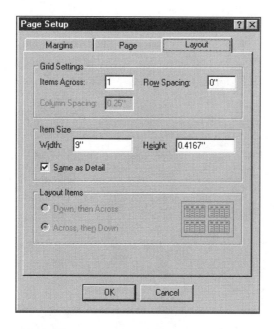

FIGURE 9.29 THE LAYOUT TAB FOR AN ORDINARY REPORT.

Notice that the Grid Settings area says that there is only 1 item across, meaning that there are not multiple columns. In addition, the Item Size area has the **Same as Detail** checkbox selected, meaning that a single item fills the entire detail area (the area of the page within the margins), because the item is not repeated on the page.

THE LAYOUT OF REPORTS WITH REPEATING ITEMS

By contrast, Figure 9.30 shows the Layout tab of for the mailing labels that you created in Chapter 5 using the Label Wizard, and Figure 9.31 shows these labels in Design View.

You can see that unlike all the other reports you have worked with, the mailing label design takes up only a small part of the page—the area of a single label. The Page Setup dialog box lets you control how the item you define in the design is laid out in multiple rows and columns on the page.

To create a multi-column report or to change the number of columns in a report, enter the number of columns you want in the **Items Across** text box.

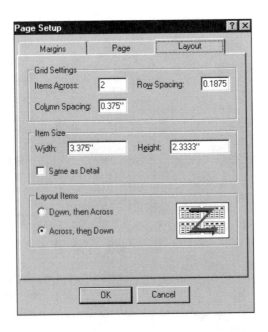

FIGURE 9.30   THE LAYOUT TAB FOR A REPORT WITH REPEATING ITEMS.

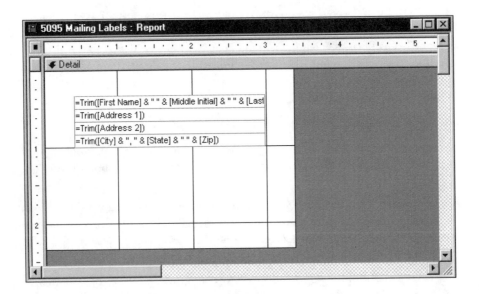

FIGURE 9.31   THE DESIGN OF THIS REPORT.

To change the spacing between items, enter the measurement you want in the **Row Spacing** or **Column Spacing** text box. *Row spacing* refers to the vertical spacing between items. *Column spacing* refers to the horizontal spacing between items, and it is disabled if you are working on single-column reports.

Use the **Item Size** area to specify the size of the item. If you are not working with a report with repeated items, you can select the checkbox to make the item the same size as the total detail area of the report. In a report with repeated items, you need a different item size: for example, if you are creating mailing labels, the item must be the right size to fit a single label, which is repeated many times in the detail area.

NOTE

When you create a multi-column report in this way, you also must be sure that the items are the right size to fit in the number of columns you specify. Take into account the width of the area of the page that is between the left and right margins, the width of the space between columns (specified in the Column Spacing text box discussed below), and the width of the items (specified in the Width text box of the Item Size area).

The Layout Items area determines if the items are printed across each row or down each column. For example, when you use the Wizard to create mailing labels, **Across, then Down** is selected, as in the illustration, so that the labels are printed across each line before going to the next line. Select **Down, then Across** if you want the labels to be printed down each column before beginning at the top of the next column.

Creating Form Letters

Though Access is easy to use in combination with Microsoft Word and other word processors to create mail merges, it can also be used to create its own form letters. A form letter is really just a report with the name, address, salutation, and body of the letter in the Detail band so that the entire letter is repeated for each record in the table or query that it is based on. It could have a letterhead in the Page Header band, or it could simply leave this band blank and print the form letters on paper with a preprinted letterhead.

You could create a form letter manually by adding expressions to the Detail band that are similar to the one you used earlier to concatenate the first and last name. Remember, though, that when you create mailing labels, the Mailing Label Wizard concatenates the fields for you.

It will be instructive for you to modify the mailing labels you created earlier to create a form letter. In addition to modifying the design in the design window, you will have to change the settings in the Page Setup dialog box because the mailing labels that you begin with are a report that uses a repeated item.

When you are working with this report, notice that the Wizard created the full name by using the expression `=Trim([First Name] & " " & [Middle Initial] & " " & [Last Name])`. When you were laying out the mailing labels, Access had no way of knowing that the Middle Initial field was an abbreviation with a period and that it would be missing in some records. As a result, the mailing labels do not have a period after the middle initial, and they skip two spaces between the first and last name for records that have no middle initial. If you want, you can edit this expression and change it to the more precise expression you used to display the full name earlier in this chapter. This exercise leaves it as is for the sake of brevity.

1. In the Database window, select the **Reports** tab, select **5095 Mailing Labels** in the Reports List, and select the **Design** button. If necessary, click the **Maximize** button to maximize the Report window.

2. Choose **Save As/Export** from the File menu. In the Save As dialog box, enter the New Name **Form Letters** and select **OK**.

3. Now, make the item in the report as large as it must be to fill an entire page: since the page is 8.5 X 11 inches with 1-inch margins, click and drag the right edge of the item until it reaches 6.5" on the upper ruler, and click and drag the lower edge of the item until it reaches 9" on the left ruler.

4. Now, change the Page Setup dialog box to print one letter on each page. Choose **Page Setup** from the File menu. In the Margins tab, enter **1 inch** in all the margin boxes. Then, display the Layout tab of the Page Setup dialog box. In the Items Across box, enter **1**. For Row Spacing, enter **0 inches**. As Item Size, click the **Same as Detail** checkbox, to automatically enter **6.5"** as the width, and **9"** as the height, as shown in shown in Figure 9.32. Click **OK**.

5. To add space for the letterhead, select **Page Header/Footer** from the View menu. Scrolling as necessary, click and drag the bottom edge of the footer so its size is 0, and click and drag the bottom edge of the header so it is 1 inch high.

FIGURE 9.32 **THE PAGE SETUP FOR THE FORM LETTERS.**

6. Finally, to make the name and address flush with the left margin, click and drag around all the text boxes that display data from the fields to select them all, and then resize them by dragging their left edges left. This also makes them large enough to display more data, if necessary.

Now that you have the basic page layout of the report, as shown in Figure 9.33, you might want to open the Print Preview window to see how the report looks. Close the Print Preview window to return to Design View when you are done.

As you can see, you created a layout with the name and address where it would ordinarily be located on the page of a business letter with a preprinted letterhead. You might have to adjust the size of the header a bit to allow for the actual size of your letterhead.

All you need to do now to create a form letter is to add a date, salutation, and a text box where you can type the body of the letter. When you first planned the Contractors table, you decided that you would address people by first name in the salutation of letters.

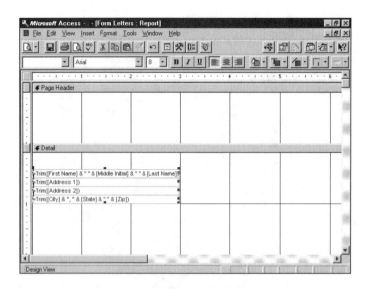

FIGURE 9.33 THE BASIC PAGE LAYOUT FOR A FORM LETTER.

If you wanted to address people by last name, you would have included a field in the table to hold a title such as Mr., Ms., Prof., Dr., and the like. You could have named this field *Honorific*, and used the expression `"Dear " & [Honorific] & " " & [Last Name]` as the salutation of the letter. For this exercise you simply use the expression `"Dear " & [First Name] & ","`.

1. To add a date, display the toolbox, then click the **Text Box** tool of the toolbox. Click and drag to place the text box in upper right of the Detail band beginning at 4.5 inches and extending to the right margin. This box should be entirely above the first line of the Name and Address fields. Click the **Property** tool to display its property sheet. Click the **Control Source** property, and type **=Date( )**. Use the drop-down list for the Format property to select **Medium Date**.

2. Next, click and drag to place a text box under the Name and Address fields, with enough space for a skipped line between them. As its Control Source property, type **="Dear " & [First Name] & ","**. Click anywhere to place the expression, and then close the property sheet.

3. Finally, to create a space for the body of the letter, click the **Label** tool, and click and drag beginning at the left margin, with enough space below the salutation for a skipped line and ending at the right margin

lower in the Detail band. Scroll back to the upper left of this text box, and begin typing **I am writing to let you know that** as the body of the letter.

4. Now, to set the font, first choose **Select All** from the Edit menu since you want all the controls to have the same typeface. Use the Font Name drop-down list on the toolbar to select a font such as **Times New Roman**, as shown in Figure 9.34.

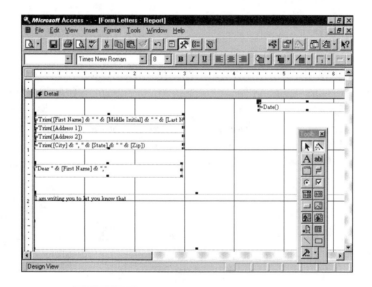

FIGURE 9.34   THE DESIGN OF THE FORM LETTER.

You may want to refine this design further by changing the size of the font and the sizing and spacing of objects in the report accordingly. You may remember that the labels on which you based this form letter were sorted by zip code. It is best to keep this sort order for the form letters to make it easier to collate them with the mailing labels.

When you want to send a form letter, you can display this report in Design View, click the label box that holds the body of the letter to place an insertion bar in it, and type the letter as usual. The main difference between typing in a label box and in an ordinary word processor is that you must use **Ctrl-Enter** rather than just **Enter** at the end of paragraphs. Since an Access label holds a maximum of 2048 characters, you may have to add additional labels if you are writing a long letter.

SHORTCUT

If you produce form letters with any frequency, it would make sense to save a dummy form letter layout like this, designed to fit your own letterhead or with a header band that contains a letterhead that it will print for you. When you begin creating a new form letter, choose **Save As** from the File menu and save each form letter you create under a different name, so that you always have this dummy letter to use as the basis of future letters.

To Sum Up

This chapter began with a review of the basics of report design, which are similar to the basics of form design, and then went on to cover more advanced features of report design.

You learned to create sorted and grouped reports, including reports that have subgroups within groups. You learned to control how groups are printed—for example, how to set up the printer and set margins for the report. You learned how to create reports that repeat the same item on the page, such as mailing labels. Finally, you learned how to use the report design screen to create form letters.

The next chapter covers advanced queries, including action queries, which let you use expressions to update groups of records in your table.

CHAPTER 10

Using Advanced Queries

In Chapter 4, you learned to use basic Select queries to specify which records and fields are displayed and their sort order. Queries offer many more features than the basics you have already learned.

Select queries include more advanced features than you learned in the earlier chapter. There is also another category of queries, *Action queries*, which are entirely different from Select queries: they let you change the data in tables, rather than just specify what data is displayed.

This chapter covers advanced features of Select queries and Action queries. You learn to:

* Use expressions rather than fields at the top of a column in the QBE grid
* Work with field properties and query properties
* Rename fields or expressions to change column headings
* Create Parameter queries
* Create Make Table queries

349

* Create Update queries
* Create Append queries
* Create Delete queries
* Create Summary queries
* Create Crosstab queries

Special Features of Query Design

Many special features of query design are accessible from the Query Type dropdown of the toolbar, as shown in Figure 10.1.

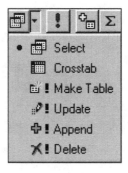

FIGURE 10.1   THE QUERY TYPE TOOL.

Both this tool and the equivalent options on the Query menu let you choose among the different types of queries. After creating a new query in the usual way, select the tool or menu option for the type of query you want. The title of the Query window changes to reflect the type of query it is:

* **Select** query is the sort of query you have already learned about, which specifies which records and fields of the underlying table or query are displayed and their sort order. Use this tool or menu option if you have converted a query to another type and want to convert it back to a Select query.
* **Crosstab** queries cross-tabulate data in the underlying table or query to summarize its data by category.

✳ The **Make Table** query makes a new table based on the underlying table or query.

✳ An **Update** query changes the values in all the fields or in a set of fields in the underlying table or query.

✳ The **Append** query adds data from the underlying table or query to an existing table.

✳ The **Delete** query deletes groups of records in the underlying table or query.

✳ A **Parameter** query lets you enter criteria each time you run the query. This type of query is accessible only from the Query menu, not from the toolbar.

Each of these types of queries are covered in detail in later sections of this chapter. The Query menu also includes an option that lets you create SQL Specific Queries, and advanced feature used primarily by programmers, not covered in this book.

In addition, the Totals tool uses features of the Design grid similar to those used in Crosstab queries. Because Crosstab queries and Totals are more advanced features of query design, they are covered near the end of this chapter.

There are a few other features of query design accessible through the toolbar that you should look at briefly now.

Using Expressions in Queries

 You can select the **Build** tool of the toolbar to display the Expression Builder, and use it to enter expressions in the current cell of the query. This tool is enabled only when you are in a cell that can hold an expression.

In Chapter 4, you looked at how expressions are used in Criteria cells to determine which records are displayed, though you had not yet learned to use the Expression Builder then.

You can also use expressions rather than field names in the Field cell of a column. For example, if you are doing a summary report on your employees and you want the result of the query to display only the year that someone was hired, rather than the exact day, you can use the expression `Year([Hire Date])` rather than the field name Hire Date in the Field cell.

You might use this expression if you wanted to sort the records by year, and sort the employees hired each year alphabetically. You could use the expression to sort even without displaying the year, by deselecting the **Show** cell in that column.

Expressions are covered in Chapter 8 of this book. The section on Crosstab queries later in this chapter uses some more advanced expressions.

Using Properties in Queries

Select the **Properties** tool, choose **Properties** from the View menu, or right-click and choose **Properties** from the shortcut menu to display a property sheet, which works in queries as it does in other objects. Property sheets were covered in Chapter 7.

FIELD PROPERTIES

If the cursor is in a column of the Design grid that has a field in it, Access displays the Field Properties sheet for that field, as shown in Figure 10.2. As you can see, it displays properties similar to those displayed in the Properties panel when you design a table, which you learned about in Chapter 2. For example, you can specify the format in which the field is displayed, as you do when you design a table.

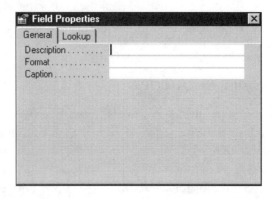

FIGURE 10.2 THE FIELD PROPERTIES SHEET.

QUERY PROPERTIES

If the Field Property sheet is open, you can select the entire query by clicking anywhere in the Query window except in a field list or in a column of the Design grid that has a field in it. Access displays the Query Properties sheet shown in Figure 10.3.

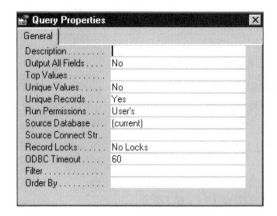

FIGURE 10.3   THE QUERY PROPERTIES SHEET.

SHORTCUT

If the Query Properties sheet is not yet open, you can open it with the properties for the entire query simply by double-clicking in the same location.

You can display help on any of these properties by moving the cursor to a property name and pressing **F1**. A few of the query and field properties are particularly useful and are covered next.

CREATING UNIQUE VALUE QUERIES

Select **Yes** for the Unique Records or Unique Values property to eliminate duplicate values in the result of the query:

✽ **Unique Records property** eliminates repetitive records. If a record has the same data in all of its fields as another record, it is not displayed in the result.

✽ **Unique Values property** eliminates repetitive data in any field. For a record to be displayed, the data in each of its fields must be unique.

You may only use one of these at a time. If you select **Yes** for one, Access automatically selects **No** for the other.

These properties are useful for summarizing data in the table. For example, if you want a list of all the states that your customers live in, you could do a query that includes just the State field, and set either the Unique Values property to

Yes. Rather than getting a long list that repeated the names of some states many times, you would get a list that includes each of the states in the table just once.

OUTPUTTING ALL FIELDS

If you select **Yes** for the Output All Fields property, all the fields in the table or tables underlying the query will be displayed in the result, rather than just the fields whose Show box is selected in the Design grid.

This is useful if you want to create a form or report based on the query, and you want to include fields that are not shown or included in the Design grid.

Changing Column Headings

By default, the name of the field is displayed as the heading of the column that holds that field in the query result. This heading might be inappropriate, particularly if you use an expression rather than a field name. You can change the column heading in two ways:

* **Caption property**: display the Field Property sheet of the field or expression, and enter the heading you want as its Caption property. As you learned in Chapter 7, the Caption property controls the label displayed for a field in a report or form and the heading displayed at the top of the column in a table or query.

* **Renaming the Field or Expression**: enter the new name followed by a colon before the field name or expression in the Design grid. Only the part of the name that is before the colon is used as the column heading.

If you use an expression in the Field cell of a query, Access assigns it an arbitrary name, followed by a colon, which it automatically adds to the expression. In this case, you must delete the arbitrary name and replace it with the name you want to use as the column heading. You look at an example of how to rename a field later in this chapter.

Parameter Queries

All of the queries you have used so far have had unique criteria entered in the query form itself, but there are also times when you might want to use a query with criteria that vary.

For example, you created a query in Chapter 4 to isolate the names and addresses of contractors from New York. In reality, though, you would not want to have to create 50 different queries to isolate the contractors from all the states.

A Parameter query lets you create a single query and enter the criterion in a dialog box that Access displays each time you run it. In this way, you could use one query to find contractors from any of the states.

Creating a Parameter Query

To create a Parameter query, you create the query design as usual, but you enter a parameter in one of the Criteria cells, rather than an actual value. It must be enclosed in square brackets, and it may not be the name of a field.

You must also choose **Parameters** from the Query menu to display the Query Parameters dialog box, shown in Figure 10.4. You use this dialog box to define the data type of the parameters. Enter the parameter in the left column, just as you typed it in the Design grid (though you may omit the square brackets around it), and select its data type in the right column.

FIGURE 10.4 **THE QUERY PARAMETERS DIALOG BOX.**

The easiest way to enter the parameter in this dialog box is by copying and pasting. Select it in the Design grid and choose **Copy** from the Edit menu (or use the shortcut keys, **Ctrl-C**), and then display the dialog box and press **Ctrl-V** to paste it. Though the menu is not accessible when you are using a dialog box, you can still paste using this shortcut key combination.

When you run the query, Access displays a small dialog box with the parameter that you specified as its prompt, where the user enters the value for the criterion. Be sure to use a parameter that is a useful prompt in a dialog box.

Criteria that you enter as parameters can be used in the same ways as values that you enter in the Design grid. For example, you can use a parameter in a logical AND or a logical OR relationship with some other value that you entered in the Design grid, just as you learned in Chapter 4.

You can also create a query with several parameters in a logical AND or a logical OR relationship with each other. When you run the query, Access displays a dialog box for each parameter, with the prompt you specified, and it uses all the values you enter as the basis of the query.

A Simple Parameter Query

Try creating a simple parameter query by changing the query that you created earlier to find names and addresses from New York so it finds names and addresses from any state:

1. Select the **Queries** tab of the Database window. In the Queries list, select **Address List of Contractors from New York**. Click the name again so you can edit it, and give it the name **Address List of Contractors by State**. Then click the **Design** button.

2. Scroll right through the Design grid until you can see the criterion under the State field. Delete the criterion that is now there, and instead type **[Enter the Name of the State]**, as shown in Figure 10.5. (The column has been widened in the illustration.)

3. Now, select the parameter you just entered and choose **Copy** from the Edit menu, and then click anywhere to deselect the parameter. Next, choose **Parameters** from the Query menu. Access displays the Query Parameters dialog box; press **Ctrl-V** to enter the parameter in it, and press **Tab** to move to the Data Type column, where Text is entered by default as shown in Figure 10.6. Select **OK**.

4. To run the query, click the **Datasheet View** tool. Access displays the Enter Parameter Value dialog box, and you can enter **CA**, as shown in Figure 10.7, and select **OK**. Access displays the query in Datasheet View with the one record from California, as shown in Figure 10.8.

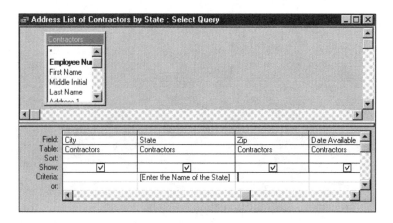

FIGURE **10.5**   ENTERING THE PARAMETER.

FIGURE **10.6**   DEFINING THE PARAMETER'S DATA TYPE.

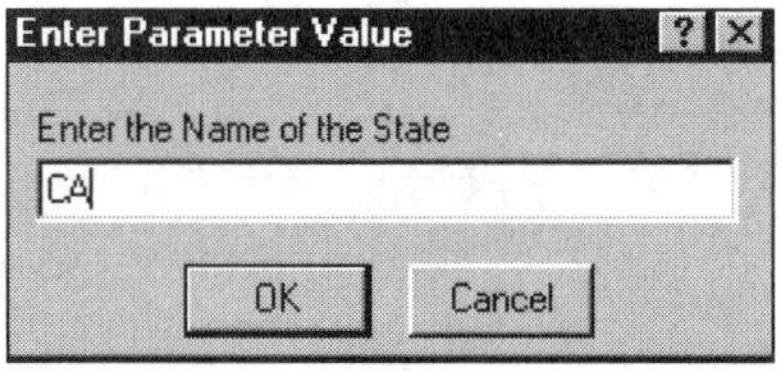

FIGURE **10.7**   ENTERING THE PARAMETER VALUE.

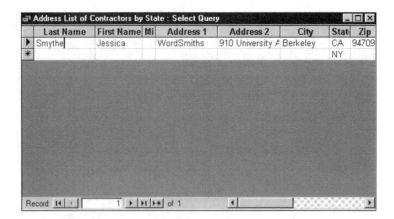

FIGURE 10.8   THE RESULT OF THIS QUERY.

5. If you want, you can try the query with other values or switch back to Design View and try entering a second parameter in a logical OR or a logical AND relationship. When you are done, close the Query window and save the changes.

Access also displays the Enter Parameter dialog box whenever you run this query by selecting it from the Database window and clicking the **Open** button.

Action Queries

Select queries, as you learned in Chapter 4, are used to determine which records and fields are displayed and their sort order, but they do not change the contents of the fields in the table. Access also lets you create Action queries, which change existing data or add new data to tables. You can use the following types of Action queries:

✳ The **Make Table** query creates a new table that holds the data that is the result of the query.

✳ An **Update** query changes the data in the table in ways that you specify.

✳ An **Append** query adds the data in records in the current table to another table.

✳ The **Delete** query deletes records that you specify.

All of these Action queries work quickly and their results are not reversible. To avoid errors, you should always back up a table before performing an Action query on it.

In addition, to avoid losing data, it is always best to run an Action query as a Select query first. After you are sure that it isolates the records you want, convert it to an Action query and run it.

The Basics

Action queries are all created in a similar way. After displaying the Query window in Design View, you can select **Make Table**, **Update**, **Append**, or **Delete** from the Query menu or use the equivalent option on the Query Type tool drop-down to convert the Select query to an Action query. The title bar changes to indicate the type of Action query you are working on.

In some cases, Access displays a dialog box before creating the query, and in some, it changes the Design grid in ways that are necessary to let you specify the action. These features are covered in later sections on the individual queries.

You can run the query from Design View by clicking the **Run** tool of the toolbar or choosing **Run** from the Query menu.

When you save an Action query, Access uses special icons in the Database window to show what type of query it is, which are similar to the icons used on the Query Type tool.

When you open an Action query from the Database window by double-clicking it or by selecting it and selecting the **Open** button, Access runs the Action query and displays the data with the changes the query made. Before opening the query, Access displays a dialog box that lets you cancel the action.

Remember that it is best to back up a table before running an Action query on it. The easiest way to do this from the Database window is to select the table and choose **Copy,** and then **Paste** from the Edit menu. Access displays the Paste As dialog box, which lets you enter a new name for the copy of the table.

Using Make Table Queries

Use a Make Table query to create a new table that holds the result of the query, or to replace all the data in an existing table with the result of the query.

When you choose **Make Table** from the Query menu or click the **Make Table** Query tool, Access displays the Make Table dialog box, shown in Figure 10.9, which you use to specify the table the data will be stored in.

FIGURE 10.9   THE MAKE TABLE DIALOG BOX.

The Current Database button is selected by default. If you want to store the data in a table in the current database, simply enter its name in the Table Name text box. If you enter the name of a new table, Access creates that table and stores the result of the query in it. If you enter the name of an existing table or use the drop-down list to select it, Access replaces the data in that table with the result of the query.

If you want to store the data in a table in another database, select the **Another Database** button, and enter the full path name of the .MDB file in the File Name dialog box. Then enter the table name.

When you finish with the Make Table dialog box, use the Query window exactly as you do for a Select query to specify the records, fields, and sort order of the new table.

If you want to change the table the results are stored in, you can do so by choosing **Make Table** from the Query menu at any time while you are designing the query to display the **Make Table** dialog box again.

Using Update Queries

Update queries let you change the values in some or all of the records of a table.

When you choose **Update** from the Query menu or click the **Update Query** tool, Access displays the Query window in the form shown in Figure 10.10. Notice that the Show and Sort rows of the Design grid have been removed because they do not apply when you are changing the data in a table. Instead, an Update To row is added, where you enter an expression that represents the new value for the field.

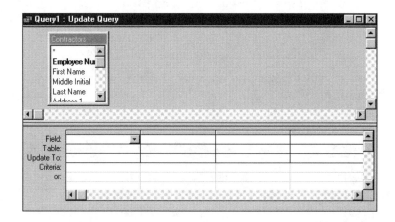

FIGURE 10.10 **THE QUERY WINDOW FOR AN UPDATE QUERY.**

If you want only some of the records updated, enter criteria in the rows to specify the records you want changed, just as you do in a Select query.

Usually, you use an expression in the Update To row that is based on an existing value in the field. For example, to give all your contractors a raise of $5 per hour, you could use the Update query shown in Figure 10.10, with the expression `[Hourly Pay] + 5` as the Update To value for the Hourly Pay field.

It is also common to include criteria for other fields to specify which records are updated. For example, you could give a pay raise only to the contractors who are writers.

You can also use an expression that uses a value from other fields in the table or in other tables that are joined to it, as long as the expression produces a unique value for the field. Thus, you can use a field from a table that the current table is in a many-to-one relationship with, but not one that it is in a one-to-many relationship with.

There are also times when you would want to use a literal as the Update To value—for example, if you have a table that requires the same value in a field in all the records that meet a specific criterion.

Using Append Queries

Append queries are similar to Make Table queries except that the data is appended to an existing table, without affecting the data already in that table.

When you choose **Append** from the Query menu or click the **Append Query** tool, Access displays the Append dialog box, which is identical to the Make Table dialog box, described earlier in the section on "Using Make Table Queries." This dialog box lets you specify the table that the data will be appended to. Use this dialog box in the same way you use it for Make Table queries.

After you specify the table for an Append query, Access displays the Query window shown in Figure 10.11. Notice that the Design grid does not have the Show row that it does in Select queries.

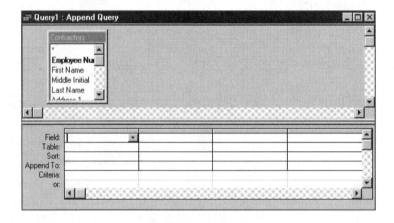

FIGURE 10.11   THE QUERY WINDOW FOR AN APPEND QUERY.

Instead, it has an Append To row, which you may use to select fields in the table you are appending the data to, in order to indicate which fields in the current table they correspond to. Click a cell in the Append To row to display a drop-down list that lets you choose among the fields in the table you are appending to.

If there are fields in the two tables that have the same name, they are displayed in these cells by default.

Use the Sort and Criteria cells as you do in Select queries to specify which records will be appended to the table and the order in which they will be added to the end of the table.

AutoNumber Fields in Append Queries

If you are using an Append query with tables that include AutoNumber fields, you can append the values in the AutoNumber fields in two ways.

If you do not include the AutoNumber field in the fields to be appended, it will be filled in automatically in sequence for all the records that are appended, just as it would be if you appended these new records by hand.

If you do this, the value in the AutoNumber field in the table that you appended to will have nothing to do with its value in the original table. Instead, it will just continue the sequence of entries that are already in that field. For example, if you have a table of employees with employee numbers from 1 to 100, and you append new records to it in this way, they will begin with employee number 101.

If you include the AutoNumber field in the Design grid as one of the fields to be appended, the values that it has in the original table will be kept in this field in the appended records. Note that this can create errors if the same value already exists in that field in the table you are appending records to, because an AutoNumber field cannot have the same value in two records. This subject is discussed later in this chapter in "Correcting Errors in Action Queries."

NOTE

In general, it is best not to include the AutoNumber field in the Design grid as one of the fields to be appended, unless you have some special reason to. If the AutoNumber is a key field, for example, it is usually best to give it arbitrary values in sequence when you append records, just as you would if you were entering new records by hand.

Using Delete Queries

It is easy to select individual records in a table and press **Delete** to delete them, and it is easy to choose **Select All** from the Edit menu and then press **Delete** to delete all the records in a table. If you have to delete records that meet some criterion, though, it is obviously easier to use a Delete query than to select the records individually.

When you select **Delete** from the Query menu or click the **Delete Query** tool, Access displays the Query window shown in Figure 10.12. It does not include the Sort or Show rows from a Select query. Instead, it includes a Delete row.

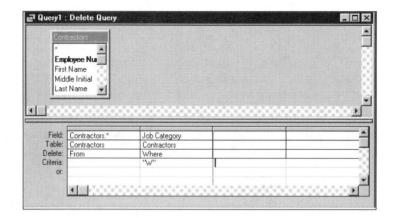

FIGURE 10.12   **THE QUERY WINDOW FOR DELETE QUERIES.**

To use a Delete query, first drag the asterisk from the field list to the Design grid. As you learned in Chapter 4, the asterisk represents all of the fields in the table, and you obviously must delete all the fields to delete the record. In addition, drag the individual fields that you will use to enter criteria.

As you can see in the illustration, the Delete row includes the word From below the table name, which was placed automatically when you dragged the asterisk, and Where below the name of the individual fields. This is simply meant to remind you that you can enter criteria only under fields.

Enter the criteria to specify which records are to be deleted just as you do for Select queries. For example, the query in Figure 10.12 would delete all writers from the Contractors table.

It is particularly important to run a Delete query as a Select query first to make sure it applies only to the records you want.

WARNING

Correcting Errors in Action Queries

The data that you can enter in a table using an Action query is limited in the same ways as the data you enter manually. When you are entering data manually, Access displays a warning that prevents you from entering invalid data in each field. When you are entering data using an Action query, Access displays a single dialog box that summarizes all the errors.

This error message is displayed before the Action query is executed. If there is an error, it is generally best to select **Cancel** so the query is not executed until you correct it.

If you select **OK**, the fields or records that contain errors will not be affected by the Action query in the way you intended. The most common errors are:

✳ **Contents of fields were deleted**: the data is not valid for the field because of data type or because a validation rule. The field will be left blank if you run the query.

✳ **Records were lost due to key violations**: there is a duplicate value or no value in the data being added to a field used as the primary key of a table. Records cannot be added to the table without a valid primary key.

✳ **Records were locked and couldn't be modified**: someone else on a network is modifying records, and they cannot be changed until that person closes them.

Remember that, despite the phrasing of the error messages, the table has not yet been changed. If an error message is displayed, you can select **Cancel** to avoid performing an Action query that creates errors.

Sample Action Queries

Action queries can save you a considerable amount of work if you use them properly, and so you should try creating one. There are times when it makes sense to use an Action query with the same criteria as a Select query that you are using, so you can modify the records that the Select query has isolated. For example, imagine you are doing a series of mailings to groups of people on a mailing list, and the mailings will depend on different types of criteria.

In practice, you would be likely to do this sort of mailing if you bought a list of prospects and you are sending them an initial letter. You might want to do mailings that depend on demographic data that comes with the list. For example, first you might send your offer to all the people who have bought a similar product previously, then to all with more than a certain income, and so on. In the exercise, you use the Contractors table and start with a mailing to all contractors who have more than a certain hourly pay rate. Then you do a mailing to all contractors who are writers.

The question is how to avoid mailing duplicate letters to people who belong to more than one category—for example, to writers who earn more than that pay rate.

It is easy to do this by adding a Yes/No field named Already Mailed To to the table. Initially, **No** is placed in this field in every record by default. Every time you use a query with certain criteria to produce the mailing labels, you can use an Action query with the same criteria to add **Yes** to its Already Mailed To field. Then, when you do later mailings, you can use two criteria: as well as meeting the actual criterion for that mailing, the record must have **No** in its Already Mailed To field to be included among the records that mailing labels are produced for.

First, design the objects you need to use in this process:

1. Add the new field to the table. Click the **Tables** tab of the Database window, select **Contractors** in the Tables list, and click the **Design** button. Scroll down to the bottom of the Field window to add a new field. Enter the field name **Already Mailed To**, select the Data Type **Yes/No**, and enter the Description **Changed By an Action Query After Mailing Labels are Produced**, as shown in Figure 10.13. Close the Table window and select **Yes** to save the change.

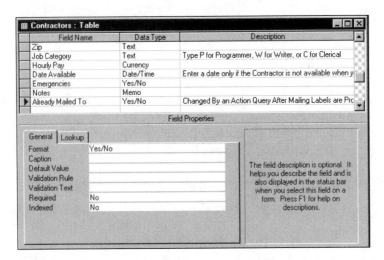

FIGURE 10.13   ADDING A NEW YES/NO FIELD.

2. Now, create the query to produce the mailing labels. Click the **Queries** tab to display the Queries List, and select the **New** button. In the New

Query dialog box, select **New Query**. From the Show Table dialog box, select **Contractors**, select **Add**, and then select **Close**.

3. In the Query window, double-click the title bar of the Field list to select all the fields, and then click and drag them to the first column of the Design grid, to place them all in the Design grid. Close the Query Window, select **Yes** to save the changes, and in the Save As dialog box, enter the name **Query Used for Targeted Mailings**.

4. The easiest way of creating mailing labels for this query is by changing the Record Source property of the mailing labels you created earlier. Click the **Reports** tab, select **5095 Mailing Labels** in the Reports list, and select **Design**. Select the **Properties** tool to display the property sheet and display its Data Properties tab. (The properties for the entire report should be displayed. If you inadvertently select some object in the report, choose **Select Report** from the Edit menu to select and display the property sheet for the entire report.) Use the drop-down list for the Record Source property to select **Query Used for Targeted Mailings**. Then close the Report window and select **Yes** to save the change.

   If you had to do mailings to the full list as well as targeted mailings, you could have chosen **Save As** from the File menu after changing the Report Source property for the mailing labels to produce two sets of mailing labels. One set would be based on the table to mail to the whole list, and the other would be based on this query.

Now that you have created the objects you need, you can try to produce a targeted mailing. First, do a mailing to the highest paid contractors on the list, and then do a mailing to all programmers (except those you already mailed to). Enter the criterion **No** in the Already Mailed To field from the beginning and save it for later use. It will not make any difference in the first mailing because all of the fields still have the value No.

1. Select the **Queries** tab, select **Query Used for Targeted Mailing** from the Queries list, and click the **Design** button. As the criterion for the Hourly Pay field, enter **>= 100**, and as the criterion for the Already Mailed To field, enter **No**, as shown in Figure 10.14. (Columns have been narrowed in the illustration to show both criteria.)

2. Select the **Datasheet View** button to run the query. Note that only one person qualifies, and he is a programmer. Choose **Save** from the File

menu to save the result of the query, and then, without closing the Query window, open the report 5095 Mailing Labels. Notice that it has only that record in it. In a real case, you would print the labels now, but for the purposes of this exercise, you can simply close the Report window.

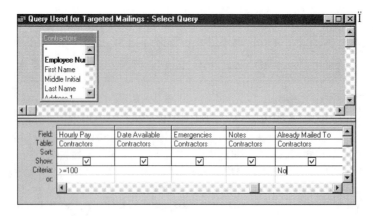

FIGURE 10.14 CRITERIA FOR THE FIRST MAILING.

3. Now, select the **Query** window, click the **View** button to display it in Design View, and choose **Update** from the Query menu to change it to an Update query. Notice that the criteria you used for the Select query are still there. Then, enter **Yes** in the Update To cell of the Already Mailed column, as shown in Figure 10.15.

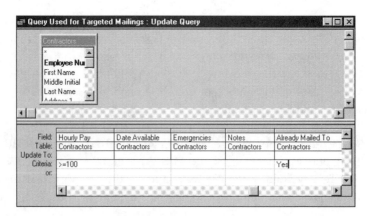

FIGURE 10.15 USING THE UPDATE QUERY.

4. Click the **Run** button and select **OK** to update the data. Close the Query window. Since you will want to use this as a Select query rather than an Update query the next time you work with it, select **No** so the changes are not saved.

5. Open the Contractors table in Datasheet View, and scroll right so you can see that the data was changed. Notice that the Already Mailed To field for one record now has **Yes** in it. Close the Table window when you are done.

6. Now, imagine it is time for the next mailing. Click the **Queries** tab of the Database window, select **Query Used for Targeted Mailings** from the Queries list, and select the **Design** button. Delete the criterion for the Hourly Pay field, and instead, enter **P** as the criterion in the Job Category column. Access adds the quotation mark delimiters around it when you move the highlight. The criterion **No** should still be entered in the Already Mailed To field.

7. Click the **Datasheet View** tool to display the result of the query. Notice that it includes the three programmers who earn less than $100 per hour, but not the programmer who earns more, for whom you already prepared a label. If you would like, you could save the query and view the mailing labels, as you would do in a real case. However, it is not necessary for this exercise since you know that they would include the labels for these three records.

8. Click the **Design View** tool to display the query in Design View. Choose **Update** from the Query menu to change it to an Update query. As you did last time, leave the criteria as is, and enter **Yes** in the Update To cell of the Already Mailed column. Select the **Run** tool and then select **OK** to run the query. Then close the Query window without saving the changes.

9. You might want to look at the table in Datasheet View again, to confirm that **Yes** is entered for all the records that you have already prepared labels for.

N O T E

Even though you tested it on just a small amount of data, you can imagine how useful this technique would be if you wanted to avoid duplication when doing a series of targeted mailings for a database with hundreds of thousands of records.

Queries with Totals and Groups

You can also use queries to produce summary data on a table, such as the average value in a field.

You can produce summary data for the entire table, but it is more common to want to group the data that you summarize. For example, you can find the average wage for all your contractors. However, you are more likely to want to know the average wage for programmers, writers, or clerical help, which involves grouping by job category.

 To create a Summary query with totals, create a query as usual, and click the **Totals** tool to add an extra Total row to the Design grid, as shown in Figure 10.16.

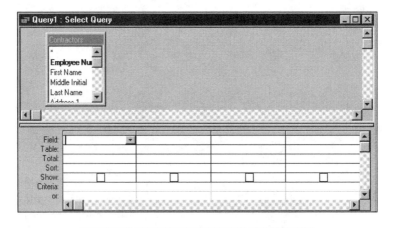

FIGURE 10.16 CREATING A QUERY WITH TOTALS.

Add the fields needed for the query to the Design grid, and use the drop-down list in the Total cell to indicate the function of each field in the query.

The name of the Total row is a bit misleading. In addition to selecting a summary operation to perform on the field, you can use this row to indicate that the field is the basis of a grouping or that it is only used to enter criteria that specify which records are included in the query. The drop-down list in a Total cell includes the following options:

✳ **Group By** means the field is used as the basis of grouping. This is the default value.

✳ **Sum** displays the total of all the values in the field.

✳ **Avg** displays the average of all the values in the field.

✳ **Min** displays the minimum value in the field.

✳ **Max** displays the maximum value in the field.

✳ **Count** displays the total number of records that have a value in the field.

✳ **StDev** displays the statistical standard deviation of values in the field.

✳ **Var** displays the statistical variance of values in the field.

✳ **First** displays the value in the field in the first record.

✳ **Last** displays the value in the field in the last record.

✳ **Expression** lets you enter an expression instead of a field name in the Field cell.

✳ **Where** indicates that this field is used only to hold criteria that determine which records are included in the query. The field is not included in the result of the query.

Though the Total row lets you include calculations, a Summary query is a type of a Select query, and you can use its other features in the same way that you do in ordinary Select queries. For example, use the Show box to specify which fields are displayed in the result, and the Sort cell to specify sort order.

Sample Queries with Totals

Summary queries are easy enough to create now that you can see how they work by creating a few sample queries. It should be easy for you to create queries to display the average hourly pay for all contractors, the average for each job category, and the average for each job category for contractors from a single state.

1. In the Database window, select the **Queries** tab, and click **New**. Select the **New Queries** tab in the New Query dialog box. Then add the Contractors table to the query, and close the Show Table dialog box.

2. Select the **Totals** tool. Use the field drop-down in the first column to select **Hourly Pay**. In the Total cell, select **Avg**. The query is shown in Figure 10.17. Click the **Datasheet View** tool to display its result, as shown in Figure 10.18.

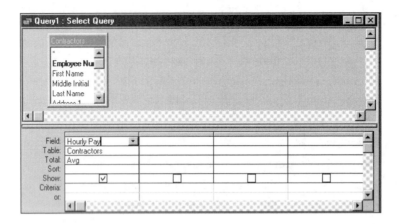

FIGURE 10.17   A QUERY TO FIND AVERAGE HOURLY PAY.

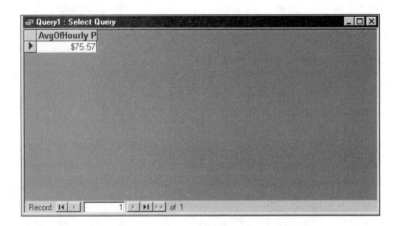

FIGURE 10.18   THE RESULT OF THIS QUERY.

3. To find the average pay by job category, click the **Design View** tool. In the second column of the Design grid, select **Job Category** as the field, and leave Group By in the Total cell. To display the columns in the correct order, click the selection box of the Job Category column to select it, and then click and drag the selection box left to make it the first column; then click anywhere to deselect it. Click the **Datasheet View** tool to display its result.

4. Finally, to restrict the query to contractors from New York state, click the **Design View** tool. In the third column of the Design grid, select **State** as the field. In its Total cell, select **Where**. In its Criteria cell, enter **NY**; Access will add delimiters to the criterion. Click the **Datasheet View** tool to display its result, and notice that it includes only programmers and clerical workers from New York state.

5. Choose **Save** from the File menu. As the query name, enter **Average Pay: Contractors from NY** and select **OK**. Then close the Query window.

Using Expressions to Group and Summarize

As with other queries, you may use expressions rather than field names in the Field cell of each column. Simply type in the expression rather than selecting a field.

You can use an expression either for grouping or to perform a calculation for the following reasons:

✽   Use an expression as the basis of a grouping to group on some value that is not the value of a field. For example, if you wanted a report that showed how much you paid your contractors each month, you could use the expression `Month( [Date Billed] )` in the Field cell of a column and select **Group By** in its Total cell.

✽   Use expressions to create summary calculations that are not available in the Total drop-down list. Enter an expression in the Field cell that uses functions, operators, and the field names to specify the calculation. Select **Expression** in the Total cell.

If you enter an expression in the Field cell and select a calculation to perform on it in the Total cell, Access automatically changes the field expression to incorporate the calculation you selected, and enters Expression in the Total cell, if possible.

You will use expressions in a Crosstab query in an exercise later in this chapter.

Grouping on Multiple Fields

You can base totals on groups that consist of multiple fields. Simply include these fields in the Design grid and select **Group By** for all of them. Access produces a separate summary calculation for each set of records that has the same values in all the fields you group by.

For example, Figure 10.19 shows the design of a query to display the average hourly pay for each job category in each state. Figure 10.20 shows the result of this query. Notice that the result has a row for every combination of job category and state in the table, but not for combinations of fields that have no value in the table.

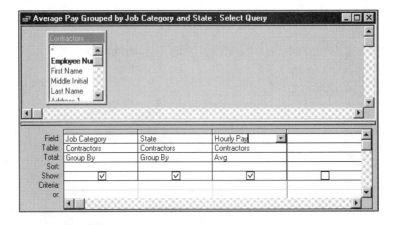

FIGURE 10.19   A QUERY GROUPED ON MULTIPLE FIELDS.

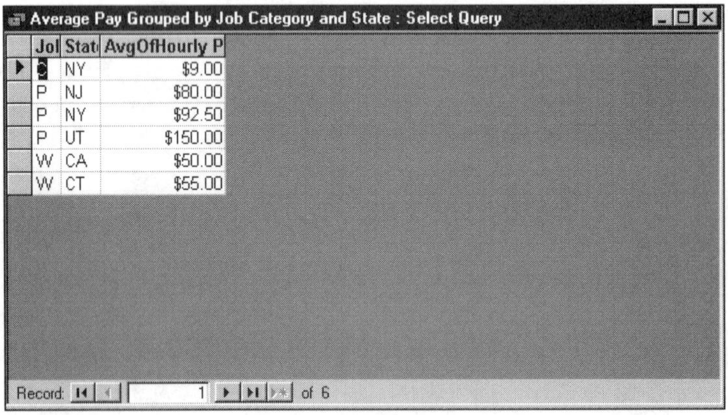

FIGURE 10.20   THE RESULT OF THIS QUERY.

Rather than grouping on multiple fields, you might prefer to display this sort of data using a Crosstab query, described in the next section.

Crosstab Queries

If you want to summarize data grouped on multiple fields, you can use a Crosstab query to arrange the summary data in rows and columns based on values in the fields.

For example, Figure 10.21 shows the result of a Crosstab query that displays average hourly pay grouped by job category and state. Each column represents a job category, each row represents a state, the cells represent average pay.

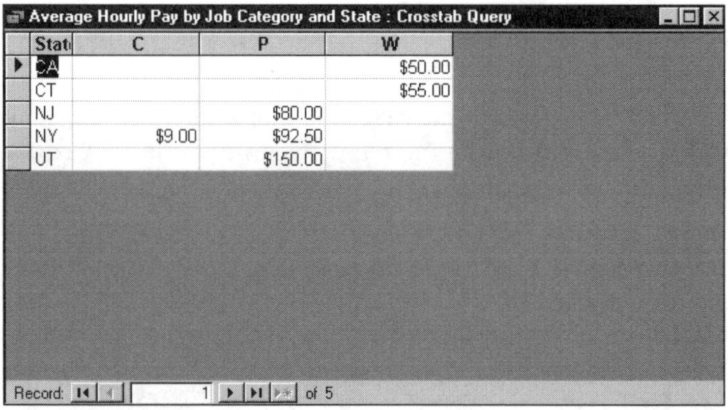

Stat	C	P	W
CA			$50.00
CT			$55.00
NJ		$80.00	
NY	$9.00	$92.50	
UT		$150.00	

FIGURE 10.21 A CROSSTAB QUERY WITH HOURLY PAY BY JOB CATEGORY AND STATE.

Unlike a Summary query based on multiple fields, a Crosstab query includes cells for all values, even if there are not entries in the table for them. For example, both the Summary query shown above and this Crosstab query show that the average pay for writers from California is $50. The Crosstab query also has cells showing there are no clerical workers or programmers from California.

You can see why this is called *cross-tabulation*. Compare the Summary query, which just lists the data in columns, with the Crosstab query, which uses one field as the basis of the row heading, one field as the basis of the column heading, and fills in the cells of the result table with summary information about all the records that fall under both the row and the column heading. Usually, a Crosstab query is much easier to understand than a ordinary columnar Summary query.

When you are working with a large database, Crosstab queries can be very valuable. For example, if you are running a mail-order business that has tens of thousands of customers, you can do a Crosstab query that shows you at a glance the average order by the customers from each state or the total number of customers you have from each state. This is information that would be very valuable for future marketing efforts.

It does not make sense to edit the values in the result of a Crosstab query because the row headings, column headings, and values are all based on values in multiple records.

Working with Crosstab Queries

You work with Crosstab queries from the Database window just as you do with other queries.

To create a Crosstab query, after creating a new query (or opening an existing one), choose **Crosstab** from the Query menu or click the **Crosstab Query** tool to convert it to a Crosstab query.

Figure 10.22 shows the Query window in Design View for the Crosstab query whose result was illustrated previously. As you can see, it has two extra rows in the Design grid:

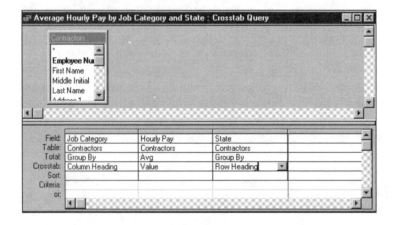

FIGURE 10.22   A CROSSTAB QUERY IN DESIGN VIEW.

✳   **Total** is used just like the Total row in Summary queries, usually to indicate that you want to group on a row or to select the summary calculation you want to perform on it.

✳ **Crosstab** indicates the function of the field in the result of the query. If you group on a field, you may select **Row Heading** or **Column Heading** in this row. If you use it for a calculation, you must choose **Value** to indicate that the result of the calculation is displayed. You may also choose **Not Shown** in this cell, as the Design grid does not have Show boxes.

In a Crosstab query, you must specify one field and only one to use as the column heading. Select **Column Heading** in its Crosstab cell and Group By in its Total cell.

You must specify at least one field to be used as row heading, with **Row Heading** in its Crosstab cell and **Group By** in its Total cell. You may use multiple fields as row headings to create more complex groupings. This is just like grouping on multiple fields in a Summary query, as described previously.

You must specify one field that the summary values are taken from. Select **Value** in its Crosstab cell and specify the value as you do in a Summary query, by selecting a summary function in the Total cell, or by selecting **Expression** in the Total cell and entering an expression in the Field cell. See "Queries with Totals and Groups" earlier in this chapter for more details.

An Advanced Sample Crosstab Query

Crosstab queries are a relatively advanced feature of Access. If you want to get a feel for them, you can do this exercise. It creates a Crosstab query to summarize how much you paid for each category of contractor each month of a year, and it also illustrates a number of more advanced features of queries.

For this exercise, you have to include two tables in this query since the Job Category field is in the Contractors table and the fields you use to calculate the pay are in the Billing table. You calculate the pay using the expression [Hours Worked] * [Billing].[Hourly Pay] and selecting **Sum** in the Total cell. Note that you must use the table name for the Hourly Pay field, because there are fields with this name in both tables.

Apart from the value, this query has columns grouped by the Job Category field and rows grouped by the expression Month([Date Billed]). Note that you cannot simply group rows by the Date Billed field because there would be a different row for every date in the table.

The Month( ) function is workable because we are only displaying results for one year. To display data from many years, you would use a combination of Year(

`[Date Billed] )` and `Month( [Date Billed] )`. In this case, it would make sense to have multiple row headings, one with each of these expressions.

However, the Month( ) function does not give you good row titles because it returns a number rather than the name of the month. After creating the query in a preliminary form, you alter it to change the row titles.

To restrict the query to one year, you have to use an additional column with Where in its Total cell, another feature that you may need in the Crosstab queries you do. The Field expression you use for the column is `Year( [Date Billed] )`, and the criterion is 1996. This is not strictly necessary because your table has data only from 1996, but it is included in the exercise because you would normally need it in practical work.

Create the query as follows:

1. Select the **Queries** tab of the Database window, and then click the **New** button. In the New Query dialog box, select **New Query**. Use the Show Table dialog box to add both the Contractors and the Billing tables, and then close the dialog box. Access automatically creates the default relationship between the tables in the Query window.

2. Choose **Crosstab** from the Query menu. Then, drag the Job Category field from the Contractors field list to the first column of the Design grid. Leave Group By in the Total cell of this column, and select **Column Heading** in its Crosstab cell.

3. In the next column of the Design grid, enter the expression used for the row heading, as explained previously. In its Field cell, type **Month([Date Billed])**. Leave Group By in its Total cell, and select **Row Heading** in its Crosstab cell.

4. In the next column, enter the value to be displayed. In its Field cell, type **[Hours Worked]** * **[Billing].[Hourly Pay]**. In the Total cell, select **Sum**. In the Crosstab cell, select **Value**. As mentioned earlier, Access changes this sort of entry.

5. In the final column, enter the expression that limits the data to one year. In its Field cell, type **Year([Date Billed])**. In its Total cell, select **Where**. In its Criteria cell, type **1996**.

6. Choose **Save** from the File menu. As the Query Name, type **Monthly Cost by Job Category** and select **OK**. The design of the query is shown in Figure 10.23. Select the Datasheet View tool to display its result, as shown in Figure 10.24.

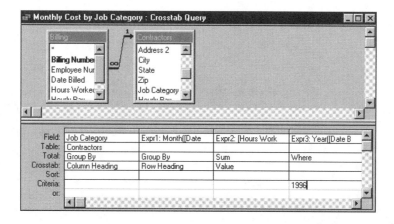

FIGURE 10.23 THE DESIGN OF THE CROSSTAB QUERY.

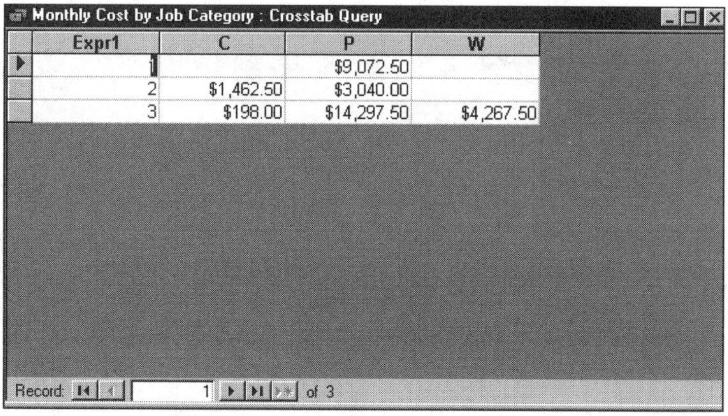

FIGURE 10.24 THE RESULT OF THIS QUERY.

All that is left to do is to give the months their proper names rather than numbers, and to put the right heading at the top of the Month column.

Changing the heading is easy. Access gives the expression `Month( [Date Billed] )` the arbitrary name `Expr1`. You just have to change Expr1 to Month to display it at the top of the column.

It is a bit more difficult to display month names in the column. You can return the names of months by using the function `Format ( [Date Billed], "mmmm")` instead of `Month( [Date Billed] )`, but if you do, the months will be sorted in alphabetical order instead of in chronological order. The solution is to use two columns, one with the Format( ) function, which is displayed as the row heading, and the other with the Month( ) function, which is not displayed but is used as the sort order:

1. Select the **Design View** tool. Edit the function that displays the row heading so it reads `Month:Format( [Date Billed], "mmmm")`. The names of months will be displayed with the title Name at the top of the column.

2. In the fifth column, which is now blank, type `Month( [Date Billed] )` in the Field cell, leave Group By selected in the Total field, and leave the Crosstab field blank so it is not shown. In the Sort field, select **Ascending**. The final query design is shown in Figure 10.25 (with the columns narrowed, to show them all). Select the **Datasheet View** tool to display its result, as shown in Figure 10.26.

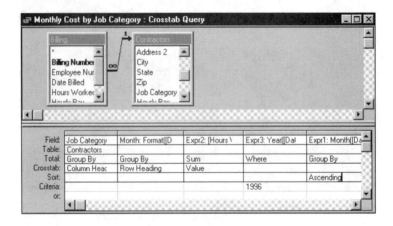

FIGURE 10.25 THE FINAL DESIGN OF THE QUERY.

When you are done looking at the result, close the Query Window and save the changes.

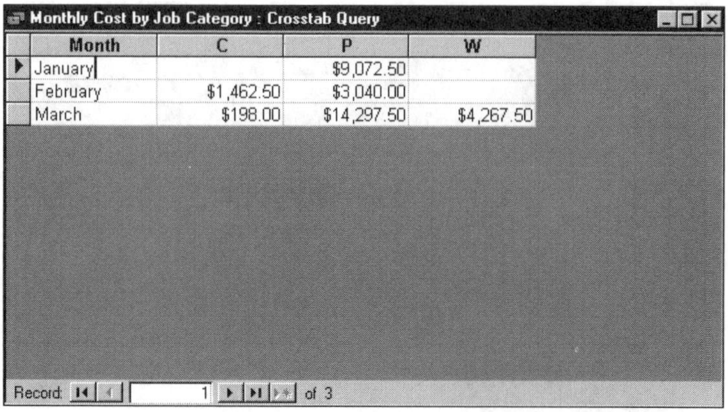

Monthly Cost by Job Category : Crosstab Query

Month	C	P	W
January		$9,072.50	
February	$1,462.50	$3,040.00	
March	$198.00	$14,297.50	$4,267.50

Record: 1 of 3

FIGURE 10.26   THE RESULT OF THIS QUERY.

The Crosstab Query Wizard

At this point, it should be easy for you to understand the Crosstab Query Wizard, which provides a graphic method of creating Crosstab queries by illustrating the result of the query as you make your selection. It automatically includes row totals. Its first step lets you select the table or query the Crosstab query is based on.

The second step lets you select the field or fields used for the row heading and displays a sample illustrating your selection. The third step lets you choose a field for the column heading and illustrates your selection.

The fourth dialog box lets you choose the field that the value will be based on and the type of summary calculation used, as shown in Figure 10.27. You can also use the checkbox to specify whether an extra column should be added that summarizes the rows.

The final dialog box lets you name and create the query. The result of a query to display the average pay of contractors in each job category by state is shown in Figure 10.28.

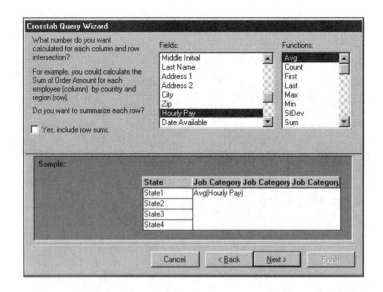

FIGURE 10.27   SPECIFYING THE VALUE DISPLAYED.

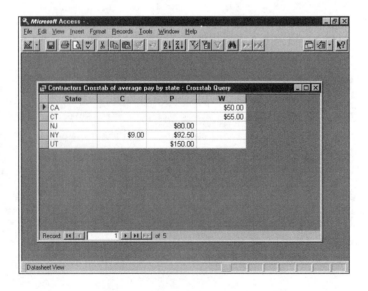

FIGURE 10.28   THE RESULT OF A CROSSTAB QUERY.

To Sum Up

In this chapter, you learned about types of queries that are more advanced than the basic Select queries that were covered in Part I of this book.

You learned to create more powerful Select queries by using expressions rather than fields at the top of columns in the Design grid, by using Field Properties and Query Properties, and by creating Parameter queries, where you enter different criteria each time you run the query. You also learned to create Action queries, including Make Table queries, Update queries, Append queries and Delete queries. Finally, you learned to create grouped queries with summary results and Crosstab queries.

Action queries let you automate your work by modifying an entire group of records at once. In the next chapter, you learn to automate your work even further by using macros.

CHAPTER 11

Saving Time with Macros

As you work with Access, you will probably find yourself doing certain tasks over and over again. You can save yourself time by creating macros to perform this sort of repetitive task, particularly if it involves a long series of actions.

A macro is a group of actions that are combined so that you can execute them using a single command. You "play" the macro to perform the entire series of actions.

In many applications, you create macros by recording keystrokes. You turn on the macro recorder and actually go through the actions that you want the macro to perform. Access uses an entirely different method of creating macros—you enter the actions in a list. After you have created macros in Access, you can run them in many ways. For most users, it is most common to run them from the Macros tab of the Database window.

Macros have many features that are useful primarily for developers. In this chapter, you'll learn the basics that are useful for the average user, and look at some more advanced features. This chapter covers the following:

✳ How to create a macro

✳ The components of macros: actions and their arguments

✳ Adding actions using drag-and-drop

✳ Adding actions using the drop-down list

✳ Specifying the arguments of an action

✳ Editing macros

✳ Using a macro to combine a query with a report or form

✳ Running macros from the menu, the macro window, a form or report, or a push button

✳ Creating macro groups

✳ Using conditional actions in macros

✳ Running a macro a single step at a time to debug it

✳ Creating a macro that runs automatically when you open a database

Creating Simple Macros

You work with macros from the Database window much as you do with other objects. Select the **Macros** tab to display the Macros list. As you can see in Figure 11.1, the buttons that you use to work with macros are similar to the ones used to work with other objects.

FIGURE 11.1   DISPLAYING MACROS IN THE DATABASE WINDOW.

✳ **New** creates a new macro.

✳ **Run** plays an existing macro. You select the macro name in the Macros list and then select the **Run** button.

✳ **Design** lets you change the design of an existing macro. Select the macro name from the Macros list and then select the **Design** button.

Only the **Run** button is different from the buttons used with other objects.

Other basic methods for managing macros are also the same as the methods used for other objects.

The Components of Macros

When you click the **New** button, Access displays the Macro window shown in Figure 11.2.

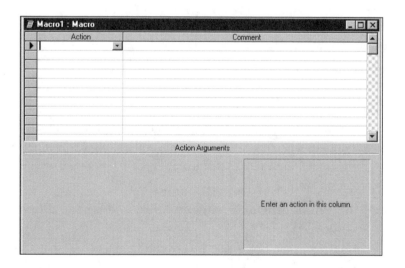

FIGURE 11.2 THE MACRO WINDOW.

In its initial form, which is all you need to use for most macros, this window is very simple:

✳ **Action**: list all the actions you want the macro to execute. The macro performs these actions in the order they are listed.

✳ **Comment**: add descriptions of the actions to make it easier to understand what the macro is doing. These comments are optional, but it can be difficult to understand and maintain older macros if they are left out.

✳ **Arguments** are displayed in the Action Arguments panel in the bottom half of the window. Most actions require arguments, which are options that control the way that actions are performed.

You can simply click and drag the line between these two columns to change their width, as you do with Access tables and other objects.

Macro Actions

There are many different types of actions that you can add to the Action list, including the following:

✳ **ApplyFilter** applies a filter or query to a form, which limits and determines the sort order of the records that the form is based on. (Filters were covered in Chapter 4.)

✳ **Beep** makes the computer beep to alert the user.

✳ **Close** closes an object.

✳ **DoMenuItem** performs any Access menu command. The command you specify must be appropriate to the situation where this action is executed.

✳ **FindRecord** finds a record that matches some criterion that you specify.

✳ **Maximize** maximizes the current window.

✳ **OpenForm**, **OpenQuery**, **OpenReport**, and **OpenTable** open the object specified.

✳ **Printout** prints the object that is currently selected.

✳ **Quit** quits Access.

✳ **RunMacro** runs the macro you specify from within the current macro.

✳ **SelectObject** selects an object that you specify. You then can perform actions that apply to the currently selected object, such as printing, to that object.

✳ **ShowAllRecords** removes all filters from the form that is currently selected, so all records in the table or query it is based on are displayed.

This is only a sample list of the actions that a macro can perform. However, it includes those actions that are most useful for beginners and it gives you an idea of some of the things macros can do.

ARGUMENTS OF AN ACTION

The arguments of an action specify the object that the action applies to and options that control the way the action is performed.

Most actions in macros require arguments. For example, if you use the OpenTable action, you must include an argument that specifies which table should be opened.

When you highlight an action in the Action list, its arguments appear in the Action Arguments panel in the bottom half of the screen—much as the properties of each field are displayed in the bottom half of the screen when you are designing a table.

Figure 11.3 shows the arguments of the OpenTable action. You obviously must specify the name of the table to be opened. You also can specify the view to open the table in (Datasheet, Design, or Print Preview) and specify a data mode of Add, Edit, or Read Only.

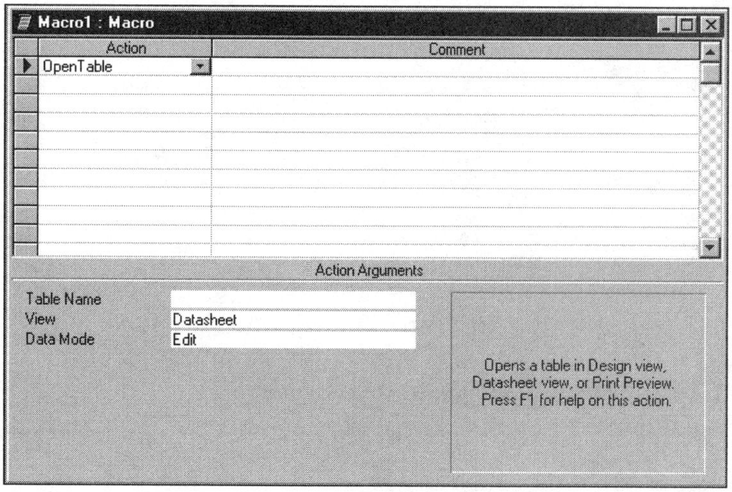

FIGURE 11.3 **THE ARGUMENTS OF THE OPENTABLE ACTION.**

HELP ON MACRO ACTIONS

This book does not list all the actions and arguments available in Access macros, but it is very easy to get help on them.

Select an action or any of its arguments and press **F1** to display context-sensitive help on that action and all of the arguments that can be used for it. Figure 11.4 shows the Help topic for the OpenTable action.

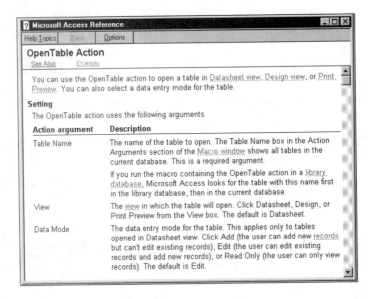

FIGURE 11.4   GETTING HELP ON AN ACTION.

Creating Macros

Designing an advanced macro can be difficult, but the mechanics of adding actions and their arguments are simple.

ADDING AN ACTION USING DRAG-AND-DROP

If you want the macro to include an action that opens an object (OpenTable, OpenQuery, OpenForm, or OpenReport) or to use the RunMacro action to run some other macro, you can add the object to the Action list using drag-and-drop.

Simply display the Database window and the Macro window so you can see both, and drag an object from the Database window to one of the cells in the

Macro window's Action list. The appropriate action for that object will be added in that cell, and the object's name will be automatically used as the first argument.

ADDING AN ACTION USING THE DROP-DOWN LIST

You can also add actions by using the drop-down lists in the Actions cells, shown in Figure 11.5, which let you choose among all the available actions in queries.

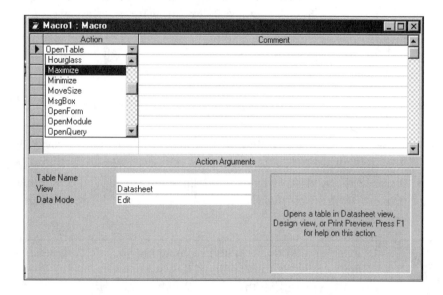

FIGURE 11.5   USE THE DROP-DOWN LIST TO CHOOSE AN ACTION.

If you know the name of the action you want to use, you can also type it in the Action cell. Access displays the first option on the list that begins with the letters you type. For example, if you type **M**, it displays Maximize, and if you go on to type **MI**, it displays Minimize.

SPECIFYING THE ARGUMENTS OF AN ACTION

When you add actions using the drop-down list, you often must specify its arguments, as some arguments have no default. For example, if you select **OpenTable** as the action, the Table Name argument remains blank until you fill it in.

Many Action Argument cells have drop-downs lists that let you choose among the available arguments. For others, you must type in the argument.

EDITING MACROS

After you have begun creating a macro, you can also edit it in the same way that you do tables and other Access objects. Simply use the mouse to place an insertion point in a cell, and follow the usual Windows editing methods, or use cursor movement keys to move among cells in the way they are always used in Access.

In addition, you can click the selection box at the left edge of a row to select the row, and then do the following:

✳ Click or drag the row to change the order in which actions are executed.

✳ Press **Delete**, choose **Delete Row** from the Edit menu, or click the **Delete Row** tool to delete the row and eliminate that action.

✳ Choose **Copy** or **Cut** from the Edit menu to copy or cut the row. Choose **Paste** from the Edit menu later, to place the row somewhere else.

SHORTCUT

To insert an additional action within a macro, click anywhere in a row to highlight it. Choose **Insert Row** from the Edit menu. Press the **Insert** key, or click the **Insert Row** tool to add a new blank row above that row.

USING A MACRO TO COMBINE A QUERY WITH A REPORT OR FORM

One very useful feature of macros is that they let you combine a query with a form or report. Though you can add a filter to a form, using macros gives you additional flexibility by letting you use a number of different queries with one or more forms.

If you use the OpenForm or OpenReport action, you see that one of its arguments is Filter Name. You can enter the name of a query here to specify which records are included in the form or report and the order they are sorted in.

This is easiest to do if the query includes all the fields that are included in the form or report. If it does not, however, you can set its Output All Fields property to **Yes**. To get to this property, display the query in Design View, select the **Properties** tool, and click somewhere in the query that is not in a field list or in the Design grid. This displays the Query Properties sheet.

NOTE

You can also limit the number of records included in a form or report by using the Where Condition argument of the OpenForm or OpenReport action to add a SQL WHERE clause or an Access expression that determines which records are displayed. SQL is not covered in this book, but simple expressions such as [State] = "NY" are all you need to filter forms or reports in most cases. This argument has the ... button to its right, which you can use to display the Expression Builder.

Running Macros

You have already seen how to run a macro from the Database window simply by double-clicking it or by selecting it and selecting **Run**. Most users only need to run macros in this way, but there are other methods of running macros that you may sometimes find convenient.

FROM THE MENU

To run a macro from the menu, select **Macro** from the Tools menu. Access displays the Run Macro dialog box, shown in Figure 11.6. Select any macro from the drop-down list (or enter its name) and select **OK** to run it.

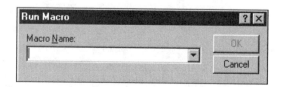

FIGURE 11.6   THE RUN MACRO DIALOG BOX.

FROM THE MACRO WINDOW

When you are designing a macro in the Macro window, a **Run** tool is added to the toolbar. Click this tool or choose **Run** from the Macro menu to run the macro you are designing. This is meant to be a quick way of testing the macro.

FROM A FORM OR REPORT

You can run a macro as an Event property of an object in a report or form. You learned in Chapter 9 that you can display the properties of an object in a form or report by selecting it and selecting the **Properties** tool, and you can use the tabs in the Properties window to display only Event properties. You can use the Event properties to select any macro, and that macro will be executed when that event occurs.

Reports have only a few Event properties because you cannot edit their data. Figure 11.7 shows the Event properties for a report as a whole. For example, you can select a macro as the On Open or On Close property, and that macro will be executed whenever the report is opened or closed. Each band of a design report also has Event properties.

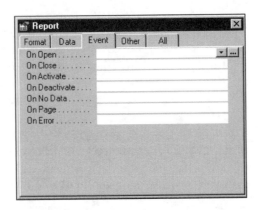

FIGURE 11.7   EVENT PROPERTIES FOR A REPORT.

Many controls on forms also have Event properties because they are meant to be manipulated by the user. For example, Figure 11.8 shows the Event properties for a text box that is used to enter or edit data in a field. You can select a macro as the On Enter or On Exit property—for example, to have it executed whenever the user moves the highlight into or out of the field.

You can select the **...** button on the right side of the Event Properties cells to display the Macro Builder window and create or edit the macro associated with that property.

To display complete information on using any of these properties, put the cursor in the property's cell and press **F1**.

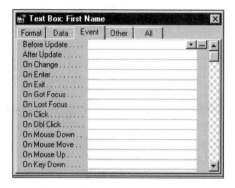

FIGURE 11.8   EVENT PROPERTIES FOR A FIELD ON A FORM.

FROM A PUSH BUTTON

In Chapter 7, you learned to add a push button to a form, and you saw that the Command Button Wizard lets you assign a large number of predefined actions to it.

You can also assign a macro to a push button by using its **On Click** property.

In general, only programmers would assign Event properties to controls in forms, but this is the one exception. Users often find it convenient to add push buttons to forms and have them execute macros in this way.

A Sample Macro

Though they have many other features, these simple techniques will be enough to create most of the macros that are needed by the typical user who is not a programmer. Before going on to look at some of the more advanced features of macros, you should do an exercise to practice the basic techniques you will find most useful.

You generally use macros to automate sequences of commands that you use frequently. The macro is simply a list of actions that you find you are going through over and over again in your work.

Let's say that you print mailing labels on a different printer than you use for most purposes, and you find that you are repeatedly selecting the mailing label object, choosing **Print Setup** from the File menu to select the printer, **Print** to actually print the labels, and **Print Setup** again to return to the default printer.

It is easy to automate this process. Try opening and closing the labels also so you can see what is being done while the macro is being executed:

1. Click the **Macros** tab of the Database window and then click the **New** button.

2. When Access displays the Macro window, click and drag its title bar to move it right so you can see the Database window to its left. Then select the **Reports** tab of the Database window, and click and drag **5095 Mailing Labels** to the first cell in the Action list of the macro. Access adds the OpenReport action to the macro, with 5095 Mailing Labels as the Report Name argument, as shown in Figure 11.9.

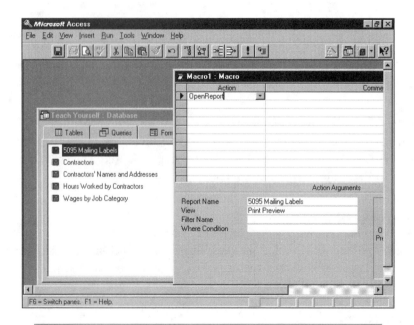

FIGURE 11.9 CLICKING AND DRAGGING TO ADD AN ACTION TO THE MACRO.

3. If necessary, click and drag its title bar to move the Macro window back to its original position. As the Comment for the first action, enter **Open the Mailing Label Report.**

4. Click the second action cell in the Macro window, click its drop-down button to display its drop-down list, and select **DoMenuItem**. Click the cell for the Menu Name property, click its drop-down button, and select

File from the drop-down list. Then click the cell for the Command property, click its drop-down button, and select **Page Setup** from the drop-down list. As the Comment for this action, enter **Display the Page Setup Dialog Box to choose the printer used for labels.**

5. Use the drop-down list for the third action cell in the Macro window to select **DoMenuItem** also. As the Menu Name property, select **File** again, and as the Command property, select **Print**. As the Comment for this action, enter **Display the Print dialog box.**

6. The fourth action is the same as the second. You must display the Print Setup dialog box again to use the default printer. Click the selection box to the left of the second action, and choose **Copy** from the Edit menu. Click anywhere in the fourth row, and choose **Paste** from the Edit menu. Finally, edit the Comment so it reads **Display the Print Setup Dialog Box to return to the default printer.**

7. As the fifth action, use the drop-down list to select **Close**. As the Object Type argument, select **Report**, and as the Object Name argument, select **5095 Mailing Labels**. As the Comment, type **Close the Mailing Label report.**

8. Choose **Save** from the File menu. In the Save As dialog box, enter the macro name **Print 5095 Mailing Labels**, and select **OK**. The final design of the macro is shown in Figure 11.10.

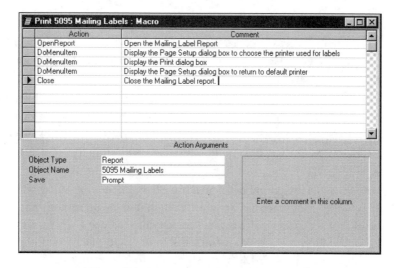

FIGURE 11.10   THE FINAL DESIGN OF THE MACRO.

9. Close the Macro window. Select the **Macros** tab in the Database window—the new macro should be selected. To test it, select the **Run** button.

This is a very simple macro, but using it saves time and effort. Most macros that you have occasion to use will be just this sort of simple, time-saving list of actions.

Using More Advanced Macro Techniques

Macros have many advanced features. Here, we look at a few that are available by using three tools that are displayed when you use the Macro window:

 Macro Names tool is used to name macros that are included in macro groups.

 Conditions tool is used to add conditional actions to macros.

 Single Step tool is used for debugging.

The uses of these tools are described below.

Creating Macro Groups

 If you select the **Macro Names** tool or choose **Macro Names** from the View menu, Access adds a Macro Name column to the Macro window, as shown in Figure 11.11. You can hide this column by selecting the tool or menu option again.

Macro names are needed only if you create a macro group, which can be convenient if you are creating a number of macros that you do not plan to run from the Database window—for example, if you create a number of macros that will be attached to push buttons and are not intended to be run from the Database window.

If you create a large number of macros of this sort, the Macros list of the Database window can become so cluttered that it is inconvenient to scroll through it to find the macros there that you actually do want. To avoid this clutter, Access lets you create groups of macros in a single Macro window, so that only the group name is added to the list, rather than creating each macro individually and having them all added to the list.

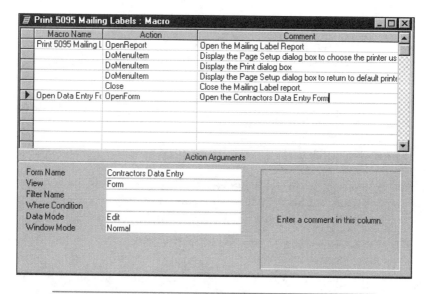

FIGURE 11.11   THE MACRO NAME COLUMN OF THE MACRO WINDOW.

To create a group of macros, simply put the name of each in the Macro Name column to the left of its first action. Each name applies to the action to its right and all the actions that follow until the next macro name. In Figure 11.11, for example, the first macro named Print 5095 Mailing Labels has the same steps as the macro you created in the last exercise. All the steps above the line with the next macro name are part of this macro.

When you create a macro group, you save and name the Macro window as usual, and its name is used as the group name. Only this name is displayed in the Database window.

If you select this name in the Database window and run it, only the first macro in the group will be run. Other macros in the group must be run in other ways, which are discussed later in this chapter—for example, by attaching them to push buttons. As you can see, grouped macros are useful primarily for application developers who might use them to hold groups of macros associated with different forms.

To run it in these other ways, you refer to a macro in a group by using the group name, followed by the dot operator, followed by the macro name. In the illustration above, for example, you can see in the title bar that the group is named Sample Macro Group, so that the first macro in it would be called `[Sample Macro Group].[Print 5095 Mailing Labels]`.

If you are developing macros in a group and you do not want any-one to run the first one from the Database window by mistake, you can create a dummy macro in the first row, which has nothing in the Action column, and you can begin the first macro that you really need in the second row.

Using Conditional Actions in Macros

If you select the **Conditions** tool or choose **Conditions** from the View menu, Access adds a Conditions column to the Macro window. You can hide this column by selecting the tool or menu option again.

Enter an expression in this column, and the action to its right will run only if the expression evaluates to true.

When you place the insertion point in a Condition cell, you can select the Build tool to use the Expression Builder to generate the expression to be entered in the cell.

If you want a series of actions to run only if a condition is true, enter the expression in the Condition column for the first of these, and enter an ellipsis (**...**) in the Condition columns for the actions that follow.

Figure 11.12 shows a simple example of a conditional macro, which is equiv-alent to using a validation rule to check if an entry is valid. The example requires the user to make an entry in the Last Name field. It is selected as the On Exit property of the text box where the Last Name field is entered, so that the macro is executed whenever the user is done making an entry in the field and leaves it.

The condition on the first row is `[Last Name] Is Null`, which evaluates as true if there is no entry in the Last Name field. The action on the first row is MsgBox, which displays a message in a dialog box. The Message argument determines what this message is—in this case *Please Enter a Last Name*, as shown in Figure 11.13. Because of the condition, this message is displayed only if there is no entry in the Last Name field.

The second row has an ellipsis in the Condition column, so its action also is executed only if the condition is true. The action is CancelEvent, which undoes the event that called this macro. Since this macro is used as the On Exit property of a field, CancelEvent places the cursor back in the field. Thus, the macro not only displays an error message if there is no entry in the field, it also refuses to let the user leave the field until there is an entry in it.

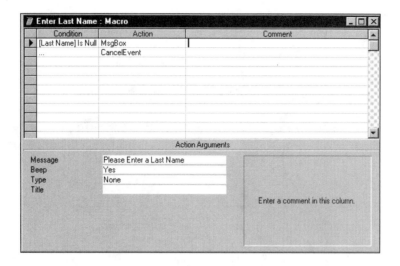

FIGURE 11.12   A CONDITIONAL MACRO.

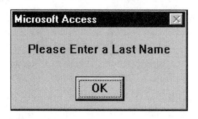

FIGURE 11.13   THE ERROR MESSAGE DISPLAYED BY THIS MACRO.

This illustration is a simple one, and you could do the same thing using a validation rule and validation text when you design the table. Programmers sometimes use much more complex macros than the On Exit Property in order to validate data.

Debugging Macros

Sometimes there are errors when you run a macro, and Access displays a dialog box like the one shown in Figure 11.14.

One common reason for this sort of error is that a macro is run from the wrong place in Access. The error message shown in figure 11.13,, for example, was produced by the macro that validates data entry in the Last Name field. When it is run as an Action property of the Last Name field as it is supposed to be, there is no error message. If you run it from the Database window by mistake, though, Access does not know what Last Name refers to in the macro so it displays this error message.

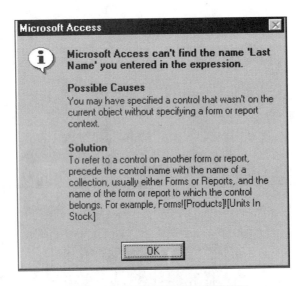

FIGURE 11.14   AN ERROR IN A MACRO.

Often, you can diagnose the problem in the macro simply by noting the error message that is displayed and looking through the macro carefully to see where it applies.

 When you are debugging a longer macro, however, it is often helpful to run the macro one step at a time to make it easier to find the error. To do this, simply select the **Single Step** tool on the Macro window toolbar or choose **Single Step** from the Run menu. As long as this option remains selected, Access runs the macro one row at a time and displays the Macro Single Step dialog box, shown in Figure 11.15, when you run a macro.

This dialog box is very easy to understand and contains the following:

✳ **Macro Name** contains the name of the macro you are running.

✳ **Condition** informs you whether the condition in the current row is true or false. (If there is no condition, this is displayed as true, meaning that the action will be performed.)

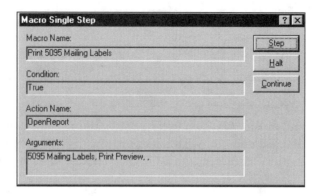

FIGURE 11.15   THE MACRO SINGLE STEP DIALOG BOX.

✳ **Action Name** is the action in the current row.

✳ **Arguments** contains the arguments of the action.

✳ **Step** performs the action of the macro that is listed in the Action Name box, and then displays this dialog box again before performing the next action.

✳ **Halt** cancels the macro. No further actions are performed after using this button, but all the actions that had been performed by the macro to that point will remain in force.

✳ **Continue** performs the rest of the macro in the usual way rather than one step at a time. Selecting this button deselects the Step Into tool of the toolbar so future macros also are not performed one step at a time, unless you select this tool or menu option again.

If you have trouble understanding the error message of a macro, run it one step at a time until you find out which action it applies to, and try to correct the error in that action.

Creating Self-Executing Macros

Access lets you automate your work even further by creating macros that execute automatically when you open a database or when you start Access.

THE AUTOEXEC MACRO

If you create any macro and save it with the name AutoExec, then that macro runs automatically when you open the database it is in.

You can bypass the AutoExec macro by holding down the **Shift** key when you open the database.

THE SENDKEYS ACTION

The SendKeys action lets you include keystrokes in a macro, which are treated exactly as if you typed them in while the macro was running. For example, you can use this action to fill in a dialog box automatically, rather than typing text into it.

This action includes two arguments:

✳ **Keystrokes** specifies up to 255 keystrokes that are sent to the application. This argument may also include symbols that represent keystrokes other than letter keys. Most users will need only **[Enter]** or ~, either of which can represent the **Enter** key. Occasionally, you may also need to use + for the **Shift** key, ∧ for the **Ctrl** key, and **%** for the **Alt** key. For example, you can use **%F** to represent **Alt-F**.

✳ **Wait** specifies whether the macro pauses until the keystrokes are processed.

If you want to use this action to fill in a dialog box, you must place the SendKeys action before the action that opens the dialog box, and select **No** for the Wait argument. When a dialog box is opened, a macro's execution is suspended until the user finishes with the dialog box. The macro would never get up to the SendKeys action if it was after the action that displays the dialog box. By using SendKeys first, you put the keystrokes in the buffer, where they are waiting to be used in the dialog box once it is opened.

Creating Applications

At this point, you have already learned enough that you can begin to set up applications for beginners who know nothing about Access.

A common way to do this is by using a *switchboard*, a group of push buttons used to perform common tasks. Before creating a switchboard, you must design all the tables, forms, reports, and other objects needed in an application.

Then, to create the switchboard, create a form with no fields in it. Add a push button to the form for each of the tasks that the user must perform. Some tasks are built into the Push Button Wizard. You must create macros to perform other tasks, and you must use the On Click properties of push buttons to attach the macros to the buttons.

For example, you could design a form with the mailing labels you need, create a macro to print them, and attach this macro to a button with the label Print Mailing Labels. You could create a data entry form, and use the **Search** option from the Push Button Wizard to let the user perform searches. You could use built-in options to perform many routine tasks after you have designed the necessary objects.

For a complex application, you could create a main switchboard, with buttons that open other, more specialized switchboards—for example, one that lets you use all the application's forms, and another that lets you print all the application's reports.

Finally, you could create an AutoExec macro in the database to open the Main Switchboard form automatically whenever this database is opened. Even a user who knew nothing about Access could use the database simply by clicking buttons on the switchboard.

Access makes it easy to develop applications in this way, without programming. Professional developers use its programming language (Access BASIC) for special tasks, but you can set up simple applications for beginners simply by creating the necessary objects, macros, and switchboards with buttons to run them. Bear in mind, though, that designing the application to make it easy for a beginning user to understand can be more difficult than creating the objects needed to implement it.

This book is meant to teach you to use Access on your own. Designing and developing applications is a study in itself. However, you have reached the point where you know enough about using Access that you can also use it to create simple applications.

To Sum Up

In this chapter, you learned to create macros that can save time for Access users, and you glanced quickly at the way that developers use macros.

You learned how to add actions and their arguments to the Macro window, both by using drag-and-drop for actions that involve objects, and by using the drop-down lists in the window. After creating some simple macros that use these features, you looked at some of the more advanced features of the Macro Window, such as macro groups, conditional actions in macros, and how to debug macros by running them a single step at a time. You also learned to create macros that run automatically, and looked at how developers would use these to create a switchboard to set up an application for a novice.

Now you have learned about all the objects you need to understand as a user of Access. In the next chapter, you look at a few additional special techniques.

CHAPTER 12

Utilities and Special Techniques

Y ou have learned all the basic features that you need to work with Access, but in order to get you up and running more quickly, the earlier chapters skipped some Access utilities and special techniques. In order to help you create and work with simple tables, queries, forms, and reports as easily as possible, the first part of this book skipped over some of the techniques that Access provides to make it easier to manage Access objects and to give you more power to work with other applications. You will learn about them in this chapter, which covers the following topics:

* Creating Windows shortcuts
* Using Access utilities to manage databases and their objects
* Creating indexes based on single or multiple fields
* Working with both embedded and linked OLE objects in Access tables and queries

✳ Working with bound and unbound OLE objects in forms and reports

✳ Attaching a table from another database application so it can be used by Access and the other application simultaneously

✳ Customizing the Access working environment using the Options dialog box

✳ Customizing Access toolbars and their buttons

✳ Importing and exporting data to share with other applications

Creating Windows Shortcuts

It is very easy to create a shortcut that lets you run any Access object by clicking an icon on the Windows desktop. Simply select the object in the Database window, and then choose **Shortcut** from the Edit menu to display the Create Shortcut dialog box, shown in Figure 12.1. The shortcut is stored in a file named in the Location box, and you can click the **Browse** button to change the name and location of this file, but there is no reason for most users to do this. Simply click **OK** to create the shortcut.

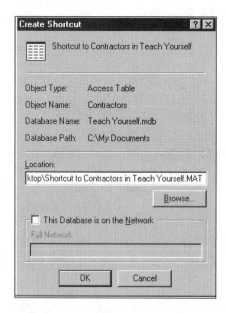

FIGURE 12.1   THE CREATE SHORTCUT DIALOG BOX.

A shortcut icon will be displayed on the Windows desktop, as shown in Figure 12.2. Simply double-click this icon to use the object. If necessary, Access will be opened automatically.

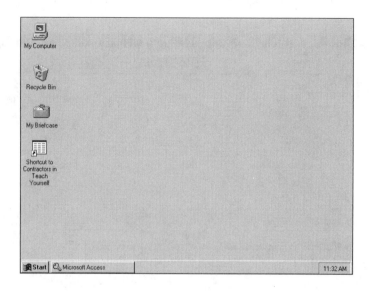

FIGURE 12.2   A SHORTCUT ICON ON THE DESKTOP.

To remove the shortcut, select the icon and press **Delete** or drag the icon to the Recycle Bin.

Using Access Utilities

Access includes two sets of easy-to-use utilities that everyone will find helpful for managing databases and for managing objects.

Utilities for Managing Access Databases

Access has a number of utilities on the Database Utilities menu of the Tools menu that are displayed only when no database is open. Most of these use two dialog boxes: the first to select the source file, and the second to select the target file for the operation.

For example, when you compact a database, as described below, Access begins by displaying the Database to Compact From dialog box, shown in Figure 12.3. Once you have selected a file and selected **Compact**, Access displays the Database to Compact Into dialog box, shown in Figure 12.4.

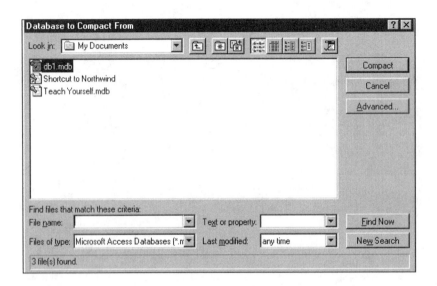

FIGURE 12.3   DATABASE TO COMPACT FROM DIALOG BOX.

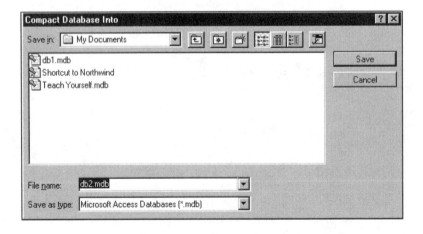

FIGURE 12.4   DATABASE TO COMPACT INTO DIALOG BOX.

As you can see, you use both of these dialog boxes to select or name a file in the same way you use the Open Database dialog box, described in Chapter 1.

As you will see, in some of the following utilities, you use the same name in the From and Into dialog box to perform the operation on the file without changing its name. In others, you must use different file names or locations in the two dialog boxes, so that the result of the operation is kept in a different file from the original.

COMPACTING A DATABASE

When you delete records from a table or delete queries, forms, reports, or other objects from a database, Access generally does not reduce the size of the database (MDB) file that they are in.

Reducing the size of the database file generally requires recopying all the objects in the file. If the file is large, this can take a considerable amount of time, and it would slow performance if Access did it every time you deleted an object. Instead, you must explicitly compact the database to eliminate this wasted space.

Before you can compact a database, you (and any other users on a network) must close it. Then choose **Database Utilities**, then **Compact Database** from the Tools menu to display the Database to Compact From dialog box. Once you have selected a file and selected **Compact**, Access displays the Database to Compact Into dialog box, which you use to enter the name and path of the file that will hold the database in compacted form. You can use the same name as the original database to compact it.

CONVERTING A DATABASE

Access version 7.0 databases use a different file format from earlier versions. To convert earlier versions of Access databases to Access 7.0 format, all users must close the database file. Choose **Database Utilities**, then **Convert Database** from the Tools menu. Select the database in the Database to Convert From dialog box, and specify the name and location of the new version 7.0 database in the Convert Database Into dialog box.

You must use a new file name or location for the new database in the Into dialog box so that you have two databases after you finish this operation. After you are sure that the operation is successful, you should delete the earlier version of the database. If you retain two versions of the same database, you are likely to enter new data or create new objects in the wrong one occasionally.

After you have converted a database to version 7.0 format, it cannot be used by older versions of Access and cannot be converted back to earlier formats. If you are working on a network, all users should update to version 7.0 before you convert databases.

REPAIRING A CORRUPTED DATABASE

A database may be corrupted if a user turns off the computer without exiting from Access, or if there is a power shortage or other system failure that prevents you from exiting Access normally.

To repair a corrupted database, choose **Database Utilities**, then **Repair Database** from the Tools menu. Select the name of the database in the Repair Database dialog box. Access repairs the database and keeps the same file name.

Access can usually detect a corrupted database and will automatically ask if you want to repair it when you open it. The **Repair Database** command is useful if Access does not detect that a database is corrupted. Use this command if the database behaves erratically.

Utilities for Managing Access Objects

In addition to the database utilities described earlier, which are displayed on the Tools menu when no database is open, Access includes a number of utilities on the Edit menu for managing the objects within a database.

RENAMING AN OBJECT

To rename an object in an Access database, first select it in the Database window, and choose **Rename** from the Edit menu or simply click the selected name. In either case, Access will display the name as text that you can edit to change it.

DELETING AN OBJECT

To delete an object in an Access database, first select it in the Database window, then choose **Delete** from the File menu or press the **Delete** key. You can select **Undo Delete** from the Edit menu immediately after deleting an object to restore it to the database.

Cutting, Copying, and Pasting Objects

You can use the Edit menu to cut, copy, and paste objects in Access databases. Simply select an object and choose **Cut** from the Edit menu to remove the object from the database and place it on the clipboard, or choose **Copy** to leave the object in the database and place a copy on the clipboard.

Select **Paste** to paste the object in a new location. Access displays a dialog box that lets you rename the object. If you are pasting an object, you must enter a name for it using the usual Access naming conventions, covered in Chapter 2.

As always, you can use the key combinations **Ctrl-X** (cut), **Ctrl-C** (copy), and **Ctrl-V** (paste) rather than using the Edit menu.

If you are pasting a table, the Paste Table As dialog box, shown in Figure 12.5, also lets you choose these options:

✳ **Structure Only**: the table you specify will have only the structure of the table you are pasting, and no data.

✳ **Structure and Data**: the table you specify will have both the structure and the data of the table you are pasting.

✳ **Append Data to Existing Table**: you must specify the name of an existing table, and the data in the table you are pasting will be added to it.

You can cut or copy and paste either within a database or between databases.

Within a database, copy and paste is an easy way of making a backup copy of an object that has a different name before you make changes to the design of the object.

You can cut or copy and paste between databases to save time creating new objects that are similar to objects in an existing database. Sometimes the easiest way to create a new table, for example, is to copy and paste a table with a similar structure from another database.

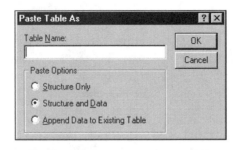

FIGURE 12.5   THE PASTE TABLE AS DIALOG BOX.

Creating Indexes

In Chapter 4, you learned to use Select Queries to determine which records are displayed and their sort order. There are times when you should index a table to speed up a query or sort. To know when to create an index, you should understand a bit about how they work.

What is an Index?

The index of a database table is very much like an index of a book.

A book's index is an alphabetical list of topics in the book, with the page number for each. It is easier to look up the topic in the index and then go the page it is on than it is to look through the entire book page by page until you find the topic.

Likewise, a table's index is an ordered list of all the values in a field (or several fields) of the table, with pointers to the record where each value appears. For example, an index could be an alphabetical list of all the last names in a table, with a pointer to the record in which each name appears. It is faster for Access to look up the last name in the index and then go to the record it points to than to read through every record in the table until it finds the name.

The primary key of an Access table is automatically indexed, and Access can use this index to speed up many of its operations. That is why it encourages you so strongly to include a primary key in each table.

You can also create indexes for other fields that are used in finds, query criteria, or sorts. If you create the index, Access uses it to speed up performance.

Advantages and Disadvantages of Indexing

Why doesn't Access just create indexes automatically when you do a find or query, so they are ready to reuse when you do the find or query again?

There is a disadvantage to creating too many indexes. When you enter or edit data, Access automatically updates indexes, and it takes a tiny amount of time to update each. If you have a few indexes, you do not notice the time it takes to update them. Updating occurs more quickly than you can type. If you have a large number of indexes in a table with many records, however, the time it takes to update them slows down Access enough that you find yourself waiting as you do data entry.

For this reason, you should create indexes for only those fields that are the basis of finds, queries, and sorts that you use frequently.

If you are always looking up people by last name, for example, you should index on the last name field to speed up the find.

If you often print mailing labels in ZIP Code order and reports in alphabetical order by name, you could create an index on the Zip field and another on the Last Name and the First Name field.

NOTE

You should not create indexes for finds, sorts, or queries that you do only occasionally.

Indexing a Single Field

To create or remove an index based on a single field, open the table in Design View and select a value for the Indexed property. As shown in Figure 12.6, there are three options for this property:

* **No** means there is no index based on the field. This is the default.

* **Yes (Duplicates OK)** creates an index based on the field and lets you enter the same value in any number of records in the field.

* **Yes (No Duplicates)** creates an index based on the field and does not let you enter a value in the field if that value has already been entered in another record.

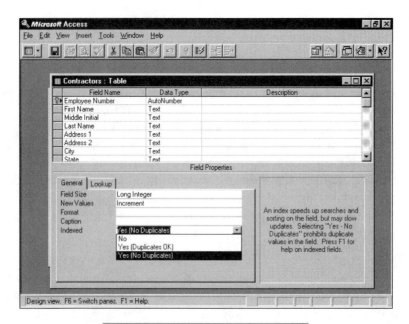

FIGURE 12.6   INDEXING ON A SINGLE FIELD.

You cannot create indexes for Memo, Yes/No or, OLE Object fields.

Yes (No Duplicates) is the type of index that is used for the primary key. You must enter a unique value for the primary key in each record. When you designate a field as a primary key, it is automatically given this index property, and you cannot change its index property as long as it remains a primary key.

You should select **Yes (Duplicates OK)** to speed up searches and sorts based on the field.

Indexes you create in this way are included in the Indexes window, discussed next.

Indexing on Multiple Fields

To create an index based on multiple fields, display the table in Design View, and choose **Indexes** from the View menu or click the **Indexes** tool. The Indexes window is displayed, as shown in Figure 12.7.

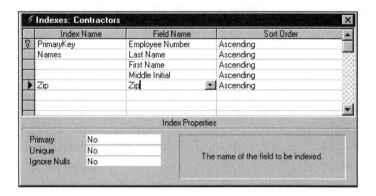

FIGURE 12.7   THE INDEXES WINDOW.

Enter a name for the index in the Index Name column. Use the drop-down list in the Field Name column to select a field on which to base the index. Use the drop-down list in the Sort Order column to specify whether the field should be indexed in Ascending or Descending order. Continue selecting Field Names and Sort Orders in the rows below the Index name. All field names and sort orders that do not have an index name are used as part of the index whose name is above them. As with sorts, the first field used is the primary field that the index is based on, and fields that follow are used as tie-breakers.

In Figure 12.7, for example, there is a primary key, an index named Names, and an index named Zip. Names is based on the Last Name, First Name, and Middle Initial fields, and is used to speed up alphabetical sorts by name. All these fields are part of the Names index because they do not have their own entries in the Index Name column.

Index Properties

You can set the following index properties in the Index window:

* **Primary**: the index is the primary key. Only one index can have this property.

* **Unique**: unique values must be entered in the field. This property is equivalent to selecting **Yes (No Duplicates)** when you create the index.

* **Ignore Nulls**: any records with a null value for the index expression will be excluded from this index.

Working with OLE Objects

Object Linking and Embedding (OLE) is a feature of many Windows applications which allows objects from one application to be used in another. For example, if you create a logo using a draw program that supports OLE, you can include it in Access forms as an OLE object.

OLE objects have many uses in databases. The most common is to hold pictures. For example, you can scan photographs of all the contractors in your table (or of the people in any other list), include the picture in an OLE field in each record, and create a form that displays it when you display the person's name and address.

OLE objects can also be used to hold sounds. For example, a music store could have a computer with a table of all the recordings it has in stock. Along with the data on each, the table could have an OLE field which you could double-click to play a sample of music. A video store could have a database table with a field that you double-click to play a sample of each video in stock.

Working with more mundane applications, you could create an Access table to keep track of all the letters you write. Include a few fields with the description, addressee, and dates of the letters, and store the letters themselves (which are documents in another application such as Microsoft Word) in an OLE object field of the Access table.

In another application, you could use a spreadsheet application to record the hours that each of your contractors worked, and you could include either an entire spreadsheet file or certain cells from the spreadsheet in each record as an OLE object. You could also use the spreadsheet application to graph the hours worked, and then you could create a form that displays the graph of the hours each contractor worked whenever it displays his or her name and address.

In any case, you must have another Windows application that supports OLE to create the picture, sound, graph, or other OLE object. Then you can use it in Access tables, forms, or reports.

Linking versus Embedding

As the name implies, OLE objects can be included in other applications in two ways:

❋ **Linking**: if the object is linked, it retains its connection with the application where it was created. Access displays the object, but it is still stored in its original file. Any changes that are made in it in the original application will also be incorporated in the application where it is included as a linked OLE object. You can also open the application from within Access and change the object.

✳ **Embedding**: if the object is embedded, a copy of the original object is made and is actually stored in your database. If you use the application where it was created and change the object, the changes are not reflected in the embedded OLE object. You must change the OLE object from within Access. You can double-click the embedded OLE object to invoke the original application to make changes in the OLE object.

Use linked objects if you want the object to change when the original changes. For example, if you have a file to keep track of letters that someone else might edit in Word for Windows, you must use them as linked objects so that changes made to them in Word are incorporated in the database.

Use embedded objects if you want to protect the object from changes or if you want the database to be portable. Because linked objects are stored in separate files, they will not be included if you copy a database to a floppy disk and give it to someone else. Embedded objects are included with the database. Of course, this also means that they require more disk space.

OLE Objects in Tables and Queries

After you have created a field of the OLE object type, you can add objects to it in several ways, described in the following sections.

EMBEDDING USING DRAG-AND-DROP

If you are working with Access and another Microsoft Office application for Windows 95, you can embed an existing object in Access by using drag-and-drop.

Size the two application windows so you can see them both. Select the data you want. Click it, hold down the left mouse button, and drag it to the OLE Object field in Access. Release the mouse button to place it in the field.

CREATING AND EMBEDDING A NEW OBJECT

You can open another application from within an Access table or query and use it to create an embedded OLE Object.

Simply select the OLE object field where you want the object to be embedded, and choose **Object** from the Insert menu to display the Insert Object dialog box, shown in Figure 12.8. The options in the Object Type list depend on the applications you have available that support OLE.

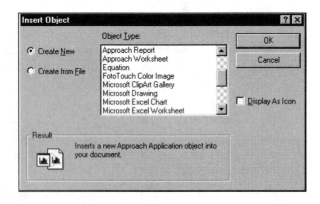

FIGURE 12.8   EMBEDDING A NEW OBJECT.

The **Create New** radio button is selected by default. Simply select the type of object you want to embed and select **OK** to open the source application, which you can use to create the object. When you are done, choose **Exit** from the File menu of the source application.

INSERTING OBJECTS IN EXISTING FILES

You can use **Insert Object** from the Edit menu if you have already created the files that you want to have embedded or linked in a table or query—for example, if you have already scanned a number of photographs and have them stored in graphics files.

Put the cursor in the OLE object field where you want the object to be added, and choose **Insert Object** to display the Insert Object dialog box. Then select the **Create from File** radio button to change the dialog box to the form shown in Figure 12.9.

You can either enter the file's name in the File text box, or click the **Browse** button to display the Browse dialog box, which you use to select a file exactly as you do with the Open dialog box. By default, the object is embedded, but if you select the **Link** checkbox, it is linked.

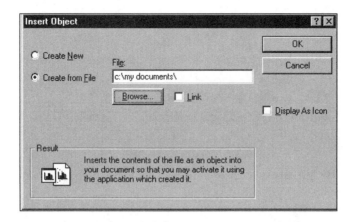

FIGURE 12.9 **EMBEDDING AN OBJECT FROM A FILE.**

COPYING AND PASTING EMBEDDED OBJECTS

You can also use copy and paste commands from most source applications to embed an object in an OLE field.

Create the object in the source application, select it, and choose **Copy** or **Cut** from the Edit menu of the source application. Then select an OLE object field in an Access table or query and choose **Paste** from the Edit menu to embed the object in the field.

If the source application does not support copy and paste, the **Paste** option will not be enabled on the Edit menu when you return to Access.

N O T E

You can use **Copy** and **Paste** to add objects from Windows applications to Access databases, even if the application does not support OLE. However, you will not be able to open the source application from Access, and the object in Access will not reflect changes in the object made in the source application. The only way to change the object is to change it in the source application, and use **Copy** and **Paste** once again to add the new version of it to Access.

ADDING A LINKED OBJECT

To add a linked object to a table or query, create the object in the source application, select it, and choose **Copy** or **Cut** from the Edit menu of the source application.

Then select an OLE object field in an Access table or query and choose
Paste Special from the Edit menu to display the Paste Special dialog box,
shown in Figure 12.10.

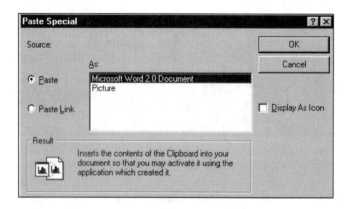

FIGURE 12.10   THE PASTE SPECIAL DIALOG BOX.

Select the **Paste Link** radio button and select **OK** to add a linked OLE object to
the table or query. The name of the source file that it is linked to is displayed at
the top of the dialog box, and any changes made in that file will also be made
in the OLE object.

Changing an Object's Format

To embed an object in a different format, create it in another application, select
it, and choose **Copy** from the Edit menu. In Access, select the OLE object field
where you want it added and choose **Paste Special** from the Edit menu to display the Paste Special dialog box.

Select the **Paste** radio button and Access displays the formats that you can
use for the object in the As list of this dialog box. In addition to the initial format, this list may include picture or bitmap formats. These formats may reduce
the amount of space that the object occupies in the database, and they let you
change its size in forms and reports. However, you can no longer use the original application to edit the object after converting it to picture or bitmap format.

EDITING AN OLE OBJECT

To edit an OLE object from within Access, double-click it or choose **...Object**
and then **Edit** from the Edit menu. Access opens the application with the object

displayed in it. The ellipsis is included before the word Object because the name of this option changes depending on the type of source application and type of object that is selected.

As you know, you can also edit linked but not embedded OLE objects from the source application.

DELETING AN OLE OBJECT

To delete an OLE object from a table or query, simply select its field and choose **Delete** from the Edit menu or press the **Delete** key. This does not affect the object in the source application.

OLE Objects in Forms and Reports

So far, you have looked at OLE objects in tables and queries, where they can be added only in fields. In forms and reports, there are two categories of OLE object controls, as there are of other controls:

✳ **Bound OLE object controls** display the OLE objects in a field. The content of the control changes when you change records. For example, you would use a bound OLE object control to display peoples' photographs that are stored in a table with their names and addresses.

✳ **Unbound OLE object controls** display OLE objects that are not stored in the table and are used purely to enhance the design of the form or report. For example, you would use an unbound OLE object control to display a company logo in a form's header. The logo remains the same as the records change.

The toolbox contains a Bound Object Frame tool and an Object Frame tool, which you can use to add these objects.

BOUND OLE OBJECTS

 You can add a bound OLE object as you do other fields. The easiest way is to display the field list and click and drag the name of an OLE object field to the form or report design.

You can also use the **Bound Object Frame** tool of the toolbox and click and drag to the form or report design to display the frame. Then use its Control Source property to indicate the field it is bound to.

You work with bound OLE objects in forms and reports using all the methods previously described for working with OLE objects in tables and queries.

For example, to add an OLE object to a table, select the **Bound Object Frame** tool in a form, and use any of the methods for adding objects described above, just as you would after selecting the OLE object field it is bound to in the table or query.

UNBOUND OLE OBJECTS

 To add an unbound OLE object to a form or report, click the **Unbound Object Frame** tool on the toolbox and click and drag to place the frame. When you release the mouse button, Access displays the Insert Object dialog box.

This dialog box was described earlier in the chapter in "Creating and Embedding a New Object" and "Embedding Existing Files." When you are adding an unbound object, you can use this dialog box in the same ways to open an application, create and embed an object, or to specify an existing file to hold the object.

To embed part of an existing object or to embed an object from an application that does not support OLE, use the Copy and Paste options, as described previously.

You can always run an unbound OLE object from Design View of a form or report, but you usually do not want people to run the object from Form View. For example, you do not want the people who are using a form to enter data to be able to redesign the logo that is displayed in an unbound object frame at the top of the form. For this reason, the Enabled property of an unbound OLE object is set to **No** by default. To run the object from Form view, set this property to **Yes**.

MOVING AND RESIZING OLE OBJECTS

You can select, move, and resize bound or unbound OLE objects as you do other objects in Form and Report designs.

Click the object frame to select it. Then click and drag the object frame or its Move handle to move it, or click and drag its Resize handles to resize it.

Scaling an OLE Object

A bound or unbound OLE object may not be the same shape or size as the frame you create for it. Of course, the way the object fits into the frame changes when you resize it.

You can use the object frame's Size Mode property to specify how Access deals with objects that do not fit in their frames properly. This property has these settings to choose from:

✳ **Clip** displays only a part of the object that can fit into the frame without changing its size or shape if the object is too large. Clip is the default setting.

✳ **Stretch** makes the object larger or smaller to fill the frame, even if this means distorting its shape. For example, if the frame is square and the object is taller than it is wide, this property compresses the height of the object more than it compresses its width, so that it fills the frame completely.

✳ **Zoom** makes the object larger or smaller to fill the frame without distorting its shape. For example, if the frame is square and the object is taller than it is wide, the zoom property compresses the height of the object to fit into the frame, and compresses the width of the object proportionately. The shape of the object is not distorted, but there is empty space beside it in the frame.

Rather than changing the size of the object to fit the frame, you can choose **Size to Fit** from the Layout menu to expand or shrink the frame to fit the object, as you can with other controls.

Customizing Access

There are two methods of customizing Access that you may find useful: customizing the working environment by using the Options toolbox, and customizing toolbars and their tools. Both of these use methods that are similar in Access and in other Microsoft Office products.

The Options Dialog Box

You can customize Access' behavior in many ways by using the Options dialog box, shown in Figure 12.11. Click its tabs to display options for controlling different features of Access's behavior.

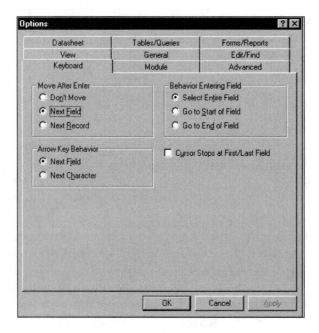

FIGURE 12.11   THE OPTIONS DIALOG BOX.

For example, the illustration shows the Keyboard tab, which lets you control keyboard behavior as follows:

✳   The Move After Enter area's radio buttons give you three options. **Next Field** is the default: you have seen that ordinarily, the highlight moves to the next field when you press **Enter**. Select **Next Record** to move the highlight down one record when you press **Enter**. If you select **Don't Move**, then pressing **Enter** will have no effect.

✳   The Arrow Key Behavior area's radio buttons give you the options **Next Field** (the default) and **Next Character**. Select **Next Character** to have the arrows act as they do in other Windows applications: deselecting the field and placing an insertion point in it rather than moving you to the next field. Other cursor movement keys also work as usual. For example, **Home** and **End** move you to the first or last field of the record.

✳   The Behavior Entering Field area determines the behavior of the field that the highlight is moved to when you press **Enter**. If the default option, **Select Entire Field**, is selected, the text in this field is highlighted, as usual. If you select **Go to End of Field** or **Go to Start of Field**, an insertion is placed at the end or beginning of the field instead.

✳ The **Cursor Stops at First/Last Field** checkbox lets you determine whether you can use the Left and Right Arrow keys to move among records. By default, it is not selected. If you are in the last field of a record, you can use the **Right Arrow** key to move to the first field of the following record, and likewise if you are in the first field of a record, you can use the **Left Arrow** key to move to the last field of the previous record. If you select this checkbox, you cannot move among records in this way. The Left or Right arrow key moves the highlight to the beginning or end of a record and no further.

There is no need to describe all the panels of the Options dialog box here. To see which of its features you would find useful, display its panels and, to find out what any of its controls is used for, click the **?** button in the dialog box's title bar, and then click that control.

Customizing Toolbars

Like other Microsoft applications, Access makes it easy for you to customize its toolbars and their individual buttons to suit the way you work.

FLOATING AND DOCKED TOOLBARS

Any toolbar can be displayed in two ways:

✳ A docked toolbar is displayed at one edge of the Access window, like the toolbar displayed at the top of the screen when you start Access.

✳ A floating toolbar is above other windows within the main Access window, like the toolbox that is displayed when you are designing a report or form.

You can convert any toolbar from one of these types to the other simply by clicking and dragging it. You can also resize any floating toolbar by clicking and dragging its edges, as you do other windows. For example, Figure 12.12 shows the toolbar that is displayed when you are working with the Database window after it has been clicked and dragged to make it a floating toolbar: notice that it has the same tools you are accustomed to seeing at the top of the Access window.

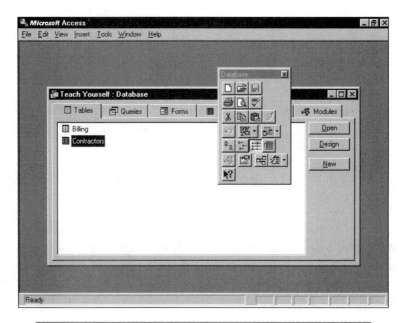

FIGURE 12.12   USING THE DATABASE TOOLBAR AS A FLOATING TOOLBAR.

At any time, you can simply click and drag this toolbar back to the top of the screen to return it to its usual location. You can also click and drag any toolbar to the sides or bottom of the Access window to dock it there.

THE TOOLBARS DIALOG BOX

The Toolbars dialog box, shown in Figure 12.13, lets you control which toolbars are displayed and a few aspects of how they are displayed.

To display the Toolbars dialog box, choose **Toolbars** from the View menu or right-click any toolbar and choose **Toolbars** from its shortcut menu. This dialog box lists the names of all of Access's toolbars and of custom toolbars that you create.

Displaying and Hiding Toolbars

By default, Access displays the toolbars that you need at any time. For example, when you are using the Database window, it displays the Database toolbar.

If you do want to specify which toolbars are displayed, however, you can simply select or deselect the checkbox to its left in the Toolbars list. If you display a toolbar when it is not needed, all of its buttons will be disabled.

FIGURE 12.13   THE TOOLBARS DIALOG BOX.

It is useful to control which toolbars are displayed after you have created custom toolbars, using the methods described below.

Controlling the Toolbar Display

The three checkboxes below the Toolbars list control how the toolbars are displayed:

* ✳ The **Color Buttons** checkbox controls whether the buttons are displayed in color or black and white.
* ✳ The **Large Buttons** checkbox lets you display the buttons so they are larger than their usual size.
* ✳ The **Show ToolTips** checkbox controls whether the name of the tool is displayed when you leave the pointer on it.

CUSTOMIZING TOOLBARS

To create custom toolbars, first display the Customize Toolbars dialog box, shown in Figure 12.14, either by clicking the **Customize** button of the Toolbars dialog box or by right-clicking any toolbar and selecting **Customize** from its shortcut menu. When the Customize Toolbars dialog box is displayed, the rest of the desktop is not completely inaccessible, as it is when most dialog boxes are displayed. Instead, with it open, you can customize toolbars in the following ways.

Removing a Button from a Toolbar

Simply click and drag any button from a toolbar anywhere on the desktop to remove it from that toolbar.

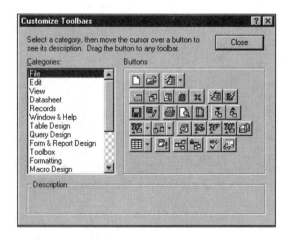

FIGURE 12.14   THE CUSTOMIZE TOOLBAR DIALOG BOX.

Moving Buttons among Toolbars

Likewise, simply click and drag any button from one toolbar to another to move it to that toolbar.

Adding Buttons from the Customize Toolbars Dialog Box

As you can see in the illustration, the Customize Toolbars dialog box has a list of categories, and you can select any one to display a selection of buttons from that category. Place the pointer on the button in the Customize Toolbars dialog box to display a description of what it does at the bottom of the dialog box, as well as displaying its name. Click and drag any button from this dialog box to a toolbar to add the button to that toolbar.

Restoring Toolbars to their Default Design

You can select a toolbar in the list of the Toolbar dialog box at any time and click the **Reset** button restore it to its original design. This removes any changes you made to it.

CREATING AND DELETING NEW TOOLBARS

To create a new toolbar, click the **New** button of the Toolbars dialog box to display the New Toolbar dialog box, shown in Figure 12.15. After you enter its name and click **OK**, Access displays a small floating toolbar with its name in the title bar.

FIGURE 12.15 THE NEW TOOLBAR DIALOG BOX.

Add buttons to this new toolbar by clicking and dragging them from other tool-bars or from the Customize Toolbars dialog box, just as you do when you are modifying an existing toolbar.

When a custom toolbar is selected in the Toolbars list of the Toolbars dialog box, you can click its **Reset** button to delete the new toolbar.

CUSTOMIZING BUTTONS

When the Customize Toolbars dialog box is displayed, you can also right-click a button of the toolbar to display its shortcut menu, shown in Figure 12.16, which you can then use to customize the button by changing the image on it.

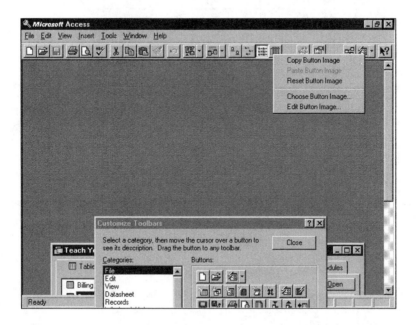

FIGURE 12.16 A BUTTON'S SHORTCUT MENU.

Choose **Copy** from the shortcut menu to copy the image on the button to the clipboard.

After copying a button image, select **Paste** from the shortcut menu of another button to replace the image on that button with the copied image.

To restore the original image of a button after it has been changed, choose **Reset Button Image** from its shortcut menu.

To choose a button image from a set of images that are distributed with Access, select **Choose Button Image** from its shortcut menu to display the dialog box shown in Figure 12.17, and select any of its images. You can also display text on the button rather than an image by selecting the **Text** checkbox and typing the text in the box to its right.

FIGURE 12.17   THE CHOOSE BUTTON IMAGE DIALOG BOX.

To edit a button's image, choose **Edit Button Image** from its shortcut menu to display the Button Editor, shown in Figure 12.18.

Click any color to select it and then click any of the squares of the picture to place that color there, or click and drag over the picture to place the color in a series of squares, drawing lines or coloring in areas.

If the selected color is already in the square, clicking it will erase it and replace it with the background color. You can erase any color by clicking the **Erase** button of the Colors area. Click the **Clear** button to remove all drawing from the picture, leaving only its background color.

If the image is too large to display in the picture area, click the buttons in the Move area to scroll and view it all.

The Preview area shows what the button will look like in actual size when you place it on the desktop.

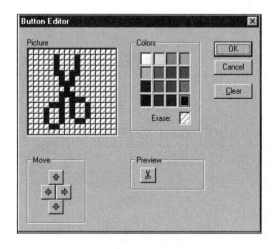

FIGURE 12.18   THE BUTTON EDITOR.

Sharing Data with Other Applications

This book has taught you how to create and work with tables in Access, but there may also be times when you want to use data in other Access database applications or when you want to let people who work with other applications use data from Access. This may be either because you want to exchange data with someone, or because you are working on a network where people use a number of database applications.

Access gives you two different ways of sharing data with other applications:

✳ **Importing and Exporting Data**: *importing* converts a table from another application into an Access table, and *exporting* converts an Access table into a type of table used by other applications.

✳ **Linking**: *linking* a table from another application lets you use its data in Access without changing the original table, so it can still be used in the application where it was created. You can edit the data in the table or create queries, reports, forms, and the like. However, you cannot modify the structure of a table.

To show that a table is linked, Access uses a special icon for it. An arrow indicates that the database is linked to an external table, and the rest of the icon indicates the table type. For example, it uses an arrow to the left of a fox head for a linked FoxPro table. Access uses the usual icon for imported tables since they are converted to ordinary Access tables.

The mechanics of importing or linking tables are very simple, but first you should understand when to use each of these options.

Importing and Exporting versus Linking

When you import a table, Access leaves the original table as is and makes a copy of it, which it converts to Access format. Likewise, when you export a table, you create a copy of it in another format. In either case, you end up with two copies of the table, and changes you make in one do not affect the other table.

When you link a table, Access does not make a copy of it. It links the currently open Access database with the table, without changing its format or location, making it easy to share the data with other applications.

The ability to link a table is one of the features that gave Access its name, since it gives you seamless access to data from other applications. You can use the data just as if it were in an Access table. Although you can change the data in the table, you do not have to change its file format. Other people on a network who use different database management programs can use the same tables simultaneously without even knowing that they are also being used by Access.

However, Access can generally work more quickly with its own tables than with linked tables. For this reason, it is best to import a table if it no longer has to be shared with other applications. Link tables only if they will continue to be used by the other application in the future.

NOTE   When you import or export a table, in order to use it in another format on your own system, you should archive the original table and delete it from your hard disk. When there are two copies of the same data available, someone is likely to update the wrong one by mistake, so that neither table is current.

Access can link or import data from a wide variety of database applications and from spreadsheet and text files. First, you should look at the general process of linking tables and of importing or exporting data, and then you can look at some of the most useful details for working with data from specific types of files.

LINKING A TABLE

To link a table, first open a database. Then choose **Get External Data** from the File menu and **Link Tables** from the submenu to display the Link dialog box, shown in Figure 12.19.

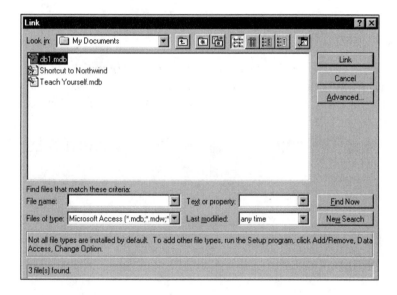

FIGURE 12.19   THE LINK DIALOG BOX.

Use this as you use the Open dialog box to display the folder and table you want to link. You can also limit which tables are displayed by using the drop-downs under the file list. You must use the Files of Type drop-down to specify the program that the file was created by.

Select the table you want in the tables list and click the **Link** button. After a moment, Access adds the file you selected to the tables list of the open database, with the appropriate icon to its left. That is usually all there is to attaching a table.

UNLINKING A TABLE

After you attach a table, you can remove it from an Access database in the same way you delete a table. First, select it in the Database window and choose **Delete** from the File menu or press the **Delete** key. This removes the table from the database but does not delete it from the disk.

> You can choose **Undo Delete** from the Edit menu immediately after unlinking a table to restore it to the database.

NOTE

IMPORTING DATA

To import data, open a database and choose **Get External Data** from the File menu and **Import** from the submenu to display the Import dialog box shown in Figure 12.20. As you can see, this dialog box works just like the Link dialog box.

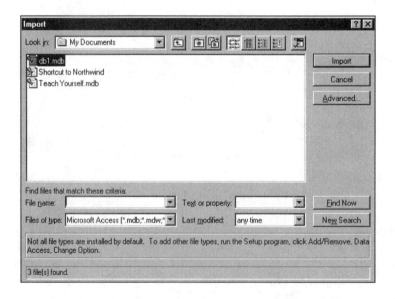

FIGURE 12.20   THE IMPORT DIALOG BOX.

When you select the table and click **Import**, Access converts the original table into an Access table.

EXPORTING DATA

Exporting data is similar to importing data or a table. First, select the table that you want to export in the Access database and then choose **Save As/Export** from the File menu. In the Save As dialog box, select the **To an External File or Database** radio button, and click **OK** to display the Save Table In dialog box, shown in Figure 12.21. Specify the folder, name, and type of the file you want to create, and click the **Export** button to create it.

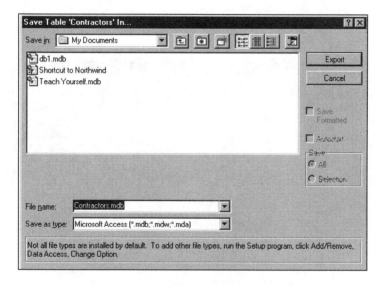

FIGURE 12.21   THE SAVE TABLE IN DIALOG BOX.

Special Technique

There are a few types of files that require special techniques of importing, exporting, or linking, which are covered below.

LINKING ACCESS TABLES

Though it is not common, there may be times when you want the same Access table included in two databases simultaneously. You can link a table from another Access database just as you attach tables from other applications. You can also import or export objects from or to other Access databases.

Unlike other database programs with which you share data, Access has multiple tables in a single MDB file. After you link or import that database file in the usual way, Access displays the Link Tables or Import Tables dialog box, which includes a list of all the tables in that database, so you can select which table or tables you want.

IMPORTING ACCESS OBJECTS

Likewise, you can import objects from an Access database by selecting the Access MDB file in the Import dialog box, as you do with other database applications. Access then displays the Import Objects dialog box, shown in Figure 12.22, which you can use to specify which objects you want to import. As you can see, you can import any type of object from an Access database, not just tables.

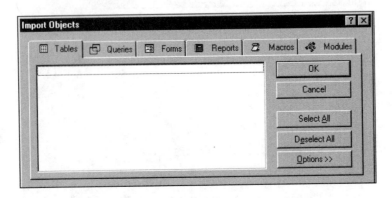

FIGURE 12.22   THE IMPORT OBJECTS DIALOG BOX.

SHORTCUT

If you want to import just one object, it is easier to copy and paste, as previously described. If you want to import a number of objects from another Access database, this method is faster.

IMPORTING AND EXPORTING TEXT FILES

Access can also exchange data with two different types of text files:

✳ **Delimited text files** have a carriage return after each record, a separator, such as a comma, between the fields of each record, and some delimiters, such as quotation marks, around character data.

✳ **Fixed-width text files** have the same size fields in every record. Extra blank spaces are used to pad fields that are shorter. Of course, with all fields fixed in size, each record must also be a fixed size.

One of these two formats must be used in order to make it clear where new records and new fields begin in the text file.

EXPORTING TEXT

If you are exporting and choose **Text Files** as the file type, Access displays the Text Export Wizard. The first step, shown in Figure 12.23, lets you choose which of the above two types you want. The data in your table in the form you choose is displayed in the sample area.

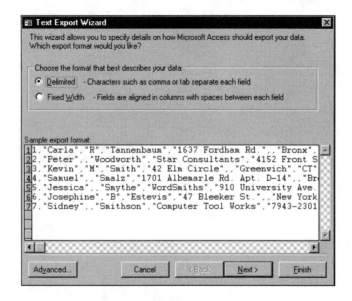

FIGURE 12.23   THE TEXT EXPORT WIZARD.

If you are exporting to a delimited file, the second step, shown in Figure 12.24, lets you choose the delimiter between fields and the character to use around text. Use the default comma and double quotation marks unless you have some special reason not to. You can also use the checkbox in this step to include the field names in the first line of the text file; do so only if the program you are using the text file in can interpret the field names. The final step lets you name the file, as in other wizards.

If you are exporting to a fixed-width text file, the second step of the Text Export Wizard lets you specify where the breaks between fields are. Simply click and drag the arrowheads to change the amount of space given to each field; you can use this if the original table has unnecessary blanks in some fields. As usual, the final step lets you name the file.

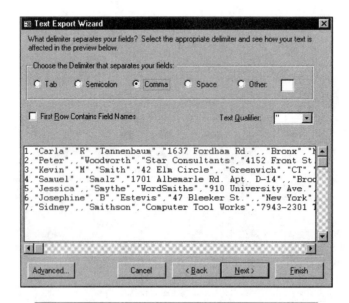

FIGURE 12.24   CHOOSING DELIMITERS AND TEXT QUALIFIERS.

IMPORTING TEXT

When you select a text file in the Import dialog box, Access displays the Text Import Wizard, which is almost identical to the Text Export Wizard.

The first step lets you choose whether you are importing a delimited or fixed-with text file.

The second step for a delimited file lets you select the delimiter and text qualifier and to specify whether the first row contains field names, just as it does in the Export Wizard.

The second step for a fixed-width file lets you click and drag to determine where the boundaries between the fields are. Though it looks the same, it differs from the second step when you are exporting, because the boundaries move through the text as you drag them. As shown in Figure 12.25, the boundaries may be in the wrong place, and you must drag them so they are actually at the dividing points between fields. You can also create breaks between fields by clicking anywhere in the sample area, or delete a break by double-clicking on it.

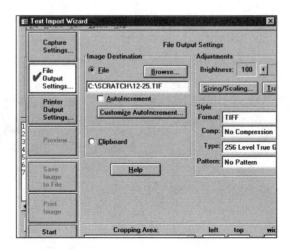

FIGURE 12.25 SPECIFYING THE EDGES OF FIELDS.

SHARING DATA WITH SPREADSHEET FILES

Access can also share data with Microsoft Excel and Lotus 1-2-3 spreadsheet files. Columns and rows in the spreadsheet are equivalent to columns and rows in an Access table.

When you export, Access simply creates a new spreadsheet containing the data in the table, with a column for each field, a row for each record, and the field names on the top row.

When you import, Access displays the Import Spreadsheet Wizard to let you specify which data should be taken from the spreadsheet and how it should be converted to fields.

The first step, shown in Figure 12.26, lets you select the data to import. Spreadsheets can be very large, and if you do not want to import all of its data, you can select the **Show Named Ranges** radio button and select a range in the box to its right; you must name the range of cells in the spreadsheet before importing its data.

The second step of the Import Spreadsheet Wizard lets you specify which row the data begins in, since spreadsheets often contain a heading of several rows before the data begins, and to specify whether the first row contains field names.

The third step lets you specify the name of each field, whether it should be used as the basis of an index, and its data type (if the data in the column can be converted to more than one data type).

The fourth step lets you specify which field is the primary key, to let Access add a new field to the primary key, or to have no primary key.

The fifth step lets you name and create the table.

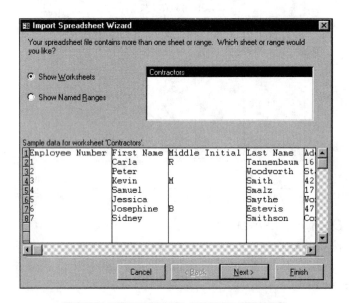

FIGURE 12.26   SELECTING THE DATA TO IMPORT.

To Sum Up

This chapter covered utilities and special techniques that let you use Access with more ease and power. It included database utilities that let you compact, convert, encrypt, and repair databases, and object utilities that let you rename, delete, cut copy, and paste. It also covered the different ways that Access shares data with other applications, importing and exporting data, attaching tables, and redirecting the output of a table, query, form or report. In addition, it covered customizing toolbars and buttons, embedding and linking OLE objects in tables, using both bound and unbound OLE objects in forms and reports, and a number of other utilities.

INDEX

HOW TO USE THE DISK
THAT ACCOMPANIES
TEACH YOURSELF... ACCESS FOR
WINDOWS 95

You can use this disk to save yourself data entry time or to skip early chapters of this book and start working with more advanced topics.

One set of exercises is used in this entire book. In Chapter 2, you create a sample table. In Chapter 3, you enter sample data in it. In Chapter 4, you perform Queries on this data. In Chapter 5, you create simple forms, reports, and mailing labels using the data. In the following chapters, you use the same data in exercises on more advanced topics.

In order to do the exercises in any chapter, you must already have done all the exercises in the preceding chapter.

You can use the files on this disk, if you are already familiar with the basics of Access and want to skip the early chapters of this book and begin with more advanced topics. For example, many readers will understand the basics of creating tables, doing queries, and using wizards, which are covered in Chapters 1 though 5, and will want to begin by learning about relational databases in Chapter 6 and then to go on to the advanced topics in Part II.

Enjoy!

INSTALLING THIS DISK

Installation

To install a file from this disk, simply copy it into the My Documents directory of your hard disk using the Windows Explorer:

1. Click the **Start** button. Select **Programs** from the menu and **Windows** Explorer from the submenu.

2. In the Explorer, be sure that the folders of your hard disk are displayed in the left panel, including the My Documents folder that is created when you install Access.

3. Double-click the disk drive that holds this disk (probably the A disk drive) in the left panel of the Explorer to display a list of its files in the right panel.

4. Click and drag the file you want from the right panel of the Explorer to the My Documents folder in the left panel. Windows will display a message saying that it is copying the file.

After you have copied it, simply use this file instead of the Teach Yourself database file when you do the exercises in the following chapters of the book.

Disk Contents

This disk contains database files with the completed exercises for Chapters 3 through 8 of this book. Each database file is named for the last chapter whose exercises have been completed. For example, the file Chapter 6.mdb is a database that includes objects created in all the exercises through the end of Chapter 6.

If you want to save yourself the tedious work of creating the database and entering sample data in it, you can use the file Chapter 3.mdb and do the exercises beginning with Chapter 4. If you only want to cover the most advanced topics in the book, use the file Chapter 7.mdb and begin working with Chapter 8 of the book.